Learning Disabilities Care

Learning Disabilities Care

A Care Worker Handbook

Tina Marshall, Layla Baker and Cathy Spencer

HODDER
EDUCATION
AN HACHETTE UK COMPANY

Orders: please contact Bookpoint Ltd, 130 Milton Park, Abingdon, Oxon
OX14 4SB. Telephone: (44) 01235 827720. Fax: (44) 01235 400454. Lines are
open from 9.00–5.00, Monday to Saturday, with a 24 hour message
answering service. You can also order through our website
www.hoddereducation.co.uk

If you have any comments to make about this, or any of our other titles,
please send them to educationenquiries@hodder.co.uk

British Library Cataloguing in Publication Data
A catalogue record for this title is available from the British Library

ISBN: 978 1 444 16326 1

First Edition Published 2012
Impression number   10 9 8 7 6 5 4 3 2 1
Year   2016 2015 2014 2013 2012

Hachette UK's policy is to use papers that are natural, renewable and
recyclable products and made from wood grown in sustainable forests.
The logging and manufacturing processes are expected to conform to the
environmental regulations of the country of origin.

Cover photo © John Birdsall/John Birdsall/Press Association Images.
Artwork by Barking Dog Art.
Typeset by Pantek Media, Maidstone, Kent.
Printed and bound in Italy for Hodder Education, An Hachette UK
Company, 338 Euston Road, London NW1 3BH.

Contents

Acknowledgements and Author Biographies

The authors and publishers would like to thank Helen Sanderson Associates for permission to reproduce illustrative material in Figures 2.6, 7.3 and 10.4.

Every effort has been made to trace and acknowledge ownership of copyright. The publishers will be glad to make suitable arrangements with any copyright holders whom it has not been possible to contact.

The authors and publishers would like to thank the following for the use of images in this volume:

Figure 1.4 © Yannis Ntousiopoulos / Fotolia.com; Figure 1.7 © Vladimir Mucibabic / Fotolia.com; Figure 2.1 © PhotoAlto / Alamy; Figure 3.1 © Paul Doyle / Alamy; Figure 3.5 © Brad Killer/iStockphoto; Figure 4.1 © Brian Jackson – Fotolia.com; Figure 4.2 © bit24 – Fotolia.com; Figure 4.3 © CANDIDEYE – Fotolia.com; Figure 4.5 © John Birdsall / Photofusion; Figure 5.4 © Silke Wolff – Fotolia.com; Figure 5.5 © pirotehnik – Fotolia.com; Figure 6.1 © Darlyne A. Murawski / Getty Images; Figure 6.2 © Zsolt Bota Finna – Fotolia.com; Figure 6.4 © St Bartholomew's Hospital, London/Science Photo Library; Figure 6.5 © Adam Gault/Science Photo Library; Figure 7.1 © Paula Solloway / Photofusion; Figure 7.2 © Roman Milert / Fotolia.com; Figure 9.3 © jscreationzs / Fotolia.com; Figure 9.6 © FPA (www.fpa.org.uk); Figure 10.2 © Jacek Chabraszewski / Fotolia.com; Figure 10.3 © Peter Atkins / Fotolia.com; Figure 10.5 © Brian Jackson / Alamy; Figure 11.1 © Dmytro Panchenko / Fotolia.com.

Author biographies

Tina Marshall started her career as an auxiliary nurse in a large psychiatric institution. She worked for several nursing agencies prior to working for an NHS trust where she qualified as an assessor and verifier. Tina has worked in many settings within the NHS and private sectors. Tina moved into education five years ago, managing NVQs and curriculum delivery. At present she project manages the e-learning training for the South West NHS based at Somerset College.

Layla Baker is Subject Leader in Health and Social Care and Lead for a range of courses at Levels 1, 2, and 3 and in Higher Education. She has extensive experience across Further Education, Higher Education, and School settings. Layla has a BA in Social Policy, Masters in Health Service Studies, PGCE in Post 16 Education, QTS and is currently studying for a Masters in Teaching and Education. She is an established textbook author as well as well as having produced learning materials for Age UK.

Cathy Spencer has many years experience of working as a qualified social worker with people with learning disabilities and autistic spectrum conditions. She has an MA in Applied Social Studies and a practice teacher/assessor qualification and has had extensive involvement in social work training. She worked from the outset on the development and implementation of the first national qualifications designed specifically for workers supporting people with learning disabilities, which form the basis of the current Level 2 and 3 Awards in Supporting Individuals with Learning Disabilities. Cathy has been employed as a consultant by Skills for Care and Skills for Care and Development to work on the revision of the awards, as well as on other projects such as common induction standards and the Diplomas in Commissioning, Procurement and Contracting for Care Services. She is currently working as a disability advisor at Sheffield Hallam University.

Walkthrough

We want you to succeed!

This book has been designed to include all the topic knowledge, assessment support and practical advice you will need for the following qualifications:

- Level 2 Award in Learning Disabilities
- Level 2 Certificate in Learning Disabilities
- Level 3 Award in Learning Disabilities
- Level 3 Certificate in Learning Disabilities

The book has been written with the work-based learner in mind. Everything in it reflects the assessment criteria and evidence based approach that is applied to this vocational qualification.

In the pages that follow you will find up-to-date resource material which will develop your knowledge, rehearse your skills and help you to gain your qualification.

Prepare for what you are going to cover in this unit, and prepare for assessment:

The reading and activities in this chapter will help you to

- Understand the importance of good hygiene
- Know how to encourage an individual to maintain personal hygiene
- Know how to support an individual to maintain personal hygiene

Reinforce concepts with hands-on learning and generate evidence for assignments

Time to reflect

 LD 201 1.3

Recall a situation when family and friends have assisted in the individual's care. What went well? What did not go so well? What could have been done differently? What benefit was person-centred thinking and planning to the situation?

Evidence activity LD 201

 1.5 Write a one-page profile to illustrate what is important for you, what people admire about you and how you would like to be supported.

Reinforce concepts with hands-on learning and generate evidence for assignments

Research and investigate

 LD 201 2.3

Read again about the tools you can use in person-centred thinking and planning. Identify which tool would be most suitable for team working and which tool would be best for individuals. Clarify why you have chosen those two tools.

Case study

LD 308 7.2 **Freda**

Understand how your learning fits into real life and your working environment

Freda has received a letter from the doctors informing her that she needs to go for a mammogram; but Freda cannot read. There were also some leaflets giving information about the procedure.

Write about how you would support Freda, identify different formats available to aid Freda's understanding of the process and where you could get these from.

Key terms

Check new words and what they mean

Preferences relates to choices, allowing the individual to express how they would like things done, in what order and the process of events.

You've just covered a whole unit so here's a guide to what assessors will be looking for and links to activities that can help impress them

Assessment Summary for Unit LD 206

To achieve the unit, your assessor will require you to:

Learning outcomes	Assessment criteria
1 Understand the importance of good personal hygiene	**1.1** Explain why personal hygiene is important See Evidence activity 1.1, p. 105.
	1.2 Describe the effects of poor personal hygiene on health and well-being See time to reflect 1.2, p. 106.

Supporting individuals with learning disabilities

Unit LD 201 Understand the context of supporting individuals with learning disabilities

What are you finding out?

According to **mencap** there are around 1.5 million people who have a learning disability within the United Kingdom. Due to advances in health and social care and the fact that people are living longer, this figure is due to increase. One of the biggest problems for people who have learning disabilities is that other people generally don't understand what it means for someone to have a learning disability. A learning disability is not an illness or a disease, and it is not always possible to tell if a person has a learning disability. Having a learning disability does not mean a person has mental health problems; however, some people who have a learning disability may develop mental health problems as a result of inadequate care and discrimination.

Learning disability is not what defines a person. It is merely a label used to diagnose people who have a learning disability. People with learning disabilities are all individuals with the right to the same life chances as other people. These people are individuals just like you and me.

The reading and activities in this chapter will help you to:

- Understand the legislation and policies that support the human rights and inclusion of individuals with learning disabilities

- Understand the nature and characteristics of learning disability

- Understand the historical context of learning disability

- Understand the basic principles and practice of advocacy, empowerment and active participation in relation to supporting individuals with learning disabilities and their families

- Understand how views and attitudes impact on the lives of individuals with learning disabilities and their family carers

- Know how to promote communication with individuals with learning disabilities

Key terms

Mencap is the leading UK charity for people who have a learning disability and their families.

LO1 Understand the legislation and policies that support the human rights and inclusion of individuals with learning disabilities

 1.1 Identify legislation and policies that are designed to promote the human rights, inclusion, equal life chances and citizenship of individuals with learning disabilities

Most of the laws which concern people who have a learning disability also apply to other people. The main laws that are likely to make a difference to the lives of people who have learning disabilities are concerned with promoting:

- human rights
- anti-discriminatory behaviour
- equality
- inclusion citizenship.

Key terms

Citizenship relates to being a citizen of a particular community with the duties, rights and privileges of this status.

Equality relates to being equal, especially of having the same political, social and economic rights.

Inclusion is a state of being free from exclusion.

Legislation aimed at promoting the human rights, inclusion, equal life chances and citizenship of individuals with learning disabilities include:

- The Human Rights Act 1998
- The Disability Discrimination Act 1995
- The Mental Capacity Act 2005
- The Equality Act 2010.

Valuing People Now is the UK Government's strategy for making the lives of people with learning disabilities and their families better by improving services. In particular, the strategy aims to make significant improvements in giving adults who have learning disabilities more choice and control over their lives through person-centred planning, advocacy and direct payments. You can find out more about Valuing People Now at www.valuingpeoplenow.dh.gov.uk.

Key terms

The **direct payments scheme** is a UK government initiative in the field of Social Services that gives service users money directly to pay for their own care, rather than through the traditional route of a Local Government Authority providing care for them.

Person-centred planning is a process of life planning for individuals, based around the principles of inclusion and the social model of disability.

Organisations that provide support for people who have learning disabilities should have policies in place which aim to reinforce this legislation. These policies set out the guidelines that all health and social care workers have to adhere to in order to ensure people who have learning disabilities are given the same opportunities as any other member of society.

Evidence activity

1.1 Legislation and policies that are designed to promote the rights of individuals who have learning disabilities

This activity allows you to demonstrate your knowledge of the legislation and policies that are designed to promote the human rights, inclusion, equal life chances and citizenship of individuals who have learning disabilities.

Take a look at the policies within your place of work and make a note of any policies which promote human rights, inclusion, equal life chances and citizenship for the service users for whom you provide support.

How do the policies support these aspects of a person's life?

1.2 **Explain how legislation and policies influence the day-to-day experiences of individuals with learning disabilities and their families**

Policies are drawn up in line with current legislation. Policies can be drawn up nationally at governmental level and also locally at an organisational level. Policy makers can influence important decisions that affect people's everyday lives. We have already established that there are around 1.5 million people who have a learning disability in the UK, so all policies will affect these people in some way.

Policies should be based on the social model of disability, aimed at empowering people. People who have a learning disability are the experts in their own lives and their views are an essential part of any evidence base. Involving these people throughout the process of policy development will help identify gaps in knowledge and give an indication of whether the policy will work in the short and long term. Understanding the perspective, needs and priorities of people who have learning disabilities will help in the development of better policies and the delivery of effective services.

Evidence activity LD 201

1.2 **How legislation and policies influence the day-to-day experiences of individuals who have learning disabilities and their families**

This activity allows you to demonstrate your knowledge of the legislation and policies that influence the day-to-day experiences of individuals with learning disabilities and their families.

Think about the legislation and policies that are relevant to the people you support. How do legislation and associated policies influence the day-to-day experiences of these people and their families?

LO2 Understand the nature and characteristics of learning disability

2.1 **Explain what is meant by 'learning disability'**

Research and investigate

2.1 What is a learning disability

Think about the service users you support. How would you define their learning disability?

Defining the term 'learning disability' is not easy, because it does not have clear-cut edges. No two people have the same level of 'ability' in the way they learn, and every person's experience of their learning disability will be individual to them.

In medical terms learning disabilities are known as **neurological disorders**. In simple terms, a learning disability may result when a person's brain development is affected, either before they are born, during their birth or in early childhood.

Key terms

Neurological disorders are disorders of the brain.

Learning disabilities are lifelong conditions that cannot be cured, and they can have a significant impact on the person's life. People with learning disabilities find it harder than other people to learn, understand and communicate. Some people with a mild learning disability may be able to communicate effectively and look after themselves, but may take a bit longer than usual to learn new skills. Others may not be able to communicate at all and may also have more than one disability. You may have heard a person's learning disability described as mild, moderate, severe or profound. If you hear these terms being used, it is important to remember that they are not separate compartments, they are simply stages along the scale of ability/disability.

mild

moderate

severe

profound

1.1 Continuum of ability/disability

Evidence activity LD 201

2.1 Explain what is meant by 'learning disability'

This activity allows you to demonstrate your knowledge of what is meant by the term 'learning disability'.

How would you explain what the term 'learning disability' means to a new member of staff within your organisation?

2.2 Give examples of causes of learning disabilities

Learning disabilities are caused by the way the brain develops, either before, during or after birth. There are several factors that can affect the development of the brain.

Before birth (pre-natal)

- Causes affecting the mother, for example rubella (German measles), excessive intake of alcohol, tobacco, recreational drugs and listeria (food poisoning).

- A child can also be born with a learning disability if certain genes are passed on by a parent. This is called an inherited learning disability. The two most common causes of inherited learning disability are Fragile X syndrome and Down's syndrome. Fragile X syndrome and Down's syndrome are not learning disabilities, but people who have either condition are likely to have a learning disability too. Fragile X syndrome is the most common cause of inherited learning disability, but not all people with Fragile X syndrome have a learning disability. All people who have Down's syndrome have some kind of learning disability.

During birth (peri-natal)

- The most common cause includes problems during the birth that stop enough oxygen getting to the brain.

Evidence activity LD 201

2.2 Causes of learning disabilities

This activity allows you to demonstrate your knowledge of the causes of learning disabilities.

Think about the service users you are supporting at the moment and, whilst respecting confidentiality, using any information that is available to you, identify the cause of their learning disabilities. Where on the continuum of learning disabilities do your service users sit?

After birth (post-natal) or during childhood

- Illness, such as meningitis, or injury in early childhood.

Sometimes there is no known cause for a learning disability. There is a lot of information about particular syndromes and conditions. Check out the useful weblinks at the end of this chapter.

2.3 Describe the medical and social models of disability

Time to reflect

2.3 How do you feel about disability?

It is important at this stage to examine how you feel about people who have a disability.

Think about the assumptions that are commonly made about people who have a disability in general. In a few words, what would you say are common assumptions often made about this section of the population? For example, would you say 'they need help?' or would you say you 'feel sorry for them?' or would you say 'people are disabled because of their environment?'.

You should not have relationships, you will never have a job, you are ill, you cannot do anything, you do not need an education, you can't walk properly, you need help

You can't play sport, you need carers

1.2 The medical model of disability

Models of disability provide a framework for understanding the way in which people with impairments experience their disability. It is commonly accepted that there are two contrasting models of disability within our society. These are known as the 'medical model' and the 'social model'.

The medical model views the person who has a disability as the problem. This model holds the belief that the person who has a disability should adapt to fit in with society. If the person cannot fit in with society then it is their problem. The emphasis is on dependence which is backed up by the stereotypes of disability that lend themselves to pity, fear and patronising attitudes. The main focus is on the disability rather than the person.

The medical model highlights that people who are disabled cannot participate in society because their disability prevents them from doing so.

The social model of disability was developed with the input of people who have a disability. Instead of emphasising the disability, the social model centralises the person. It emphasises dignity, independence, choice and privacy.

This model makes an important distinction between impairment and disability.

Impairment is seen as something not working properly with part of the body, mind or senses, for example, a person may have a physical impairment, a sensory impairment or a learning impairment.

Disability occurs when a person is excluded by society, because of their impairment, from something that other people in society take for granted. That might be the chance to attend an event, access a service or get involved in an activity. The exclusion may affect a person's choices to live independently, to earn a living, to be kept informed, or just to make choices for themselves.

The social model of disability says that disabilities are created by barriers in society. These barriers generally fall into three categories, these are:

- The environment – including inaccessible buildings and services.
- Attitudes – including discrimination, prejudice and stereotyping.
- Organisations – including inflexible policies, practices and procedures.

Some people wrongly assume that the impairment causes the disability. However, the social model believes that it is the choices society makes that creates the disability. If things are organised differently, these people are suddenly enabled – though their impairment hasn't changed.

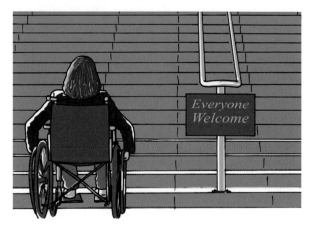

Everyone Welcome

1.3 The social model of disability

Evidence activity LD 201

2.3 The medical and social models of disability

This activity allows you to demonstrate your knowledge of the medical and social models of disability.

Look at the assumptions you made within the Time to reflect box. Would you say your beliefs support the medical model of disability or the social model of disability?

Take a look at the environment in which you work – are there any aspects of the environment that could disable a person? If so, what changes could be made to make the environment more enabling?

Evidence activity LD 201

2.4 The proportion of individuals with a learning disability for whom the cause is not known

This activity allows you to demonstrate your knowledge of the approximate proportion of individuals who have a learning disability for whom the cause is not known.

Think about the service users you support. Do any of them have a learning disability for which the cause has never been identified? How do your findings compare to those identified by BILD?

2.4 State the approximate proportion of individuals with a learning disability for whom the cause is 'not known'

There are a number of reasons for finding out the cause of a person's learning disability. Firstly, individuals and their families want to know and also have a right to know. There are also health factors as some forms of learning disability or syndromes can increase the likelihood of certain health problems occurring. Genetic counselling may also be required both for the family and for the person with the learning disability, especially where there is a wish to start a family.

We have identified some of the causes of learning disability within section 2.2. However, the British Institute of Learning Disabilities (BILD) identifies that amongst people who have a mild learning disability, in about 50 per cent of cases no cause has been identified. In people who have severe or profound learning disabilities, cases which are of unknown cause are fewer, but still high at around 25 per cent.

2.5 Describe the possible impact on a family of having a member with a learning disability

Over 60 per cent of people with learning disabilities live with family carers who often make sacrifices in their own lives in order to support the person.

Family members who provide care for those with a learning disability can suffer immense emotional and physical strain, and respite from their role can be made difficult by the adverse effects it can have on the person they are caring for.

While every family can have stresses and strains, these are very often exacerbated in families where a member of the family has a learning disability. Depending on the family members, the amount of support they receive, and the person who has the learning disability, this can impact on every aspect of the families' needs, including economic needs, domestic needs, healthcare needs, relationship needs and self-identity needs. This can also impact on other aspects of family life leading to significant extra costs and complications.

A child who does not have a learning disability will usually mature and become more independent, eventually leaving the family home. A child with a learning disability, however, may not follow this pattern, and is more likely to remain within the family home into adulthood. This person may also require prolonged periods of intensive care. This could impact upon everyday occurrences such as family outings, which could become complicated or even impossible.

LO3 Understand the historical context of learning disability

3.1 Explain the types of services that have been provided for individuals with learning disabilities over time

Little is written about the lives of people with learning disabilities before the eighteenth century. There are however references to 'village idiots'. It is thought that these people represent a small minority of the people we would describe today as having a learning disability. Literacy skills were less in demand than labouring skills, so mild learning disabilities would easily go unnoticed.

The Poor Laws of 1834 led to the building of purpose built institutions called 'asylums' to house people described as 'mad' or 'mentally weak'. These were workhouses with harsh and rigid regimes, and contained many people who had learning disabilities. These people had little choice and were not valued as people. The asylums became overcrowded, and conditions worsened as attitudes changed and the people who were housed there began to be regarded as dangerous and a drain on society.

The development of institutions continued into the early 20th century, though the purpose of moving people to institutions changed. Laws were passed that encouraged the building of schools for 'mentally disabled' children, and in 1908 the Radner Commission stated that: 'Feeble-mindedness is largely inherited'. It was suggested that such people were genetically inferior and needed to be segregated from the rest of society.

1.4 Institutionalisation

The 1913 Mental Deficiency Act stated that any person admitted to an institution had to be certified as 'mentally defective'. The institutions were now renamed 'colonies', and their purpose was to separate their residents from society. In 1929, the Wood Committee suggested that such people were a threat to society.

During the periods between the two World Wars, the numbers of people admitted to institutions increased. Laws were passed to further segregate all people who had learning disabilities and their families from the rest of society. Proposals were introduced to round up and separate all families of 'feeble minded people', including 'insane, epileptics and drunks', to name but a few.

It was suggested that such people would 'take over' and 'infect' others and that a 'racial disaster' would ensue. Cyril Birt was a member of the Eugenics Society, a group that believed there was a problem of 'degeneracy' in society and that there was a need to separate those with learning disabilities, keeping men and women apart so they would not procreate. History shows that the theories of eugenics have justified many atrocities committed against people with a learning disability and the mentally ill, as well as the millions of victims of the Holocaust.

Fortunately, this country drew back from such unthinkable measures. However, this ideology continued to affect the huge numbers of people admitted to institutions right up until the late 1980s. In the 1930s, the IQ test was introduced – people scoring low on the test were categorised as 'mentally defective' and unable to learn.

The introduction of the National Health Service in 1946 and the development of the medical model of disability had an impact. The term 'mentally handicapped' came into use, and the 'institutions' turned overnight into hospitals, with the emphasis now on caring for their residents. Society had moved from seeing the 'mentally handicapped' as dangerous and degenerate to viewing them more sympathetically, as people in need of treatment, although still a drain on the public purse. People with a learning disability remained segregated and isolated, and the standard of care was extremely poor. This remained the case right up until the closure of the long-stay hospitals.

In 1959, the Mental Health Act began the idea that some people might not need to be cared for in a hospital. It was also the first time that people with a 'mental illness' were distinguished from those described as having a 'mental handicap'.

In 1967, national newspapers started to draw attention to the bad conditions in 'mental handicap' hospitals. In 1971, the Government published a paper, 'Better services for the Mentally Handicapped', in response to continued reports about appalling conditions in the hospitals. This paper laid the foundations for 'Care in the Community', with the expectation that half of the people in hospitals should be living in the local community by 1990.

During the 1980s, the concept of 'normalisation' began to influence the delivery of care for people who had a learning disability. Normalisation theory emphasises the 'value of the individual', their right to choice and opportunity, and the right to any extra support they need to fulfil their potential. At this time there was also recognition that institutions were a major barrier to inclusion.

The idea that everyone in society has the right to a life with choice, opportunity and respect, with extra support according to their needs, helped to change the way services were planned and delivered. The National Health Service and Community Care Act 1990 recognised the right of disabled people to be an equal part of society, with access to the necessary support.

We might like to believe that the task of de-institutionalising the care of people with a learning disability is now complete. Nearly all the long-stay hospitals are now closed, and many rights are now law as detailed in the Disability Discrimination Act.

However, the reality is that many people are still denied the things that most people take for granted, such as a decent income, somewhere appropriate to live, the chance to work, leisure opportunities and choices in education.

Evidence activity LD 201

 3.1 The types of services that have been provided for individuals with learning disabilities over time

This activity allows you to demonstrate your knowledge of the types of services that have been provided for individuals with learning disabilities over time.

Find out about the history of your service users. Were any of them 'cared for' within an institution?

Make a note of the differences between the care that was provided within institutions and the support provided by your organisation.

Today's services aim to enable people and promote equal treatment and inclusion. This brings with it new challenges and responsibilities, the greatest of which is to change public attitudes towards people with a learning disability and raise understanding.

www.mencap.org.uk

3.2 Describe how past ways of working may affect present services

People who have worked in health and social care for some time may remember some of the institutions, and may have indeed worked in them. Some health and social care workers may therefore have adopted the medical model approach to disability. This will, without a shadow of a doubt, affect the care and support that these health and social care workers are delivering.

3.2 How past ways of working may affect present services

This activity allows you to demonstrate your knowledge of how past ways of working may affect present services.

How do you think past ways of working may affect present ways of working?

3.3 Identify some of the key changes in the lives of individuals who have learning disabilities

There have been major key changes in the lives of individuals who have a learning disability. We have already discussed the institutionalised medical model approach to care and support. Person-centred planning has generally led to positive changes for people who have learning disabilities. However, mencap report that people who have a learning disability are still treated differently.

Where people live

There have been major changes in the living arrangements of people who have a learning disability. With a move away from an institutionalised approach to care, more people are being empowered to maintain their independence for as long as possible. Whilst over 60 per cent of people who have a learning disability live with their family, there are also a significant number of people who maintain their independence within their community through supported living.

Daytime activities

With the introduction of self-directed support, service users are able to make choices about where they go and what they want to do during the day time. Self-directed support should enable service users to decide:

- how to live their lives
- where to live and who with
- what to do during the day
- how to spend their leisure time

- what to spend money on
- who they are friends with.

Employment

Mencap report that only 1 in 10 people who have a learning disability are in employment. They are more excluded from the workplace than any other group of disabled people. Where they do work, it is often for low pay and part-time hours. Research shows that 65 per cent of people with a learning disability want to work, and that they make highly valued employees when given the right support.

Research and investigate

 3.3 Why?

Using any information that is available to you, take a look at why people who have a learning disability find it difficult to get paid work.

Sexual relationships and parenthood

Discussions surrounding sexuality are uncomfortable for 'able bodied' people. This is a very private area of a person's life and one which we choose not to discuss openly. It is now recognised that people who have learning disabilities also have sexual feelings and may want to engage in close personal relationships. Some organisations run courses for people who have learning disabilities where they are taught about social and personal development. Because people with learning disabilities are a vulnerable group of people there are many aspects that need to be considered to ensure any relationship remains a safe and healthy relationship.

All too often support services start with the belief that people who have a learning disability won't make good parents and that their children should be taken away. Mencap also identify that this is backed up by research that shows that 40 per cent of parents who have a learning disability do not live with their children. Not all parents with a learning disability can look after their own children and the welfare of the child is essential. However, if parents who have a learning disability are provided with adequate support, they should be able to keep their children.

Case study

 (3.3) Frank

Frank is a young man who has learning disabilities. He confides in his support worker about the difficulties he is having with his girlfriend. Frank and his girlfriend (who also has learning disabilities) want to have sexual intercourse but they are unsure about 'safer sex'. The worker advises them of the different organisations that have up-to-date information in user friendly format that would provide them with some knowledge of 'safe sex'. The worker also advises them that these organisations can provide support and help in talking over the issues.

What responsibility does the support worker have at this stage?

What responsibility does the person with learning disabilities have?

Who else has responsibilities and what are they?

Provision of healthcare

People who have a learning disability generally experience poorer health and poorer healthcare than other members of the public. However, as we are well aware, these people have just as much of a right to receive good healthcare. They will need healthcare in the same way that everyone else will, and some people with a learning disability will have additional health needs (for example, people with a learning disability are more likely to have epilepsy). Often, they need more support to understand information about their health, to communicate symptoms and concerns, and to manage their health.

LO4 Understand the basic principles and practice of advocacy, empowerment and active participation in relation to supporting individuals with learning disabilities and their families

4.1 Explain the meaning of the term 'social inclusion'

The term 'social inclusion' has come to replace older terminology, such as 'community development work'. In practical terms, social inclusion means working within the community to tackle and avoid circumstances and problems that lead to social exclusion, such as poverty, unemployment or low income, housing problems and becoming housebound and isolated due to illness.

Historically, people with learning disabilities have faced poor life chances, largely due to social exclusion. They have not been accepted by mainstream society, facing stigmatisation, prejudice and even fear, and this has led to these people becoming socially excluded within society.

Promoting social inclusion is closely linked to empowering the individual. This means giving people with learning disabilities a voice, allowing them to make choices for themselves about the direction of their own life based on their wishes and aspirations.

Evidence activity LD 201

(3.3) Key changes in the lives of individuals who have learning disabilities

This activity allows you to demonstrate your knowledge of key changes in the lives of individuals who have learning disabilities.

Make a poster which identifies the key changes in the lives of people who have learning disabilities. The poster should take into account where people live, daytime activities, employment, sexual relationships and parenthood and the provision of healthcare.

1.5 Social inclusion

4.2 Explain the meaning of the term 'advocacy'

The term 'advocacy' is concerned with 'speaking up for, or acting on behalf of, yourself or another person'. The other person is often receiving a service from a statutory or voluntary organisation. Some people require the assistance of an advocate because they are not clear about their rights as citizens, or have difficulty in fully understanding these rights. Other people may find it difficult to speak up for themselves. Advocacy can enable people to take more responsibility and control for the decisions which affect their lives.

Advocacy can help service users to:

- make their own views and wishes known
- express and present their views
- obtain independent advice and accurate information
- negotiate and resolve conflict.

4.3 Describe different types of advocacy

All people are very different from each other. Their needs for support are different, and may also change at different stages throughout their life. All advocacy types are of equal value. Which type of advocacy is used, and when, should depend on what is best suited to the person who seeks it. A single person may ask for different types of advocacy support at different times in their life.

What is essential to all types of advocacy is that it is the person who has a learning disability who is always at the centre of the advocacy process. Advocacy can therefore be described as a process which is personcentred. It is about the person's needs, what that person wants, and finding the best way of getting that across to the people who need to know.

Advocacy can be likened to a box of tools. Different types of advocacy can be used together or they can be used separately depending on the job that needs to be done.

Professional advocacy

Professional advocacy is frequently described as the 'case-work' model. It is used for short to medium term involvement, which often supports people in finding a solution to a problem. Professional advocacy may be required where an individual requires support with issues requiring specific expertise, for example child protection, education, housing, employment and financial matters.

Citizen advocacy

The advocate in this relationship is usually called the 'citizen advocate', and the person receiving the service is called the 'advocacy partner'. An advocacy partner is someone at risk of having choices, wishes and decisions ignored, and who needs help in making them known and making sure they are responded to. A citizen advocate is a person who volunteers to speak up for and support an advocacy partner and is not paid to do so. The citizen advocate is unpaid and independent of service providers and families and is a member of the local community. The advocacy relationship is based on trust and confidentiality.

Crisis advocacy

Crisis advocacy provides support that aims to give the person a voice in a situation that requires a quick response. It is usually short term and aimed at helping the individual solve a problem.

Peer advocacy

Peer advocacy is usually provided by a person who has experienced a similar situation. It is based on the fact that people who have experienced the same things feel they have a better understanding and can be more supportive. In the past, peer advocacy occurred when people with learning disabilities lived in isolated hospitals. They were often separated from others in their community and only had each other for company. There was no one else to speak up for them other than their fellow peers. As people with learning disabilities began to learn more about their rights and the obligations of citizenship, more of them began to speak up for each other. Peer advocacy is often of great support to an individual but is not recognised as being independent or unbiased.

Self advocacy

Self advocacy is what most of us do most of the time. It is about speaking up for yourself. This type of advocacy should always be encouraged wherever possible. Many people who have learning disabilities have a good ability to speak up for themselves. However, they sometimes find it hard to get others to accept this or even to listen to them. Self advocacy groups are a good way to encourage this. Self advocacy groups are run by people who have learning disabilities. These are often groups of people who use services or have the same interests locally. They work together to

make sure they have a say in how those services are run. Self advocacy groups are a very good way for people to support each other and they can help to build confidence so that people feel more able to speak up for themselves.

Time to reflect

4.3 Self advocacy

How do you enable your service users to self advocate?

1.6 Self advocacy

Legal advocacy

As the name suggests, legal advocacy is concerned with using the services of a lawyer or ombudsman to support an individual with specific legal issues.

Evidence activity   LD 201

4.3 Different types of advocacy

This activity allows you to demonstrate your knowledge of the different types of advocacy.

Give examples to demonstrate times that the different types of advocacy have been used within your organisation.

4.4 Describe ways to build empowerment and active participation into everyday support with individuals with learning disabilities

Empowerment is a word we hear a lot, and has become an important aspect of delivering health and social care services. Empowerment for people with learning disabilities is the process by which individuals develop increased skills to make decisions and take control over their lives. This helps individuals to achieve their goals and aspirations, thus maximising their quality of life.

A key feature in empowering people is giving them a voice and actively listening to what they have to say. Empowerment is, therefore, closely linked to the concept of person-centred care and various forms of advocacy.

For the person who has a learning disability, the subjective experience of empowerment is about rights, choice and control which can lead them to a more **autonomous** lifestyle. For the health and social care worker, it is about anti-oppressive practice, balancing rights and responsibilities and supporting choice and empowerment whilst maintaining safe and ethical practice.

Key terms

Autonomous means independent, not controlled by others.

Person-centred planning places the individual at the centre of all processes and uses techniques to ensure meaningful participation is key to empowering individuals in this way.

LO5 Understand how views and attitudes impact on the lives of individuals with learning disabilities and their family carers

5.1 Explain how attitudes are changing in relation to individuals with learning disabilities

People who have a learning disability and their families have always been affected by the way they are viewed and treated by society. Sadly, the history of public and private attitudes to learning disability over time has been one of intolerance and lack of understanding.

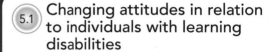

Evidence activity — LD 201

5.1 Changing attitudes in relation to individuals with learning disabilities

This activity allows you to demonstrate your knowledge of how attitudes are changing in relation to individuals with learning disabilities. We have already established that attitudes towards people who have learning disabilities have changed over time. With a move away from institutionalisation and an emphasis on inclusion, today's services aim to enable people who have learning disabilities, and promote equal treatment and inclusion.

Why do you think attitudes towards people who have a learning disability are changing?

Evidence activity — LD 201

4.4 Building empowerment and active participation into everyday support

This activity allows you to demonstrate your knowledge of the ways to build empowerment and active participation into everyday support with individuals who have learning disabilities.

Explain the processes that are in place within your organisation to ensure the people you support are empowered and enabled to actively participate in decisions on a daily basis.

5.2 Give examples of positive and negative aspects of being labelled as having a learning disability

The way people with learning disabilities have been portrayed has often been with a 'label'. Terms like 'the mentally handicapped', 'the blind' and 'the mentally ill' place the person in a group which risks a stereotypical view. Being labelled as 'disabled' and 'inadequate' also creates barriers to things that 'able-bodied' people enjoy and take for granted, for example, relationships, employment, education, housing, transport and many more. In addition, it perpetuates **prejudice** and **discrimination**. Anti-discriminatory legislation is helping to remove barriers and shake off negative attitudes and discrimination, but there is still a long way to go.

In some respects, it is important to apply a 'label' to a certain condition as this will ensure the person who has a learning disability is given any support and care that is required to ensure they lead a good quality of life. It is the type of label that is applied that makes all the difference.

Key terms

Discrimination is the acting out of negative prejudices.

A **label** is a 'tag' that we use to describe someone and is usually based on their appearance and behaviour.

A **prejudice** is an attitude or way of thinking based on an unfair pre-judgement of a person, rather than on a factual assessment.

The most important aspect to remember, with any label, is that the person is an individual with individual needs. This sometimes tends to be forgotten. If this view is not upheld, the more profound perception of the disability will result. Using the right positive language goes a long way to defining people with a learning disability as a person first.

5.3 Describe steps that can be taken to promote positive attitudes towards individuals with learning disabilities and their family carers

It is now accepted that the way people are portrayed within the media can greatly influence public perception and attitude. The recognition of the social model of disability has gone a long way in changing the attitudes of health and social care workers towards people who have learning disabilities and recognising that the person comes first.

Some employers undertake disability awareness training as part of their general staff training programmes, and this can go a long way in changing attitudes towards people who have learning disabilities.

More people who have learning disabilities are now using mainstream community facilities, such as colleges, hospitals, libraries and leisure centres. This sends out a clear message that segregation is no longer acceptable but more could be done to ensure that people are positively welcomed and included.

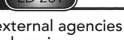
5.4 Explain the roles of external agencies and others in changing attitudes, policy and practice

External agencies have an important role in facilitating changes in attitude, policy and practice. For example, support groups such as the Learning Disability Coalition, who are a group who represent 14 learning disability organisations and over 140 supporter organisations who have come together to form one group with one voice.

They believe that people with a learning disability have the right to live independent lives, with the support that they need. Their aim is to ensure the government provides enough money so that people with a learning disability have the same choices and chances as everyone else. They do this by:

- Providing a unified voice to government and other key decision-makers.
- Gathering evidence on cuts to services at local level.
- Raising awareness of the financial pressures on services for people with learning disabilities, and campaigning for better funding.
- Achieving an evidence-based assessment of the long-term resource requirements for people with learning disabilities.

www.learningdisabilitycoalition.org.uk

LO6 Know how to promote communication with individuals with learning disabilities

6.1 **Identify ways of adapting verbal and non-verbal communication when communicating with individuals who have learning disabilities**

Communication is a two way process in which messages are sent, received and understood between people or groups of people. It is a basic human right upon which we build relationships, make friends and control our existence. It is the way we become independent and make choices. It is the way we learn and express our thoughts, feelings and emotions. The British Institute of Learning Disabilities (BILD) estimates that between 50 and 90 per cent of people who have learning difficulties also experience difficulties with communication. People who have learning disabilities do not have one recognised tool to help them communicate and every person is different. It is therefore essential that an assessment is undertaken to ensure effective methods of communication are identified for each individual person.

Generally, people in societies develop common languages in order that they can live together with a shared method of communication. In fact, communication is fundamental to being a part of society.

People who find it difficult to communicate, or are undervalued in their societies, will automatically feel excluded unless those around them are prepared to adapt their method of communication. Effective communication is therefore essential in order to promote the principles associated with independence, choice, rights and inclusion.

1.7 Accessible communication

Methods of communication vary and can either be verbal or non-verbal. A high percentage of communication is non-verbal.

- When communicating verbally it is important not to overestimate language skills. Equally it is important that the pace of communication is consistent with the person's level of understanding.
- Objects, pictures, signs and symbols are all powerful ways of communicating meaning.
- British sign language (BSL) has long been established as a language used by people who have a hearing impairment.
- Braille enables people who have a visual impairment to be able to read.
- People with more complex learning disabilities may not be able to use any recognised means of communication and will therefore be dependent on others to interpret their needs and choices through observation and response to their communicative behaviour.

6.2 Explain why it is important to use language that is both 'age appropriate' and 'ability appropriate' when communicating with individuals with learning disabilities

When communicating with people who have a learning disability, it is essential that the communication takes place at a pace and in a manner that the individual can process. This means that the information should be both 'age appropriate' and 'ability appropriate'. Communication must also take into account the person as a whole and sensitive consideration should be given to the person's cultural and religious beliefs.

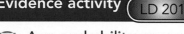

Evidence activity · LD 201

6.2 Age and ability appropriate language

This activity allows you to demonstrate your knowledge of the importance of using language that is both 'age and ability appropriate' when communicating with individuals who have learning disabilities.

Explain why it is important to use language that is both 'age appropriate' and 'ability appropriate'.

How do you ensure you take these factors into account when communicating with service users?

What could be a consequence of not taking these factors into consideration?

6.3 Describe ways of checking whether an individual has understood a communication, and how to address any misunderstandings

When communicating with a person who has a learning disability it is essential that the person understands what has been communicated. If the person has understood, this may be immediately obvious.

Within your role as a care worker you will want to help individuals communicate to the best of their ability and promote understanding of their needs and preferences whenever appropriate. However there will be times when you find that you are having difficulty with communication and you are unsure whether an individual has understood what you have communicated to them. Hopefully you will know your service users well, but it is also important to seek advice from a senior member of staff when misunderstandings occur. Individuals who are unable to successfully communicate with you, or understand what you are communicating to them, may become distressed.

The extent of the frustration and distress will vary from person to person but will be apparent through verbal communication, body language or facial expression.

Evidence activity LD 201

6.3 Checking understanding and addressing misunderstandings

This activity allows you to demonstrate your knowledge of the importance of checking whether an individual has understood communication and how you address any misunderstandings.

How do you check understanding when you are communicating with service users?

How do you address any misunderstandings as they arise?

Assessment summary

Your reading of this chapter and completion of the activities will have prepared you to demonstrate your learning and understanding of supporting individuals who have a learning disability in your workplace. To achieve the unit, your assessor will require you to:

Learning outcomes	Assessment criteria
1 Understand the legislation and policies that support the human rights and inclusion of individuals with learning disabilities by:	**1.1** Identifying legislation and policies that are designed to promote the human rights, inclusion, equal life chances and citizenship of individuals with learning disabilities See Evidence activity 1.1, p. 2.
	1.2 Explaining how legislation and policies influence the day-to-day experiences of individuals with learning disabilities and their families. See Evidence activity 1.2, p. 3.
2 Understand the nature and characteristics of learning disability by:	**2.1** Explaining what is meant by 'learning disability' See Evidence activity 2.1, p. 4.
	2.2 Giving examples of causes of learning disabilities See Evidence activity 2.2, p. 4.
	2.3 Describing the medical and social models of disability See Evidence activity 2.3, p. 6.
	2.4 Stating the approximate proportion of individuals with a learning disability for whom the cause is 'not known' See Evidence activity 2.4, p. 6.
	2.5 Describing the possible impact on a family of having a member with a learning disability. See Evidence activity 2.5, p. 7.

Learning outcomes	Assessment criteria
3 Understand the historical context of learning disability by:	**(3.1)** Explaining the types of services that have been provided for individuals with learning disabilities over time See Evidence activity 3.1, p. 8.
	(3.2) Describing how past ways of working may affect present services See Evidence activity 3.2, p. 9.
	(3.3) Identifying some of the key changes in the lives of individuals who have learning disabilities in: a) where people live b) daytime activities c) employment d) sexual relationships and parenthood e) the provision of healthcare. See Evidence activity 3.3, p. 10.
4 Understand the basic principles and practice of advocacy, empowerment and active participation in relation to supporting individuals with learning disabilities and their families by:	**(4.1)** Explaining the meaning of the term 'social inclusion' See Evidence activity 4.1, p. 11.
	(4.2) Explaining the meaning of the term 'advocacy' See Evidence activity 4.2, p. 11.
	(4.3) Describing different types of advocacy See Evidence activity 4.3, p. 12.
	(4.4) Describing ways to build empowerment and active participation into everyday support with individuals with learning disabilities. See Evidence activity 4.4, p. 13.
5 Understand how views and attitudes impact on the lives of individuals with learning disabilities and their family carers by:	**(5.1)** Explaining how attitudes are changing in relation to individuals with learning disabilities See Evidence activity 5.1, p. 13.
	(5.2) Giving examples of positive and negative aspects of being labelled as having a learning disability See Evidence activity 5.2, p. 14.
	(5.3) Describing steps that can be taken to promote positive attitudes towards individuals with learning disabilities and their family carers See Evidence activity 5.3, p. 15.
	(5.4) Explaining the roles of external agencies and others in changing attitudes, policy and practice. See Evidence activity 5.4 p. 15.

Learning outcomes	Assessment criteria	
6 Know how to promote communication with individuals with learning disabilities by:	**6.1**	Identifying ways of adapting verbal and non-verbal communication when communicating with individuals who have learning disabilities See Evidence activity 6.1, p. 16.
	6.2	Explaining why it is important to use language that is both 'age appropriate' and 'ability appropriate' when communicating with individuals with learning disabilities See Evidence activity 6.2, p. 17.
	6.3	Describing ways of checking whether an individual has understood a communication, and how to address any misunderstandings. See Evidence activity 6.3, p. 17.

Weblinks

Office for Disability Issues	**www.officefordisability.gov.uk**
Understanding Individual Needs	**www.understandingindividualneeds.com**
About Learning Disabilities	**www.aboutlearningdisabilities.co.uk**
mencap	**www.mencap.org.uk**
Learning Disability Coalition	**www.learningdisabilitycoalition.org.uk**
The Foundation for People with Learning Difficulties	**www.learningdisabilities.org.uk**
Easyhealth	**www.easyhealth.org.uk**

Support person-centred thinking and planning

2

Unit LD 202 Support person-centred thinking and planning
Unit LD 302 Support person-centred thinking and planning

What are you finding out?

We are going to explore what person-centred planning and thinking means to you as the carer, to the individual, to their relatives and to outside agencies. We will identify the different tools available for implementation, their effectiveness and how they empower individuals.

To explore person-centred thinking and planning we need to know its origins, the legislation and the tools that enable us to implement the process effectively. We need to understand the importance of person-centred planning and identify how useful this tool is in helping us care for/assist the individual.

The reading and activities in this chapter will help you to:

• Understand the principles and practice of person-centred thinking, planning and reviews

• Understand the context within which person-centred thinking and planning takes place

• Understand own role in person-centred planning, thinking and reviews

• Be able to apply person-centred thinking in relation to own life

• Be able to implement person-centred thinking and person-centred reviews.

Key terms

Person-centred means allowing the individual to be the focus, and in control of, their care.

Person-centred caring is about identifying who the person really is, where we as carers fit into their lives, and what we are able to do together to improve their lives now and in the future.

In the past care plans were used to identify what care was needed to support the individual. The care planning approach made assumptions. It did not ask or involve the individual, or if it did it was only to inform them of what the carers were going to do.

The need for individuals to have control and become empowered is of the highest importance in achieving a good outcome. To do this we need to be clear on what they want to achieve. By doing this we value and reinforce their beliefs and include them in our society as equal members.

Key terms

Value can be defined as worth. In person-centred planning it is to demonstrate the importance of the individual.

Advocate means to act on behalf of the individual to support their wishes.

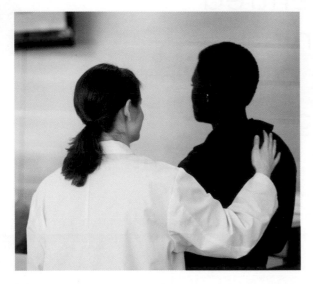

2.1 What is person-centred care?

choices heard is a human right (Human Rights Act 1998). With person-centred thinking and planning we are addressing their individual choices, needs and rights.

Person-centred thinking derives from the concept of the individual being at the centre of decisions and in control. Previously, care planning was often carried out without the individual being involved in the process. Professionals decided what was needed and the views of the individual or others involved in their care were not encouraged. Many care plans were templates and only slight adjustments were made for each individual. The care plans were often not communicated to the carers or support workers, leading to failure. Care plans were not individualised or agreed by the majority of people involved in caring for an individual and so frequently had little or no effect.

It was recognised that changes were needed. Person-centred planning was developed on the basis of empowering individuals with learning disabilities.

As individuals we can explain the difference between the old way of care planning by thinking of how we react to situations ourselves. If we are told to do something with no explanation as to why, we may be less likely to do it. If we are involved in the process of the task, and understand why we are being asked to do it, we are more likely to follow the instructions.

LO1 Understand the principles and practice of person-centred thinking, planning and reviews

1.1 **LD 202** **Identify the beliefs and values on which person-centred thinking and planning is based**

We are all aware of the concept individuals have of care, due to experience or media information. Try to recall your understanding of care before you started working in the sector. The role of the carer was seen as practical assistance, the need to help the individual with personal care and dietary needs. When we had this view, how much thought went into how this was to be achieved?

The history of care for those with any form of learning disability prior to the 1970s was unacceptable; the aim was to keep them out of sight and treat them as a lower class citizen. The development of community care and legislation has dramatically changed the way individuals are cared for.

The importance of the individual receiving the right care and being empowered to have their

Time to reflect

LD 202 **1.1**

Think about how you like to be treated in your everyday life. Imagine if it was your day off from work and you had decided to relax all day. Your parents or friends decide that you are going to do an extra shift. They have not discussed this with you and the first thing you know about it is when they enter your room at 6 am and start pulling you out of bed and preparing you for work. You would not be happy. Think how they could have done this in a manner that would be agreeable for you, as in person-centred thinking. Explain why this approach would be better.

1.3 **LD 302** **Explain how the beliefs and values on which person-centred thinking and planning is based**

Person-centred thinking originated in the 1950s from psychologist, counselor and theorist, Carl Rogers, who identified the need to assist individuals and that doing this required identifying their wishes, not those of the carer or institution. This concept was later developed in Canada and the USA by a group of individuals including Michael Smull, who refined the process due to the service response of disability care at that time.

A clear understanding of the individual having rights and abilities is at the core of their findings. The aim is to promote the individual's rights and enable them to live their life as they would want. Through this simple idea of individuals planning their own care, outcomes are easily achieved. Person-centred planning empowers individuals, ensures their rights and acknowledges support from others.

Belief is the idea that something is true and we have confidence and understanding in it, whilst value is a sense of worth. Therefore in person-centred thinking the belief is that to assist with an individual's care needs we need to clearly understand the individual's wishes and needs. We reinforce this by identifying the value of the individual's needs. This is done by involving the person, hence the title of person-centred, to clarify their thinking on the care they want and then identifying how we can put these wishes into practice.

Research and investigate

LD 302 **1.3**

Carry out research into the theories regarding person-centred thinking and planning and describe how these theories are put into practice in your workplace, emphasising the individual's beliefs and values.

1.2 **LD 202** **Define person-centred thinking, person-centred planning and person-centred reviews**

1.1 **LD 302** **Explain what person-centred thinking is, and how it relates to person-centred reviews and person-centred planning**

As we have established, person-centred thinking, planning and reviewing aims to empower the individual and increase the involvement of the individual and those they wish to help them in their journey. The medical model of care planning involved only professionals who were asked to proscribe the best way of assisting an individual. We all prefer to make our own decisions and be in control of our lives, to do as much as possible for ourselves and make our own dreams and ambitions. We will require support at times on this journey and as an adult we know who we could ask to support us.

Persons with learning disabilities have the same visions and aspirations, and have the right to be treated as an equal. With learning disabilities there may be many more obstacles than we would face to achieve our goals, which is why planning is required and support needs to be obtained. This still should be the individual's choice. As support workers we are the advocates for the people we support and need to ensure their rights are met. Person-centred thinking and planning puts the individual in the centre of their care and enables them to take charge of the direction they wish for their care to be delivered.

Evidence activity LD 202

1.2 In the table below, in each column list words that describe person-centred planning, person-centred thinking and person-centred reviews

Person-centred thinking	Person-centred planning	Person-centred reviews

Time to reflect

LD 302 **1.1**

Write down your experience of person-centred thinking, describing how this has assisted with person-centred planning and reviewing. What went well and what did not go so well?

1.3 **LD 202** ## Describe the difference that person-centred thinking can make to individuals and their families

1.2 **LD 302** ## Explain the benefits of using person-centred thinking with individuals

The need for the individual to be at the centre of their own planning appears obvious to us now and the more person-centred thinking and planning is used, the more the culture in how individuals are treated will change. The medical model of planning care and the lack of involvement for families and carers left the individual's family detached from the process and feelings of helplessness must have occurred. With person-centred thinking and planning the family and carers are seen as vital to ensuring that the ambitions of the individual can be achieved.

By taking this approach to care, other benefits can occur. An example of this would be when an individual has requested to go to church on Sunday; unfortunately a member of staff has phoned in sick and the home has reduced resources and cannot help the individual with their wishes. The individual becomes cross and frustrated and you as the support worker have a more difficult shift. By involving family and friends in their care, extra resources are available to the individual, reducing frustrations they may come across.

Time to reflect

LD 202 **1.3**

Recall a situation when family and friends have assisted in the individual's care. What went well? What did not go so well? What could have been done differently? What benefit was person-centred thinking and planning to the situation?

1.2 Review a person-centred care plan you have been involved in. Explain how the family/carers/friends were involved. Highlight their role in the process and list the benefits of their input.

1.4   LD 202   Describe examples of person-centred thinking tools

1.7   LD 302   Describe examples of person-centred thinking tools, their purpose, how and when each one might be used

To aid the process of person-centred thinking, planning and reviewing, tools have been developed to enable this process and record the information in a format that all can understand. These tools put the individual at the centre of the process and in the driving seat to progress the plan. There are four basic types of tool for person-centred thinking, planning and reviewing:

- Essential Lifestyle Planning
- PATH (planning alternative tomorrows with hope)
- MAPS (making action plans)
- Personal Futures Planning

Essential Life Planning

This approach identifies seven tools to plan person-centred thinking:

- **Sorting importance to/for**. This tool asks the individual what is important to them, to make them both happy and socially included. Contrasted against the environment they live in, restrictions, health and safety. From this guide and identifying any obstacles, you have a basis to clarify information you need to find out or support you need to gain for the individual to achieve their wants.
- **The doughnut sort**. This tool identifies roles and responsibilities for the individual and identifies different people involved in their care.
- **Matching staff**. This identifies skills in performing care, identifies any extra staff/carers/family members that may be needed and the role they will perform.
- **Relationship circle**. This identifies all the people involved with the individual, the support needed and the level of involvement from people that the individual requires.
- **Communication charts**. These identify the individual's preferred means of communicating and identify any frustrations or communication problems.

2.2 Tools have been developed to assist person-centred planning

- **Learning log**. The learning log identifies the development process, what has worked well for the individual, who has supported/visited and the impact that this has had, and also identifies things that have not gone so well.

- **Sorting what's working/ not working**. This tool clearly identifies what is working, to allow enhancement/maintenance of these aspects, and what is not working for the individual. It gives a clear picture of how things are for the individual at that moment in time.

PATH (Planning alternative tomorrows with hope)

The aim of this tool is to identify what the individual's goals are and steps to achieve them. This is broken into eight steps:

- **What are the goals/dreams?** This can be a long term or short term goal/dream.

- **First steps**. What small changes are needed to help the individual achieve their goal/dream?

- **Now**. Where are they now in relation to their goal/dream?

- **Enrol**. Who can help them achieve their goal/dream? The circle of support of family/friends/carers.

- **Keeping strong**. How are they being supported/responsibilities?

- **Action plan**. The full plan on how to achieve these goals and dreams.

- **Next steps**. The long term changes that need to be implemented.

- **First steps**. What small changes are needed to help them achieve their goal /dream?

2.3 MAPS can be drawn from different areas of an individual's life

2.4 Personal Futures Planning

MAPS (Making Action Plans)

Maps are pictures and are drawn from different areas of the individual's life, again in seven stages:

- **What is the individual's history?** The need to listen to past experiences, events that have occurred that have been a positive or negative influence on the individual.
- **The dream.** What the individual would like to happen/occur.
- **The nightmare.** Identifying the anxieties and obstacles in the way of achieving the dream.
- **Gifts and capacity.** Recognising their abilities, their strengths and achievements; this will then be a tool to help them achieve their goal.
- **Needs.** The need to identify what support and help the individual requires from others. Paid or unpaid support.
- **Action.** Action plan to achieve their individual care needs, a very simple plan clearly stating what, how, when and where.

Personal Futures Planning

The aim of this approach is to identify those that wish to be involved in helping the individual towards the future they want, their family, friends, and social contacts. Meetings are arranged at a suitable time for all who want to be involved and at a location suitable for all those attending. There are five steps to planning.

1. All involved recognise and share the individual's gifts and strengths.
2. All involved develop a common understanding of the future/dream for the individual.
3. The group agrees to meet and share ideas on how to achieve the dream.
4. This group identifies a champion who will advocate and organise.
5. At least one care deliverer is committed to supplying and implementing the dream.

This is not an exhaustive list of the tools available, just the main ones. With these tools it is easy to identify patterns and the need for person-centred thinking.

Evidence activity LD 202

1.4 From the list above, identify a person-centred tool that you use in your workplace and write a brief explanation of why you use this tool.

Research and investigate

LD 302 1.7 Models of dementia

Research the above person-centred tools and in the table below identify a scenario where you would use each tool.

Tool	Scenario
Essential Lifestyle Planning	
PATH (planning alternative tomorrows with hope)	
MAPS (making action plans)	
Personal Futures Planning	

1.4 LD 302 **Explain how the beliefs and values on which person-centred thinking and planning is based differs from assessment and other approaches to planning**

We have briefly discussed the other models of planning that have been used in the past, such as the medical model which looks at the symptoms and interventions needed. This created care planning which the carer or support worker would derive in isolation from the individual or any others involved in their care.

Case study

 LD 302 **1.4**

Joseph has learning disabilities and has been cared for in a shared house with six other residents, which has staffing input 24 hours a day. Joseph has lived here for four years and is very dependent on support with his daily living. Risk assessments have been completed and these identified that he cannot be left in the kitchen by himself. This assessment was completed on the medical model.

The main outcomes of the assessment were:

* Joseph needs to get up in time for breakfast and be washed and dressed in time for his medication, which cannot be taken on an empty stomach.
* Joseph is likely to have seizures and therefore cannot go out without a support worker.
* Joseph has eczema and requires bathing in emollient at least twice a week.

Write an account of the difference person-centred planning could offer Joseph from this medical model.

1.5 **LD 202** **Explain what a 'one-page profile' is**

1.8 **LD 302** **Explain the different ways that one page profiles are used**

A one-page profile should consist of all the things that are important to the individual. The one-page profile should include details of how the individual likes to be supported, what other people like about them and what makes the individual really happy.

Evidence activity

LD 202

 1.5 Write a one-page profile to illustrate what is important for you, what people admire about you and how you would like to be supported.

Evidence activity

LD 302

1.8 From the description of a one-page profile above, write a short essay with the three titles:

* Support
* What makes me happy/ is important for me
* What do people admire about me.

With each heading explain how this can be used in person-centred planning.

1.5 **LD 302** **Explain how person-centred thinking tools can form the basis of a person-centred plan**

We have explored the one-page profile and how they may be used in the planning process. The other tools we have discussed are all vitally important to the process of planning with the individual. It is very difficult to achieve the individual's goals and ambitions if we are unsure of what the individual wishes to achieve.

Evidence activity

LD 302

1.5 Explore some of the person-centred planning you have been involved in. Identify the different tools used and which of the tools you would use initially to assist in the person-centred planning and explain why.

1.6 **LD 202** **Describe the person-centred review process**

We have looked at person-centred planning tools and their application. Any planning will require reviewing on a regular basis to ensure it will achieve the goals set or if whether the goals have changed and therefore the plan may need to be altered. An effective tool for reviewing is the learning log; this should be completed on a regular basis with the individual involved. The learning log will then become the focus point for the review process. An example is included below.

One page profile

Photo

Each one page profile has a current photo of the person.

Appreciations

This section lists the positive qualities, strengths and talents of the person. It can also be called 'like and admire'.

What's important to the person

This is a bullet list of what really matters to the person from their perspective (even if others do not agree). It is detailed and specific. This section needs to have enough detail so that someone who does not know the person can understand what matters to them. It could include:

• Who the important people are in the person's life, and when and how they spend time together.

• Important activities and hobbies, and when, where and how often these take place.

• Any routines that are important to the person.

How to support the person

This is a list of how to support the person, and what is helpful and what is not.

The information in this section includes what people need to know, and what people need to do.

2.5 An example of a one-page profile. Reproduced by permission of Helen Sanderson Associates.

Date	Activity [what, where, when, how long etc]	Who was there [staff, individual, others]	What worked well about the activity? What should continue?	What didn't work well? What must be different? What did you learn?

The review process will be assisted if you have a structured format. Some useful questions to consider are:

- Who contributed to the review?
- What we like and admire about the person?
- What is important to the person now?
- What is important for the person in the future?
- What support and help the person needs to stay healthy and safe?
- Which questions and issues we are struggling with now?
- What is working and what is not?

Finally, from this an action plan should be derived. [Smull and Sanderson 2001]

 1.6 LD 302 **Describe the key features of different styles of person-centred planning and the contexts in which they are most useful**

We have explored different types of person-centred tools and which are more suitable for particular tasks. Person-centred planning is as individual as the person using it.

Evidence activity LD 302

 1.6 Identify two individuals you support. Describe their plans and the person-centred tools used. Explain why different tools were used and the effectiveness of both types of tools.

Evidence activity LD 202

1.6 Examine your work place reviews and identify the tools used and how they were used.

LO2 Understand the context within which person-centred thinking and planning takes place

The need for planning to involve the individual and for the individual to feel in control has been highlighted in LO1. We now need to look at the practicalities of where person-centred planning takes place.

The easiest answer to this is where the individual would like this process to take place. The individual needs an environment where they feel comfortable and safe to do this. The need for planning to ensure everyone involved in their care can attend and support the process is also vital. The individual must be supported prior to this process so they remain in control. The importance of ensuring all those involved in the care are able to attend can be quite difficult and a major task in itself. This reinforces the need for forward planning.

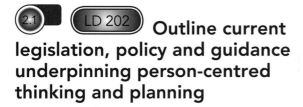 **Outline current legislation, policy and guidance underpinning person-centred thinking and planning**

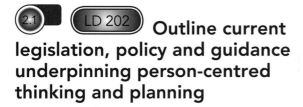 **Interpret current policy, legislation and guidance underpinning person-centred thinking and planning**

Valuing people: a new strategy for learning disability for the 21st century: planning with people towards person-centred approaches – guidance for partnership boards (January 2002) was introduced to explicitly ensure that those needing help had a say in the way their care was going to be delivered, with the emphasis on how the individual could achieve their goals and how they were to be included in society. Care plans and reviews used to be built on the medical model: you have an infection, here is a prescription, and the nurse will give you your tablets four times a day for seven days. Person-centred thinking addresses this differently by clarifying what you are feeling, how you would like treatment to be achieved and who you would like to support you. It is a very simple concept, but by using person-centred thinking we give choices and encouragement to the individual to enable them to achieve the outcome they wish. The role for a person-centred thinker is to assist with looking at the support the person needs, involving the individual, carers/family/friends and health professionals if needed. As with any plan, it needs to be reviewed. Again, with person-centred thinking the review primarily involves the person who is receiving the care, and the people who are assisting them with their care (who are not always paid professionals; the majority of care delivered is by unpaid carers and family members).

The Department of Health has researched the value of person-centred planning and has published their findings on their website www.dh.gov.uk; they also published *Personalisation through Person-centred Planning* in March 2010.

Research and investigate

Read through your policies and local procedures on Person-centred thinking and planning and review them against legislation.

 Describe the relationship between person-centred planning and personalised services

 Analyse the relationship between person-centred planning and the commissioning and delivery of services

Person-centred thinking is about asking questions and listening to the individual's responses, how much help they require and how they would like their personal needs delivered. This is the beginning of planning their care and ensuring inclusion for the individual.

We are all aware that some people are 'morning people' and enjoy getting up and being active first thing, while others are late risers and are more active later on in the day. We may be aware of this in our own family and circle of friends. Are we aware of this with the individuals we care for? Imagine if you needed care how you would like to be cared for. If you are a late riser, how would you feel about being woken at 6am and assisted with your personal needs? This is a small example but clearly illustrates attitudes we have all seen in the past when delivering any personal care.

Part of this process looks at what resources we need to ensure are available to support the individual. By completing these plans we can ensure the resources are there. After completing the planning, details of the resources needed are forwarded via the care manager to specialist boards, known as partnership boards, who influence budgets and ultimately governments on needs for the local person.

Partnership boards consist of persons with disabilities, friends, carers, support workers and adult social services and PCT staff.

Time to reflect

Think of someone you support, whether they live independently or in a support house, and explain how person-centred planning and personalised budgets work together.

Write up about a time you have supported an individual through their person-centred planning, receiving resources to enable them to achieve their goals. Write about what went well, what did not go so well and what you would do differently next time.

  Identify ways that person-centred thinking can be used:

- **With individuals**

- **In teams**

Person-centred thinking is focused on listening and understanding the individuals' needs and wishes. With person-centred planning the emphasis is put on everyone being involved in their care. The need to identify all persons involved in their care includes families and carers and there is a big emphasis on their knowledge and skills.

Imagine you have walked into a shop and been told you have to buy an article, you don't want the article but you still have to buy it. How would this make you feel? If the scenario was different and people were using person-centred thinking, and family and friends had identified places you like to shop and taken you there, how different would you feel?

When individuals are listening or know you well enough to identify your likes and dislikes, this demonstrates that they care and understand you; the same principle applies to person-centred thinking and planning. As the name says the thinking and planning is about the person.

Involving families and friends (later this will be classed as the relationship circle) actually reduces the amount of input/work you need to do, as they can identify areas they wish to be involved in, with the agreement of the individual.

Research and investigate

Read again about the tools you can use in person-centred thinking and planning. Identify which tool would be most suitable for team working and which tool would be best for individuals. Clarify why you have chosen those two tools.

 Describe how person-centred planning and person-centred reviews influence strategic commissioning

We have looked at commissioning partnership boards and the need to ensure they have the correct information to enable the resources needed.

Evidence activity

Review the last person-centred planning you were involved in. Identify from that plan any resources that were needed and investigate how these resources were met with the commissioning partnership boards.

 **Explain what a person-centred team is**

The concept of person-centred teams was developed to create structure and support. Persons are identified as team members due to their strengths and interest. All team members are encouraged to support others and ensure all are heard.

Research and investigate

Look at your own workplace policies and procedures. Find out who is on your person-centred team and discuss the process with them.

 Explain how person-centred thinking can be used within a team

With person-centred thinking it is vital for all to be involved and share the vision.

Time to reflect

LD 302 2.5

Reflect on a situation in your own workplace when you have used person-centred thinking as part of the team. Describe what went well, what did not go so well and what you may do differently next time.

2.6 LD 302 **Analyse how to achieve successful implementation of person-centred thinking and planning across an organisation**

Case study

LD 302 2.6

A new member of staff has begun to work in your setting and as senior support worker your role is to complete the induction. The new person has never been involved in care before and has the belief that the most important function is to do things for the individual. They have little knowledge that the individual is able to do their own tasks with support and no concept of person-centred thinking. How would you introduce this and monitor their understanding of person-centred thinking and planning?

2.7 LD 302 **Describe the role of the manager in implementing person-centred thinking and planning**

Case study

LD 302 2.7

Following on from the case study in 2.6 above, the new support worker has developed the skills of person-centred thinking. She has been involved in her first planning session and has come to you for advice. The individual she supports needs support in transporting herself. The obstacles are the lack of funds available for transport and that the local bus does not go to the venue she wishes to attend every Friday evening. As a new support worker she does not know where to take these problems. How would you advise her and how would you inform her of the manager's role in this process?

2.8 **LD 302** **Explain how this relates to the role of a facilitator**

The role of the support worker involved in the person-centred planning process is to support and enable the individual's wishes to be heard and acted upon. They are also responsible for the organisation of the planning event and inviting of all persons involved.

Evidence activity **LD 302**

 2.8 Read up your own workplace policies and procedures. Identify the facilitator's role and describe when you have been a facilitator and how successful your facilitating of events was.

LO3 **LD 202** Understand own role in person-centred planning, thinking and reviews

LO3 **LD 302** Understand own role in person-centred planning

Person-centred thinking, planning and reviewing are now established as necessary to enable individuals to live the life they wish to have and to have the right to choose the level of support they require. Your role or job description in your workplace will determine the amount of input and responsibility you have in planning and reviewing. All staff have a duty to use person-centred thinking.

3.1 **LD 202** **Describe own role in person-centred thinking, planning and reviews when supporting individuals**

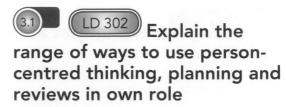 **3.1** **LD 302** **Explain the range of ways to use person-centred thinking, planning and reviews in own role**
- **With individuals**
- **As a team member**
- **As part of an organisation**

As a support worker, your role is to advocate for the individual you are supporting and ensure their voice can be heard. Person-centred caring is about identifying who the person really is, where we as support workers fit into their lives, and what we are able to do together to improve their lives now and in the future.

It is vital that we think about how the person can be central throughout the process, from gathering information about their life, preparing for meetings, monitoring actions and on-going learning, to reflection and further action. There is a danger that efforts to develop person-centred planning simply focus on having better meetings. Any planning without implementation leaves people feeling frustrated and cynical, which is often worse than not planning at all.

Very often you will only be caring for and supporting people when they are in a vulnerable position. The quality of care that you can provide will be improved if you have knowledge of the whole person, not just the current circumstances: for example, knowledge can help us to understand better why people behave in the way they do. A care plan, based on a person-centred approach, will help in understanding some of this, but what else might help? Person-centred planning, then, demands that you see the person whom you are supporting as the central concern. You need to find ways to care and support individuals, not 'one size fits all'. The relationship should move from being one of carer and cared for towards one based on a partnership: you become a resource to the person who needs support.

Research and investigate

LD 202 **3.1**

Read through your job description and your workplace's policies and procedures and describe your role in person-centred thinking, planning and reviewing.

Time to reflect

 LD 302 **3.1**

Identify when you have used person-centred thinking, planning and reviews, with individuals, as a team member or as part of an organisation, write what went well, what did not go so well and what you would do differently next time.

Time to reflect

 LD 202 **3.2** **LD 302** **3.3**

Identify a time when you have come across a challenge in implementing person-centred thinking, planning or reviews. Write about what went well, what did not go so well and what you would do differently next time.

 3.2 **LD 202** **Identify challenges that may be faced in implementing person-centred thinking, planning and reviews in own work**

 3.3 **LD 302** **Identify challenges that may be faced in implementing person-centred thinking, planning and reviews in own work**

Sometimes, especially when we are facing a new process, obstacles can occur. An example of this may be that everyone in the supported house would like to get up at the same time and each individual needs individual support with their daily living skills. This is when we need to pool our resources and look at what compromises can be made so that we can achieve the desired outcome.

One way may be to discuss shift changes to ensure more staff are available in the morning when needed. It may be that family members would like to be involved. The other option might be an agreement of slightly later times for individuals to get up.

 3.2 **LD 302** **Explain the different person-centred thinking skills required to support individuals**

Person-centred thinking is a skill in itself. Excellent communication and listening skills are paramount. Sometimes persons with learning disabilities have difficulties in communicating their needs, so it is important to look at alternative communication skills. Frequently the easiest way of commencing the thinking skills to support the individual may consist of paper and pens. Another important person-centred thinking tool would be the hospital passport. This is a clear document written or drawn to show the way they would like to be supported if admitted to hospital.

Time to reflect

LD 302 **3.2**

Think of the last person you supported to complete a plan for hospital. Describe the plan. Was it written or drawn? What was easy to do and what was more difficult? Has the hospital passport been used in hospital and if so was it effective? What would you do differently next time?

 **Describe how these challenges might be overcome**

Case study

Alex is 30 years old and has lived in care for several years. He has severe developmental dysphasia due to brain injury from an accident when he was three years old. His father has died and his mother visits frequently, although she is not physically well herself and has recently been diagnosed with terminal cancer. Alex has a great interest in modern music and enjoys interacting with others. However, sometimes social interaction causes him frustration due to his communication problems caused by his developmental dysphasia. Alex has been used to care delivery and supervision with his mother assisting. Alex has limited social contacts and has never been employed.

Using person-centred thinking and planning, describe how you could overcome some of the obstacles Alex is facing.

3.4 **LD 302** **Describe how challenges in implementing person-centred thinking, planning and reviews might be overcome**

You will often come across obstacles during the planning process. It is vital to act in a positive manner and explore all avenues to resolve these obstacles. If you still have problems overcoming these obstacles you may need to seek support.

Time to reflect

LD 302 **3.4**

Think of an occasion when you have had difficulties in overcoming obstacles. Describe what the situation was, what you did, what went well, what did not go so well and what you would do differently next time. Think of where you could have obtained additional support.

LO4  Be able to apply person-centred thinking in relation to own life

To fully understand person-centred thinking and planning it is important to identify where you may use it in your own life. To some extent we all use person-centred planning every day; for example, when planning a holiday you would contact a travel agent, go to the bank to change currency, ensure that transport is booked, etc. When using person-centred planning in our own lives we may not necessarily write it down or think of this as planning in the same way.

4.1 **LD 202** **LD 302**

Demonstrate how to use a person-centred thinking tool in relation to own life to identify what is working and not working

To fully understand the process and how an individual may feel using person-centred thinking and planning it is sometimes useful to apply the principles to yourself. I am sure we have all been in a position when someone has told us what to do. Recall how that felt, having no say. Imagine wanting to go shopping, with an idea of an item you want to purchase and the store you would be able to get this from, and someone stopping you by taking you to the wrong store and making you spend your money on something they feel is more suitable. How would this make you feel? Remember this feeling when supporting others with their choices.

4.1 Use a person-centred tool to plan a shopping trip, identifying the key things needed and support required from others. Explain how the process made you feel.

4.2 LD 202 **Describe own relationship circle**

We all need support to achieve positive outcomes. Recall from activity 4.1 who you selected to go with you on the shopping trip. You may have chosen someone whose judgement you respect or it may have been someone who could help you with the finance. In everyday life we all rely on others to support us in our goals. As children the support comes from our parents and family to guide us on what is right and what is wrong. Encouragement from them to achieve our goals will help to build self-confidence and self-esteem. As children we need the support to learn and develop into adults.

Learning disabilities requires that support. The level needed will depend on each individual's abilities. This does not make the individual with learning disabilities weak; this enables them to learn and develop, increases their confidence and self esteem.

To understand your own relationship and network support, complete the following activity.

4.2 Using the Essential Life Planning tool, use the relationship circle and identify who you would include in your circle.

4.2 LD 302 **Describe what other person-centred thinking tools would be useful in own life**

Within this chapter we have explored the main person-centred thinking, planning and reviewing tools. There are variations on these tools and it is important to explore all tools to find the one most suitable for the individual concerned. Some workplaces identify the types of tools that should be used within the setting. You will need to explore your workplace's policies and procedures relating to this.

The important thing to remember is the tool is just a vehicle to achieve the individual's choices and assist them to achieve their goals. Any plans used should be shared with all those involved. The plan should be in a format that the individual can understand. The tool needs to work for the individual concerned.

Research and investigate

LD 302 **4.2**

Research all person-centred tools and identify which tool you would use when planning a holiday.

4.3 LD 202 **Describe how helpful using a person-centred thinking tool was to identify actions in relation to own life**

From the activities in this section, you should have gained some concept of the process of person-centered thinking and identified areas that are more difficult to plan and those that were easier to plan. It is important to think of these activities when assisting an individual to complete them. It is also important to note how empowering this was for you and hopefully will be for the individual.

Evidence activity LD 202

 4.3 Complete the 'what's working and what's not working' tool in relation to your personal development.

 4.3 LD 302 **Evaluate which person-centred thinking tools could be used to think more about own community connections**

When looking at community connections, we need to explore with the individual the amount of involvement from others they require and to revisit the gifts the individual can offer. Individuals are living in the community and are part of that community. Our role in supporting the individual is to ensure they feel part of the community and that the community includes the individual. Within person-centred thinking a large emphasis is put on community involvement.

Research and investigate

LD 302 4.3

Review all person-centred tools and identify the tool that would assist more with community connections and explain why you believe this is so.

4.4 LD 202 **Describe how to prepare for own person-centred review**

When assisting individuals in person-centred reviews, we need to ensure they understand the process and are clear on what outcomes they want and that someone they trust is there to be an advocate for them. All of the people the individual wishes to be involved should be present. The venue and time should be agreed on by everyone involved.

 Evidence activity LD 202

 4.4 Write an account of the type of support you would require for your review. Who you would want to be present and where would you like it to be held?

 4.4 LD 302 **Evaluate which person-centred thinking tools or person-centred planning styles could be used to think more about own future aspirations**

To achieve our goals and aspirations, we need to make plans on how the individual is going to achieve these goals and the support that they will need along the way. Sometimes the goals are very large and will take time to achieve; to promote success we need to assist the individual to identify and make a plan of small steps needed to achieve their goals. With small steps (manageable and achievable during a short period of time) the individual can feel they are moving towards their main goal, which then becomes achievable and realistic, increasing the individual's motivation and increasing their confidence.

Research and investigate

LD 302 4.4

Research person-centred tools and describe which tool would be better for planning future aspirations. State why you have come to that conclusion.

LO5

Be able to implement person-centred thinking and person-centred reviews

The next section looks at ways of ensuring the implementation of the person-centred planning process. As a support worker your role as the individual's advocate is vital. You should also be aware of outside advocates such as family members, who the individual may choose as their advocate. Your role will be to support them in the process.

 **LD 202** ## Use person-centred thinking to know and act on what is important to the individual

As the support worker, you may have worked closely with the individual and be aware of their communication skills and ways of preference of being treated.

Case study

LD 202 5.1

Jane is unable to communicate her needs clearly by verbal means. If Jane is unhappy she will make a short murmur; if she is happy she will make a very sharp high pitched noise. Jane is due to go clothes shopping. Generally her sister takes her and Jane comes back with dated clothes. You have noted that Jane does not wear the clothes she has bought. Her sister feels she is helping and that this is a task she can support Jane with. The relationship is very strained and Jane's sister attends once a month to take her shopping.

Write down what actions you should take to support Jane and her sister using person-centred thinking.

5.2 **LD 202** **Establish with the individual how they want to be supported**

5.1 **LD 302** **Demonstrate the person-centred thinking and styles of person-centred planning that can be used to help individuals move towards their dreams**

When supporting an individual it is important to be clear what their ambitions or goals are. Sometimes this can be difficult if they have limited life experiences.

Case study

LD 202 5.2 **LD 302** 5.1

Read again the case of Alex on page 36. Use MAPS to try to work out a plan to help Alex with his social interaction, identifying some of the obstacles you may encounter.

Use Personal Futures Planning to work out the process for planning with Alex how to manage with his mother's illness.

5.2 **LD 302** **Show that the plan and process are owned by the individual**

The value of the plan depends on the involvement of the individual. It is important that the individual owns the plan. The purpose of person-centred planning is to listen, understand and support the individual to achieve their goals and dreams. The plan should be an active tool that is frequently visited and reviewed to ensure the achievement of the plan.

As we have already seen, the need for the individual to be in the centre of the plan is paramount. As a support worker you need to ensure the individual understands the process and the plan. This may be a time to look at alternative forms of communication. There are other ways of preparing the plan as well as writing it, for example the individual may draw the plan or it could be recorded as an audio file.

Person-centred planning has no one format. It must be as individual as the person the plan is serving.

■ Research and investigate

LD 302 · **5.2**

Identify the varieties of person-centred planning and explain how you can demonstrate involvement of the individual.

5.3 · **LD 202** Use person-centred thinking to know how and respond to how the individual communicates

Person-centred planning is an effective tool if used correctly and frequently. The person-centred plan must be in a format for the individual to understand. It is important to start a communication chart as soon as possible so that this can be shared with all involved.

Evidence activity — LD 202

5.3 In the table below, think of a person you support and complete the communication chart. In the example below the individual to be supported is named Rufus.

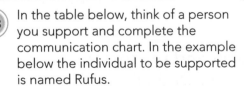

When this is happening	Rufus does this

5.3 · **LD 302** Demonstrate how person-centred thinking tools can be used to develop a person-centred plan

Person-centred thinking, planning and reviewing is about listening, understanding and communicate an individual's wishes to others.

Evidence activity — LD 302

5.3 Using a communication chart and a learning log from one of the individuals that you support, write a PATH plan and explain how these two tools will help you complete the plan.

5.4 · **LD 202** Be responsive to how an individual makes decisions to support them to have maximum choice and control in their life

Person-centred thinking allows us to deliver care in a manner that the individual chooses. Through listening we find out what is important to the individual and what would make them happy and content. We also need to be aware of the limitations that the service has and find agreeable compromises.

■ Time to reflect

LD 202 · **5.4**

Recall an incident where someone became angry or distressed when you were trying to assist them. This may have been a time when you were seeing to their personal needs. Recall if you discussed with them beforehand how they would like to be attended to. Remember this is not the communication made when you enter the room, stating 'I am going to wash you now'. What could you have done differently? What went well? What did not go well? What would you do differently?

 **Use information from a person-centred review to start a person-centred plan**

Case study

  LD 202 5.2 LD 302 5.1

Rufus has completed his review. His wishes were listened to and the outcomes he wants to see are included in the review notes below:

What Rufus would like to happen	Action
Rufus would like to learn to swim	
Rufus wants to have a lie in on Sundays	
Rufus would like to do his own cooking once a week and would like to make cakes	
Rufus would like to extend his social interactions	

Evidence activity LD 302

 5.4 In the table above add the actions needed to reach the outcomes Rufus would like to achieve. Explain how in a person-centred planning these can be planned.

Time to reflect

LD 202 5.5

Think of an individual you support and describe the actions and planning you have done in including the individual into the community. Write about what went well, what did not go so well and what you would do differently next time.

 5.5 LD 202 **Support the individual in their relationships and in being part of their community using person-centred thinking**

Community person-centred planning uses the same tools but with different slants on the questions. This is called the community connecting approach. It begins with learning about the person and identifying their networks, and includes a passion audit about likes and dislikes. The next step looks at community mapping, the main focus being on exploring the gifts and capabilities of the individual, allowing identification of areas in the community that are accessible and where the individual will be able to participate and feel happy.

 5.5 LD 302 **Use a person-centred thinking to enable individuals to choose those who support them**

An important part of this process is to identify who the individual wishes to support them. Sometimes this will not be their allocated support worker. You should not take this personally as we are all different and personalities have a big impact on outcomes. Persons with learning disabilities may have difficulty in expressing who they want to support them and the first time you might notice this is when reviewing their learning log. An example of this may be that the task they are trying to perform is not done well when they are working with certain people. It is important that we explore the relationship circles as soon as possible.

Research and investigate

LD 302 **5.5**

Look around your workplace and the surrounding neighbourhood for barriers that prevent people with particular needs from living as normal and fulfilling life as possible. What does this tell you about some of society's attitudes to people with a disability?

Research the different tools to identify who should support the individual, explain how the process works and when you would use the tool.

5.6 **LD 202** ## Ensure that the individual is central to the person-centred review process

To ensure the individual remains at the centre of the process, they need to be fully supported in the review process. As their support worker you will be aware of any difficulties they may have. You will need to ensure that someone attending their review will advocate for them.

Time to reflect

LD 202 **5.6**

Think of an individual you have supported in the person-centred planning process. State what you did to support the individual, what went well, what did not go so well and what you would do differently next time.

5.7 **LD 202** ## Explain how to ensure that actions from a review happen

5.6 **LD 302** ## Support the individual and others involved to understand their responsibilities in achieving actions agreed

The review process is there to kick start the outcomes the individual has stated they want to achieve. Whilst reviewing we can identify any obstacles, problems and hopefully solutions to these obstacles. This is only one part of the review process. As with any tool, the review process is only effective if it is used. At a review plan actions to move the programme forward are made with whose responsibilities to ensure those actions are followed. These actions should be recorded and checked off when completed.

Case study

LD 202 **5.7** **LD 302** **5.6**

Review a recent review plan of someone you support. Identify the actions made and the persons responsible for completing them. Look for any actions not followed up and describe what actions you can take to support the individual in this process. If all of the actions have been completed, reflect on what you could do if they were not completed.

5.7 **LD 302** ## Demonstrate a successful person-centred review

How would we know if a review was successful? The action plan would be completed and the individual would achieve their outcomes. Any plan can be measured if it has objectives to be met.

Case study

LD 302 **5.7**

Identify two individuals that you support and who have recently been reviewed. Write about the individual process for each one, explore why they were successful and your role in the process. Reflect on what went well and what you may do differently next time.

Assessment Summary for Unit LD 202

Your reading of this chapter and completion of the activities will have prepared you to demonstrate your learning and understanding of supporting individuals who have a learning disability in your workplace. To achieve the unit, your assessor will require you to:

Learning outcomes	Assessment criteria
1 Understand the principles and practice of person-centred thinking, planning and reviews	**1.1** Identify the beliefs and values on which person-centred thinking and planning is based See Time to reflect 1.1, p. 22.
	1.2 Define person-centred thinking, person-centred planning and person-centred reviews See Evidence activity 1.2, p. 24.
	1.3 Describe the difference that person-centred thinking can make to **individuals** and their families See Time to reflect 1.3, p. 24.
	1.4 Describe examples of **person-centred thinking tools** See Evidence activity 1.2, p. 27.
	1.5 Explain what a 'one page profile' is See Evidence activity 1.5, p. 28.
	1.6 Describe the person-centred review process See Evidence activity 1.6, p. 30.
2 Understand the context within which person-centred thinking and planning takes place	**2.1** Outline current legislation, policy and guidance underpinning person-centred thinking and planning See Research and investigate 2.1, p. 31.
	2.2 Describe the relationship between person-centred planning and personalised services See Time to reflect 2.2, p. 32.
	2.3 Identify ways that person-centred thinking can be used: • with individuals • in teams See Research and investigate 2.3, p. 32.

Learning outcomes	Assessment criteria	
3 Understand own role in person-centred planning, thinking and reviews	**3.1**	Describe own role in person-centred thinking, planning and reviews when supporting individuals See Research and investigate 3.1, p. 34.
	3.2	Identify challenges that may be faced in implementing person-centred thinking, planning and reviews in own work See Time to reflect 3.2, p. 35.
	3.3	Describe how these challenges might be overcome See Case study 3.3, p. 36.
4 Be able to apply person-centred thinking in relation to own life	**4.1**	Demonstrate how to use a person-centred thinking tool in relation to own life to identify what is working and not working See Evidence activity 4.1, p. 37.
	4.2	Describe own relationship circle See Evidence activity 4.2, p. 37.
	4.3	Describe how helpful using a person-centred thinking tool was to identify actions in relation to own life See Evidence activity 4.3, p. 38.
	4.4	Describe how to prepare for own person-centred review See Evidence activity 4.4, p. 38.

Learning outcomes	Assessment criteria
5 Be able to implement person-centred thinking and person-centred reviews	**5.1** Use person-centred thinking to know and act on what is important to the individual See Case study 5.1, p. 39.
	5.2 Establish with the individual how they want to be supported See Case study 5.2, p. 39 and Case study 5.2, p. 41.
	5.3 Use person-centred thinking to know and respond to how the individual communicates See Evidence activity 5.3, p. 40.
	5.4 Be responsive to how an individual makes decisions to support them to have maximum choice and control in their life See Time to reflect 5.4, p. 40.
	5.5 Support the individual in their relationships and in being part of their community using person-centred thinking See Time to reflect 5.5, p. 41
	5.6 Ensure that the individual is central to the person-centred review process See Time to reflect 5.6, p. 42.
	5.7 Explain how to ensure that actions from a review happen See Case study 5.7, p. 42

Assessment Summary for Unit LD 302

Your reading of this chapter and completion of the activities will have prepared you to demonstrate your learning and understanding of supporting individuals who have a learning disability in your workplace. To achieve the unit, your assessor will require you to:

Learning outcomes	Assessment criteria
1 Understand the principles and practice of person-centred thinking, planning and reviews	**1.1** Explain what person-centred thinking is, and how it relates to person-centred reviews and person-centred planning See Time to reflect 1.1, p. 24.
	1.2 Explain the benefits of using person-centred thinking with **individuals** See Evidence activity 1.2, p. 25.
	1.3 Explain the beliefs and values on which person-centred thinking and planning is based See Research and investigate 1.3, p. 23.
	1.4 Explain how the beliefs and values on which person-centred thinking is based differs from assessment and other approaches to planning See Case study 1.4, p. 28.
	1.5 Explain how person-centred thinking tools can form the basis of a person-centred plan See Evidence activity 1.5, p. 28.
	1.6 Describe the key features of different styles of person-centred planning and the contexts in which they are most useful See Evidence activity 1.6, p. 30.
	1.7 Describe examples of person-centred thinking tools, their purpose, how and when each one might be used See Research and investigate 1.7, p. 27.
	1.8 Explain the different ways that one page profiles are used See Evidence activity 1.8, p. 28.

Learning outcomes	Assessment criteria
2 Understand the context within which person-centred thinking and planning takes place	**2.1** Interpret current policy, legislation and guidance underpinning person-centred thinking and planning See Research and investigate 2.1, p. 31.
	2.2 Analyse the relationship between person-centred planning and the commissioning and delivery of services See Time to reflect 2.2, p. 32.
	2.3 Describe how person-centred planning and person-centred reviews influence strategic commissioning See Evidence activity 2.3, p. 32.
	2.4 Explain what a **person-centred** team is See Research and investigate 2.4, p. 33.
	2.5 Explain how person-centred thinking can be used within a team See Time to reflect 2.5, p. 33.
	2.6 Analyse how to achieve successful implementation of person-centred thinking and planning across an organisation See Case study 2.6, p. 33.
	2.7 Describe the role of the manager in implementing person-centred thinking and planning See Case study 2.7, p. 33.
	2.8 Explain how this relates to the role of a facilitator See Evidence activity 2.8, p. 34.
3 Understand own role in person-centred planning	**3.1** Explain the range of ways to use person-centred thinking, planning and reviews in own role: • with individuals • as a team member • as part of an organisation See Time to reflect 3.1, p. 35.
	3.2 Explain the different person-centred thinking skills required to support individuals See Time to reflect 3.2, p. 35.
	3.3 Identify challenges that may be faced in implementing person-centred thinking, planning and reviews in own work See Time to reflect 3.3, p. 35.
	3.4 Describe how challenges in implementing person-centred thinking, planning and reviews might be overcome See Time to reflect 3.4, p. 36.

Learning outcomes	Assessment criteria	
4 Be able to apply person-centred planning in relation to own life	4.1	Demonstrate how to use a person-centred thinking tool in relation to own life to identify what is working and not working See Evidence activity 4.1, p. 37.
	4.2	Describe what other person-centred thinking tools would be useful in own life See Research and investigate 4.2, p. 37.
	4.3	Evaluate which person-centred thinking tools could be used to think more about own community connections See Research and investigate 4.3, p. 38.
	4.4	Evaluate which person-centred thinking tools or person-centred planning styles could be used to think more about own future aspirations See Research and investigate 4.4, p. 38.
5 Be able to implement person-centred thinking, planning and reviews	5.1	Demonstrate the person-centred thinking and styles of person-centred planning that can be used to help individuals move towards their dreams See Case study 5.1, p. 39 and Case study 5.1, p. 41.
	5.2	Show that the plan and process are owned by individual See Research and investigate 5.2, p. 40.
	5.3	Demonstrate how person-centred thinking tools can be used to develop a person-centred plan See Evidence activity 5.3, p. 40.
	5.4	Use information from a person-centred review to start a person-centred plan See Evidence activity 5.4, p. 41.
	5.5	Use person-centred thinking to enable individuals to choose those who support them See Research and investigate 5.5, p. 42.
	5.6	Support the individual and others involved to understand their responsibilities in achieving actions agreed See Case study 5.6, p. 42.
	5.7	Demonstrate a successful person-centred review See Case study 5.7, p. 43.

Communication in health, social care or children's and young people's settings

3

Unit SHC 21 Introduction to communication in health, social care or children's and young people's settings
Unit SHC 31 Promote communication in health, social care or children's and young people's settings

What are you finding out?

This chapter is about how to identify ways of communicating with individuals on difficult, complex and sensitive issues. This chapter is about the importance of communication in such settings, and how we can overcome barriers to meet individual needs and preferences in communication.

You will need to be aware of the different ways of communicating, including verbal and non verbal. You will also need to be aware of the impact of confidentiality on your role.

The reading and activities in this chapter will help you to:

- Understand why effective communication is important in the work setting

- Be able to meet the communication and language needs, wishes and preferences of individuals

- Overcome barriers to communication

- Be able to apply principles and practices relating to confidentiality, especially at work.

LO1 Understand why effective communication is important in the work setting

1.1 Identify the reasons people communicate

Communication between workers and individuals

As a worker you can provide a range of information to individuals who use services, to enable them to understand the support that is available to meet their needs. You could ask the individual for their opinions about the provision available and encourage them to make choices. Exchanging information is important in order to develop your understanding of the needs of an individual, so that you can provide the support that the client requires and improve the quality of service provision. If the information exchanged is inaccurate, mistakes can be made, for example, an individual could be prescribed the wrong medication if the GP did not know they were allergic to it. If information is not exchanged, individuals may not feel supported and workers will not be able to carry out their job roles as effectively as they could.

Developing and promoting relationships

You will establish many different relationships across the sector, some of which will be formal and others more informal. Two-way communication is required to form relationships and establish the boundaries. It will help to ensure that everyone concerned understands the purpose of the relationship and what they are aiming to achieve.

3.1 Developing relationships

The relationships between workers and service users, and also between colleagues, have a significant impact on the ability to provide effective care and support. Respect for each other can be developed through communication. Getting to know people by talking and listening to them will enable you to develop an understanding and awareness which will lead to stronger relationships in the longer term. Relationships are developed between workers and service users when they communicate effectively and appropriately, and trust is established. In order to maintain effective support and achieve success, each person involved in a relationship should know exactly what their responsibilities are and what the other person's expectations are. The targets for effective communication are to form a good working relationship or partnership where each contributor is valued. This involves:

- respecting individuals' rights
- maintaining confidentiality
- considering the person's beliefs and cultural views and opinions
- supporting individuals in expressing their views and opinions
- respecting **diversity** when individuals do not behave in the same way or have the same views as you.

Key terms

Diversity means variety, particularly in relation to people. You must understand that each individual is unique.

Evidence activity   SHC 21   SHC 31

1.1 Reasons for communication

Think about all the people you communicate with. Reflect back over your day, or think about yesterday. How many people did you communicate to? Consider all the purposes you communicated with them for.

1.2 How effective communication affects all aspects of the learner's work, including relationships

Relationships with supervisors

Good communication affects your relationship with your supervisor. The last thing any learner would want is a relationship with their supervisor which is negative, unsupportive or sarcastic. Creating a relationship which is mutually beneficial, supportive and open where you can share ideas, receive support and advice and receive feedback honestly is the best scenario. It can be difficult at times to take on board any negative comments about one's behaviour, abilities and progress, but as long as learners remember that this constructive criticism is there to help them, and they accept this, reflect on it and take it on board, criticism can be a very useful tool.

Relationships with individuals with learning disabilities

Effective communication can also ensure that relationships with individuals are improved. For individuals with learning disabilities this can be even more important, as ability to communicate could be an area where specific needs exist. Improved communication can have direct and indirect effects.

- Directly – better communication will allow for needs to be better understood and hence better care to be given.
- Indirectly – the individual (as well as learners themselves!) will feel a lot better about their role and situation if communication is good. An individual's self-esteem could be improved as there may be feelings of being *actually listened to*, and understood.

It is vital for learners to build rapport with individuals in their care, but it needs to be remembered at all times there is only the opportunity to develop professional relationships, that is ones that although they can be friendly, are not essentially friendship. There may be times when rules need to be explained and behaviour challenged, and a relationship which shows respect towards care professionals is needed. Learners must therefore be able to use communication to instil any boundaries.

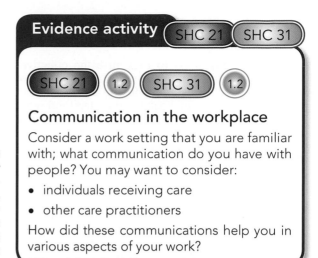

Evidence activity

SHC 21   SHC 31

SHC 21   1.2   SHC 31   1.2

Communication in the workplace

Consider a work setting that you are familiar with; what communication do you have with people? You may want to consider:

- individuals receiving care
- other care practitioners

How did these communications help you in various aspects of your work?

1.3   SHC 21   Importance of observing an individual's reactions when communicating with them

Conversations are such common, everyday events that people often think they do not require any specific or specialist skills. Some interactions will be informal, such as speaking with friends or family members. Other conversations will be more formal, for example, having a conversation with a health specialist, colleague or employer.

Communication in work settings may be complex. This means that it may have several purposes. As a practitioner, you will need to be aware that each individual has their own way of interpreting what is said, and observation can help you with this. How are they responding, does their body language match their spoken words? Effective communication means more than just passing on information, it means involving or engaging the other person or people with whom you are interacting.

Communicating has to be a two-way process where each person is attempting to understand and interpret, or make sense of, what the other person is saying. Often it is easier to understand people who are similar to us, for example, a person who has the same accent as us, or is in a similar situation. The decoding equipment in our brain tunes in, breaks down the message, analyses the message, understands it and interprets its meaning, and then creates a response or answer. When a practitioner is speaking with an individual they are forming a mental picture of what they are being told.

Listening attentively and responding

Active listening helps to maximise the effectiveness of communication. It is important to show not only that you are listening to the individual, but that you have actually heard and understood what has been said. By listening actively, you will pick up on an individual's reactions, verbal or non verbal. A slight twitch at the mention of something, a glance away when someone is around; these reactions can be observed by close active listening. Facial expressions in particular are used to convey meaning in communication. They can be an indication of the emotional state of the person communicating. Facial expressions include smiling, frowning, raising an eyebrow or pulling the mouth into particular shapes. A quizzical expression can show that a person has misunderstood or wants to ask a question. A sad expression can indicate that something is wrong. Facial expressions can also show pain or surprise.

3.2 Facial expressions

Evidence activity SHC 21

Observing while communicating

This activity will help demonstrate that you understand why it is important to observe an individual's reactions when communicating with them. What can observing an individual tell you about how they feel?

LO2 Meeting the communication and language needs, wishes and preferences of individuals

2.1 Show how to find out an individual's communication and language needs, wishes and preferences

As a practitioner, it is important that you become familiar with the needs of individuals to ensure you can communicate effectively with them. You can do this by:

- Asking the person – they know best!
- Looking at the care plan.
- Speaking to a family member, or a close friend.
- Asking other practitioners.
- Use reference books, if appropriate.

For example, in many cultures the use of touch or gestures and the use of personal space may differ. The ways in which people express themselves might also be different; or the way that men address women or the use of first names might be different. How people are addressed is important too. Some people prefer to be called by their first name while others may request to be called Mr or Mrs.

There are two particular ways a practitioner can communicate effectively to help establish the needs, wishes and preferences of individuals:

1 Using active listening

In your role you are encouraged to use active listening techniques in order to encourage effective communication and maximise the communication process. Active listeners focus on:

- what is being said verbally, that is content
- how the person is saying it, that is the tone of voice
- what is being communicated non verbally, that is body language.

2 The use of questioning

Only about 10 per cent of our communication is actually spoken, and it is very important that you make the most of your conversations with individuals and their families, as this will enable you to establish relationships and accurately identify their needs and feelings. Much of this information can be collected through careful questioning, and it is important that you consider the different techniques that might be used to accurately and effectively collect information without creating too much distress. For example, you might use:

- *Closed questions* – for example 'Would you like an extra pillow, Mr Smith?' The breathless person need only reply 'Yes' or 'No'. A more complex question would need a longer answer, and cause further breathlessness and discomfort.

- *Open questions* – for example 'Tell me about your family, Mr Smith.' This will enable you to start up a conversation.

- *Process questions* – for example 'What did you think the doctor was saying, Mr Smith?' This type of questioning can give you an indication as to how the individual understands his or her situation.

- *Clarification* – for example 'I think you said that this made you feel worse. Is that right, Mr Smith?' This is a useful way of checking or summarising the outcomes of a conversation, and shows that you are listening.

Evidence activity SHC 21 SHC 31

 Finding out about someone's preference

Level 2 How would you collate the needs, wishes and preferences of individuals in a care setting you may be familiar with?

Level 3 Write a report demonstrating how you did this in practice

This activity helps demonstrate that you understand how to find out an individual's wishes and preferences.

2.2 SHC 31 **Describe the factors to consider when promoting effective communication**

Communication makes the world go round. On a lower level, communication, or being able to communicate effectively, is what gets you through each day, in both your career and personal life. No matter what your age, background or experience, communicating effectively is something that every person can achieve. It requires self-confidence, good **articulation** and knowledge of how communication can be made more effective.

Key terms

Articulation is the formation of clear and distinct words when communicating through speech.

Choose the right moment and the right place. If you need to discuss something in private with a person, make sure that the choice of venue is private and that you do not feel uncomfortable about the possibility of being overheard. On the other hand, if you need to make your point before a group of people, ensure that the location is somewhere that your discussion will be audible to all who are present, to ensure that you engage everyone in the group.

Organise and clarify ideas in your mind before you attempt to communicate them. Decide on some key points and stick with these to avoid your message becoming garbled, which can happen if you feel passionately about a topic. A good rule-of-thumb is to choose three main points and keep your communication focused on those. That way, if you wander off topic, you will be able to return to one or more of these key points without feeling flustered.

Time

Communication should never be rushed, as this may make an individual feel that they are not important, or that you lack respect for them. Also, taking too much time can be seen as dragging out the conversation and can make people feel uneasy. Timing should be appropriate for the purpose of the communication and take into account the needs of the individuals involved. It is important to give individuals time to say what they want to; this ensures that they feel respected and that their personal interests have been considered fully. Individuals should not be interrupted when they are speaking as this may make them feel that they are not being listened to properly.

3.3 Listening

Evidence activity | SHC 31

2.2 Helping an individual

Alice is a new member of staff and speaks very quietly and slowly. Not all individuals understand her. How can you help Alice to communicate more effectively?

2.2 | SHC 21 | Demonstrate communication methods that meet an individual's communication needs, wishes and preferences

2.3 | SHC 31 | Demonstrate a range of communication methods and styles to meet individual needs

Non-verbal communication

Eye contact

Eye contact is a way of showing that the person who is listening is interested in the conversation. Eye contact will help the person you are communicating with realise that you are concentrating on what they are saying rather than on other conversations or activities that may be going on around you. Eye-to-eye contact can also help you to know how the other person is feeling. If either the individual or the practitioner is angry or upset, they might have a fixed stare that can send

out that message; if they are excited or interested in someone, then their eyes will get wider. This means that when you are talking to an individual, the person can tell whether you like what you are hearing or not.

As a practitioner, you need to understand that eye contact conveys different meanings for people from different cultures. For example, direct eye contact is considered to be rude in some cultures and should be avoided. It is important to understand what is and what is not acceptable for the people with whom you are working. Also, some individuals may be unable or unwilling to make and/or maintain eye contact because of a disability.

Touch

Touch can assist communication. A gentle hand on a shoulder, the holding of a hand, a reassuring touch, can communicate the message that the care practitioner is listening to the individual and is there to support them. Clearly touch needs to be appropriate and not infringing on anyone's rights.

Physical gestures

Gestures are hand or arm movements that can portray a message to another person. Usually gestures are used to enhance the understanding of what is being said verbally, but some gestures carry their own meaning and can be misinterpreted by others. People who cannot use sign language may be able to relay a message to, or understand a message from, a person with speech impairments by using or watching gestures. Gestures can be used to convey both positive and negative responses. For example, 'thumbs up' can mean 'OK', 'success' or even 'yes please'. Putting a hand up with the palm facing a person gives the meaning of 'stop that'. Shrugging shoulders can mean 'not sure'. However, you should be aware that these gestures can mean different things to people from different cultural groups, for example, in some cultures the thumbs-up sign can have negative connotations.

Body language

The non verbal signals you use when talking to people, such as gestures, facial expressions, body positioning and movement of the body, are known as 'body language'. Body language is a way of giving messages to those with whom we are speaking, for example smiling will convey friendliness. First impressions are often made from observing an individual's body language. A person can convey confidence or lack of confidence through their body language, which can have an impact on the effectiveness of the communication. By developing an awareness of the signs and signals of body language, you will find it much easier to understand other people and to communicate more effectively with them. Increasing understanding of body language can also help you to become more aware of the messages you are conveying to others.

There are subtle, and sometimes less subtle, movements, gestures, facial expressions and even shifts in individuals' whole bodies that indicate something is going on. The way they talk, walk, sit and stand all say something, and whatever is happening on the inside can be reflected on the outside. There are also times when mixed messages are sent – a person says one thing and their body language displays something different. This can be confusing, so it is important to understand the messages being sent to others as well as those being received.

Take care not to assume meanings, particularly when communicating with individuals from other cultures. For example, not making eye contact may, for some, be read as 'having something to hide', while others may see it as a mark of respect.

Behaviour

An individuals' behaviour can tell you a lot about them. An individual who is rushing or is very slow may give indications about motivation, nerves or even well being. An individual who is displaying different behaviour to their normal characteristics may give you a message about how they are feeling.

Verbal communication

Vocabulary

Care practitioners need to ensure that the language and vocabulary they choose is appropriate:

- **Age appropriate**

  Language used should always consider the age of the individual, and as may be the case for many with learning disabilities, not just the biological age, but possibly the learning age.

- **Ability appropriate**

  Language used should be too difficult or technical that it is confusing. Further, it should not be too simple or 'childish' that it can be seen as condescending to an individual.

- **Offensive**

  Words which are racist, sexist, disablist, ageist and so on should all be avoided.

- **Profanity**

  Any words which are viewed as being 'swearwords' should not be used as they may cause offence.

Linguistic tone

Tone is not what you say, but how you say something, the attitude of how it is said. Many a teacher or parent has often said 'don't take that tone!'. The same word or sentence can have very different meanings depending on how it is said. Even a simple 'yes' can be said excitedly, sarcastically, aggressively, sadly and so on. Therefore it is vital that care practitioners listen to not just what is said, but also how it is said.

Pitch

Pitch is an integral part of the human voice. The pitch of the voice is the rate of vibration of the vocal folds. The pitch of someone's voice can also be affected by emotions, moods and inflection. Someone with a high pitched language may come across as being stressed, nervous or possibly less serious, more frivolous or 'unprofessional'. Conversely, an individual with a deep, lower pitched voice, may be seen as too formal, serious, possibly even intimidating.

Use of technology, JAWS

Electronic forms of communication are now a well-established way of everyday life. In recent years the development of electronic mail (email) has proved to be a significant form of communication. Emails can be formal or informal, depending on their purpose. The internet is also being used increasingly as a source of information for a variety of purposes. An advantage of emails is that they provide a very quick way of interacting with other people or organisations, as answers can be received in a matter of minutes, rather than having to wait several days for a letter. A disadvantage is that on some occasions emails are lost and, as a consequence, the sender has to repeat the process.

In the health and social care and community justice settings, computers can be used for networking between one organisation and another. A GP surgery could use the computer to send information about a patient to a consultant at a hospital or to send a prescription to a pharmacy. Similarly, an internal system can enable employees within one setting to be linked with others to share information.

JAWS is a computer program that reads information on the screen and speaks it aloud through a speech synthesiser. It works with any PC to provide access to software applications and the internet. It also outputs to refreshable Braille displays, providing Braille support for screen readers. Where the use of technology is appropriate to assist with communication, this should be encouraged so that everyone feels actively involved and no one is struggling to hear what others are saying or is unable to present their ideas or opinions.

Technological aids can be used to enhance communication with people who may otherwise have difficulties. Some people may use word or symbol boards to support their speech so that a picture enhances the listener's understanding of what has been said. Others may use speech synthesisers, which replace speech either by producing a visual display of written text or by producing synthesised speech that expresses the information verbally. Hearing aids, hearing loops, text phones, text messaging on mobile phones and magnifiers are also forms of technological communication devices. Voice recognition software can be purchased for any computer which supports the communication of individuals who find writing difficult. Computers can also be used to present information with graphics and sound.

Use of special methods of communication

Sign language

British Sign Language (BSL) is used by a large number of people within the UK. It is thought that nearly 70,000 people use sign language in the British Isles. The government officially recognised BSL in March 2003. Children find sign language fascinating and, as a result, learn the signs quite easily. BSL has a phrase, 'make your fingers count', which appeals to children. Sign language can be taught at any age and is used by many of those with hearing impairment. It is a language that has developed over hundreds of years and enables interaction between people who otherwise might experience difficulty. It may or may not be the first language of those using it. If a care practitioner is able to respond using signing, they should.

Makaton

Makaton is a large collection of symbols that can help people who have a hearing impairment, or who have a learning difficulty, to communicate with others. It is a system that uses signs, speech and symbols. Those using Makaton may use all three methods to help them communicate with others. Makaton uses an established set of hand movements to convey meaning. It is usually taught to children when they are young, as soon as it is realised that they have a need.

Braille

The communication system known as Braille was first introduced in 1829, by a blind man called Richard Braille. The system is one of raised dots that can be felt with a finger. For people who have limited vision or who are blind the system provides the opportunity for independent reading and writing as it is based on 'touch'. It is possible, with the correct computer software, to change the printed word into Braille and to print out using special printers.

As well as being used to read books and magazines to satisfy the intellectual needs of people who have poor sight, Braille can be used for leaflets and handouts, for example, giving information about the person's treatment.

Research and investigate

SHC 21 **2.2** Communication methods

Investigate the range of communication methods used in a specific setting, such as a nursery or learning disability provision, and list the benefits of each method.

| MAKATON | is | used | with |
| manual signs | graphic symbols | and | speech. |

3.4 Makaton symbols

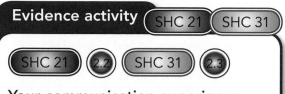

Evidence activity — SHC 21 · SHC 31

SHC 21 2.2 **SHC 31** 2.3

Your communication experience and needs

Produce a report which describes the various communications methods which you have used, or are available in a care setting you are familiar with.

  2.4 · SHC 31

Demonstrate how to respond to an individual's reactions when communicating

At all times, care practitioners need to remain interested, neutral and non judgemental when communicating. Indivduals need to feel relaxed and comfortable about what they are saying. It is not the care practitioner's job to express opinions or make comment.

Non verbal communication

Posture, facial expressions, eye contact, gestures and so on can all be used when responding. Giving a reaction of being bored (hands on hips, slouched, yawning etc.) when an individual is communicating will not be helpful. Giving a reaction to being shocked (open mouthed, raising hands, opened eyes, etc.) may make a person think they are being judged and they may decide to stop communicating. Giving a reaction of disapproval (shaking head, tutting, etc.) may make an individual feel they are in the wrong.

Care practitioners need to be relaxed, with open body language and whatever their own personal opinions about what they are discussing might be, they cannot place their own perspectives on the communication.

Verbal communication

Verbal communication is an important method of communication between workers and service users across the sectors. People talk to each other and have conversations regularly, receiving and giving information quickly and effectively. Ideas can be exchanged and decisions made there and then. If there is any confusion about what has been said, this can be clarified at the time so that everyone knows and understands exactly what

has happened or is going to happen in the future. Service users will be able to find out about the treatment or procedures they are going to have. Instructions can be given to other workers so that they know what their duties are. Activities can be carried out and problems solved, using speech as the method of communication.

Again, care needs to be taken to not be judgemental. A care worker's tone, language and so on cannot change. If an individual with learning disabilities is explaining that they do not want to live independently, they want to live with their parents and the care practitioner disagrees, the care practitioner should not be sighing, saying 'really?!', or using language such as 'pathetic', 'childish' and so on or using a disappointed or disapproving tone.

Evidence activity — SHC 31

2.4 **Communicating about a difficult or sensitive issue**

Produce a leaflet for future care practitioners on how to be neutral and objective when caring for an individual as regards an issue which is difficult or sensitive.

2.3 · SHC 21

Show how and when to seek advice about communication

If there are problems identified with communication there are a range of services which can be accessed. Never presume that you or anyone else can be heard, understood and responded to, without first thinking about the person involved. Check first to ensure you are supporting someone to communicate as effectively as possible by working with them to overcome as many challenges and barriers as possible. It may be necessary to access additional support or services to help make communication better or clearer. People may have problems in communicating with others due to:

- Intellectual impairment leading to problems comprehending and processing information.
- Sensory difficulties (hearing, vision).
- Problems in understanding social interaction (for example autism).
- Speech problems (for example articulation problems).
- Others not listening and valuing what they are trying to communicate.

Many different professionals may be involved in this, but a person's motivation and efforts are equally important. Key experts likely to be encountered include speech and language therapists to help with communication problems, advocates, interpreters and clinical psychologists to help with problems affecting mental processes and emotions.

Health professionals need to:

- Take time and have patience.
- Value what is being communicated.
- Recognise non verbal cues.
- Find out about the person's alternative communication strategies if verbal communication is difficult (for example their typical non verbal cues, use symbols, sign language).
- Explain things clearly in an appropriate way (verbally and with pictures etc).
- Be prepared to meet the person several times to build up rapport and trust.
- Use the knowledge and support of people's carers.

Use of advocates or interpreters

An advocate is a person who tries to understand the needs and preferences of an individual and speaks on their behalf. Advocates are often needed when someone has a disability which makes it difficult for them to speak for themselves. An advocate should try and get to know the service user and develop an understanding of their culture and background, so that they can represent them accurately. The advocate should understand the person's needs and communicate these to practitioners or professionals involved with them. To ensure that they are unbiased, advocates are independent of the professional carers who work with the individual.

Interpreters can help people for whom English is not their preferred or first language. In the past interpreters may have been family members of the person in question, but this is now discouraged as far as is possible for reasons of confidentiality. For example, a mother whose daughter was interpreting for her may not want her daughter to know that she had cancer. Interpreters communicate the meaning of one spoken language to another, while translators change written material from one language to another.

There are drawbacks to using translators and interpreters, as it may sometimes be difficult to grasp the exact meaning of a message or to express the meaning in the other language.

Where an interpreter is used, it is important to remember to communicate with the service user rather than the interpreter, to ensure that the individual is empowered and feels valued.

In many services, leaflets concerning health topics or health facilities are produced in several other languages in addition to English, so that people from ethnic minorities can access the information. If information is not readily available in the relevant language it will need to be translated.

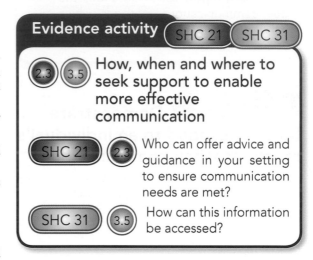

Evidence activity · SHC 21 · SHC 31

2.3 · 3.5 **How, when and where to seek support to enable more effective communication**

SHC 21 · 2.3 Who can offer advice and guidance in your setting to ensure communication needs are met?

SHC 31 · 3.5 How can this information be accessed?

LO3 Be able to overcome barriers to communication

3.1 · SHC 31 **Explain how people from different backgrounds may use and/or interpret communication methods in different ways**

3.5 Overcoming barriers

Respecting cultural preferences and differences

It is important to respect the fact that people have different cultural preferences and values, and therefore different priorities. You will need to recognise the diverse attitudes of those with whom you come into contact, and must not condemn or treat people differently if their values are different from yours.

Body language can be interpreted differently by different cultures. Certain cultures use gestures or touch much more than others, and gestures can mean different things in different cultures. In some cultures, touching someone shows understanding and empathy, but in British culture it might be considered unacceptable in a work situation. Making direct eye contact when communicating may be considered acceptable and even desirable in one culture (e.g. British), but rude and totally unacceptable in another (e.g. Greek). In order to avoid causing any offence or misunderstanding, it is worth taking time to find out about an individual's cultural background.

It is important to develop your knowledge and understanding of different cultures. For example, you should know that in some cultures, young women can only receive medical attention if they are accompanied by an older family member. Also, decisions about whether to have treatment or care are often made collectively by the senior members of the family rather than by the individual. These considerations may not at first seem to be directly linked to communicating with services users, but they do have an impact on the way people communicate and with whom.

Tips for communicating with people from different cultures include:

1. **Understand the individual's values**: Understand that people from other cultures might have entirely different value systems from yours. It is useful to check the person's records for information, or speak to a member of their family or a friend if appropriate or possible. Ask someone else from the same culture, either another worker or an advocate. Use reference books and/or the internet if necessary.

2. **Give the appropriate amount of personal space**: Different cultures have different norms regarding a person's public space (in which others can stand and converse with you) and their private space (reserved only for people who are close to you). For example, people from Arab countries do not share the British concept of 'personal space' – for them

it is considered offensive to step or lean away while talking to someone. Make sure you leave the correct amount of space between yourself others when you talk to them.

3. **Do not belittle their religion**: Remember, most people believe passionately in their religion, and they may have different beliefs from yours. If you have trouble dealing with this, you may wish to avoid discussing the topic of religion altogether.

4. **Learn to recognise physical cues**: Physical gestures that are acceptable when communicating vary widely between different cultures.

5. **Know relationship differences**: Many foreigners think British relationships are superficial (with a brief, 'Hi, Jim', and never a backward glance). British people might think relationships in other cultures are too sentimental. So, know that if a person strikes you as too outspoken or withdrawn, it may be considered normal in their culture.

6. **Learn about their culture**: Learn about greetings, goodbye rituals, before-meal ceremonies, food and clothes. This will help you understand people from other cultures and improve your communication with them.

7. **Accept that there may be lapses in communication**: Even the best communicators fall short when jumping across the large gap that exists between different cultures. Humour and non-defensiveness are the best way of dealing with these situations.

8. **Ask**: There is no better tool for effective communication than asking a question. If something strikes you as funny or inappropriate, if you feel the other person is neglecting you or is offended, simply ask them what you can do to change the situation. Misunderstandings can create big problems unless they are discussed openly.

Evidence activity SHC 31

3.1 How different backgrounds may use and /or interpret methods in different ways

Produce a 'Guide to different backgrounds' booklet to help individuals working in care settings understand different backgrounds better. Explain how these differences can affect communication.

 **3.1** Barriers to
communication

Identify barriers to effective communication

Research and investigate

SHC 21 **3.1** Barriers to communication

You are working in a care setting. There is a lot of noise going on, with new staff and new service users. What barriers do you think there are?

Barriers are features which can hinder or stop something happening. Barriers to communication make communication less effective. There are many reasons why this can happen; some due to the practitioner, some due to the individual, some due to the environment or setting.

Attitude of the worker

Your attitude can affect the way others communicate with you. When a worker is abrupt towards an individual, that person could feel intimidated and not want to communicate. They may feel that the worker is not interested in them and does not want to help. An insincere approach or lack of empathy may make an individual feel that they are wasting their time, and could make them reluctant to divulge personal information. A sincere and polite attitude is likely to promote more open communication from the service user. Practitioners may have their own emotional issues that can create barriers. The practitioner may not be able to focus or may be tired due to worrying and lack of sleep. Listening and empathising takes mental energy, which may not be available if the practitioner has their own concerns.

Limited availability and use of technology

Some individuals need technological aids to support their communication. When there is limited availability of a technology, communication may be more difficult. For example, the absence of a **hearing loop** could be a barrier to an individual who uses a hearing aid. Workers who have limited experience of using technology (e.g. computers, fax machines or other technological devices) could find that this interferes with their ability to communicate, for example they may not

be able to communicate via email or use a fax machine. This could ultimately delay messages being received and responded to, and could undermine someone's authority if they need to ask for help.

Key terms

A **hearing loop** provides information on an induction loop system, to assist the hearing impaired by transmitting sound from a sound system, microphone, television or other source, directly to a hearing aid.

Sitting too far away or invading personal space

Sitting too far away from a person may make them feel that they are not important or that the practitioner is not interested in what they have to say. It may also mean that they need to speak more loudly, which could compromise confidentiality or make them feel uncomfortable about communicating. Invasion of personal space (getting too close) can also make people feel uncomfortable. Most people prefer to get to know someone first, and often only allow those who are close to them into their 'intimate zone'.

Emotional distress

3.6 Distress

Emotional issues, especially those that cause worry or distress, can make people behave erratically and unpredictably. When individuals have serious emotional needs they can be afraid or depressed because of the stresses they are experiencing. They may lack self-awareness or appear to be shy or aggressive, which has an impact on their ability to communicate. Listening involves learning about frightening and depressing situations, which can mean that practitioners sometimes avoid listening to avoid feeling unpleasant emotions. The practitioner can become emotionally distressed by the needs of the individual and can also make assumptions, or label or stereotype others.

When individuals are depressed, angry or upset, these emotions will influence their ability to understand what is being communicated to them, and their ability to communicate their own needs. Additionally, individuals who do not trust service providers or practitioners are less likely to share information with them.

Not giving individuals time to say what they want to

Some individuals need more time than others to express themselves. This may be due to a lack of confidence or because they have communication difficulties. When individuals are not given the time they need to express themselves, they may feel that they are being rushed. They get annoyed when, for example, someone else finishes off their sentences for them, or they may 'clam up' and not talk at all.

Poor or unwelcoming body language (non verbal communication)

A worker who displays negative body language in the form of crossed arms or legs, using inappropriate gestures, poor facial expressions, poor body positioning or constant fidgeting creates barriers to communication.

Poor interpersonal skills

A worker who has poor **interpersonal skills** does not make an individual feel welcome. They may use inappropriate language or rely too heavily on technical terminology. Their manner and demeanour may be off-putting, which can create a barrier to successful communication. If the worker is not paying attention to the individual or is not listening properly they may miss important information. It is inappropriate to then ask for this to be repeated, as it will make the individual feel that they are not being valued.

Lack of privacy

Conversations should not be held in a public place where others can overhear what is being said, as this lack of privacy can feel disrespectful. Interruptions by other people may make the individual feel intimidated and unimportant. A person is likely to communicate much more freely if they feel that what they are saying is being taken seriously and kept private.

Lack of respect for individual

An individual is unlikely to communicate if they feel that they are not being respected. Addressing someone as 'dear' or 'lovey', or invading their personal space shows a lack of respect. Any action that is going to be taken should be clearly explained before actually carrying it out, and the opinions and choices of the individual should be respected. If someone feels that they are not being respected they may withhold information which could be vital.

Stereotyping

Stereotyping means describing everyone in a particular category as being 'the same', or describing aspects of their behaviour or characteristics as 'the same'. It is an easy way of grouping people together. For example, it is stereotyping to believe that everyone over 70 years old is less mentally able or needs a walking aid, or that all children below the age of 4 are unable to make decisions for themselves. Sometimes individuals are stereotyped because of their language or the colour of their skin. Some people may assume that anyone who is not white cannot speak English, so they speak in 'broken English' to the individual without first finding out if they can speak English or if English is their preferred language.

Key terms

Interpersonal skills are the skills we use to interact with others.

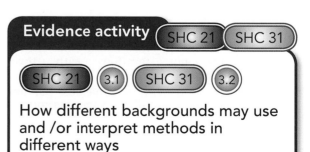

Evidence activity SHC 21 SHC 31

SHC 21 (3.1) SHC 31 (3.2)

How different backgrounds may use and /or interpret methods in different ways

This activity will help demonstrate that you can identify barriers to effective communication.

In a care setting of your choice, using the list above, produce a report identifying all the potential barriers to communications which you can identify.

Demonstrate ways to overcome barriers to effective communication

A good care practitioner will do all they can to remove barriers to communication. There are many ways this can be done.

Respecting cultural preferences and differences

Cultural differences can influence communication. Culture is much more than just the language that is spoken, it includes the way people live, think and how they relate to each other. In some cultures children are not allowed to speak if certain adults are present. Other cultures do not allow women to speak to men they do not know. Cultural differences can sometimes make relationships difficult; therefore workers across the sectors need to make sure they prepare well for this.

You must make sure that you acknowledge culture when communicating. For example, certain hand gestures are acceptable in this country but would not be in others. To show friendliness, in one culture you may say hello with a smile on your face; in another, you may make a silent formal bow; and in a third, you may even embrace the people warmly. Looking straight into the eyes of the person you are speaking to is desirable in most conversations in this country, but would be considered rude in others. These cultures believe that looking down shows proper respect for another individual. A practitioner who feels that eye contact is important must learn to accept and respect this cultural difference.

When communicating it is important to remember the following points:

- Do not make assumptions when meeting a person – they could appear to be demanding simply because they feel insecure or because they are not familiar with their surroundings.
- Treat a person with a same-sex partner accompanying them in the same manner as everyone else.
- Show respect for the values of individuals.
- Do not invade personal space – often people feel uncomfortable with this until they develop trust.
- Acknowledge the beliefs and differences of individuals from other cultures.
- Develop knowledge and understanding of different cultures in order to avoid making mistakes or causing offence.

Asking questions to clarify points, aiding understanding of communication

- Ask an individual to summarise their understanding of the situation so that further explanation can be given if necessary.
- Always ask if there is anything that is not understood – this can prevent mistakes being made or something being interpreted in the wrong way.
- Ask questions relating to timing, place and procedures to enhance understanding.

Using a level appropriate to individual's understanding

- If possible, check the approximate age of the individual before communicating with them.
- Read through their records to find out what level of understanding they are likely to have.
- Never use technical terminology which has not been explained to the individual.
- Never use acronyms without explaining what they mean.
- Do not assume that an individual will understand what you have said, or that they must have understood because they did not state otherwise.

A comfortable, safe environment

- Make sure that the environment is at the right temperature – not too hot and not too cold.
- Check the environment for any hazards and take precautions to reduce these risks before the communication takes place.
- Make sure the layout of the room is appropriate for the communication to take place.
- Make sure the environment has adequate ventilation – not too draughty or too stuffy.
- Check suitability of seating arrangements – some people prefer chairs with arms so that they can push up to get out of them, some may prefer softer seating, and others may prefer lower/higher chairs.

Respecting dignity and privacy

- Ask what name the individual prefers to be called by.
- Do not speak to the pusher of a wheelchair and by-pass the wheelchair user.
- Involve children in conversation – do not presume they do not understand the discussions.

- Talk to the child and ask their opinions.
- Offer choices wherever possible.
- Allow preferences to be expressed.
- Use a private room where appropriate.
- Do not discuss personal issues where others can overhear.
- Use passwords on the computer.
- Never disclose information over the telephone unless the identity of the caller can be established.
- Ask people to leave the room when appropriate to respect the privacy of the individual.
- Ask permission from the individual before sharing information with others.
- Explain who will have access to personal information.

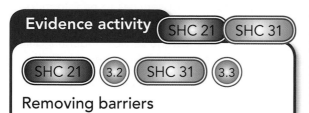

Evidence activity   SHC 21   SHC 31

SHC 21   3.2   SHC 31   3.3

Removing barriers

There are three new service users at the care setting:

1. Hamid who speaks little English but is keen to get to know people.
2. Joan is who very nervous and doesn't like big groups of people.
3. Andrew who is quite aggressive and presents challenging behaviour.

How can the service, and you, help the three new individuals to integrate and participate in full communication?

3.3   SHC 21   3.4   SHC 31

Demonstrate strategies that can be used to ensure understanding and clarify misunderstandings

However you choose to send a message, you must try to ensure that those who are receiving it are aware that it is genuine and purposeful. However, there may be occasions when a message is misinterpreted because potential barriers to the communication process have not been duly considered.

Using verbal communication

Asking questions to clarify points, aiding understanding

Asking the right questions without being too intrusive is an important skill to develop. It will help you to clarify important points and understand the communication. Questions should be short and to the point. Using language and vocabulary that is easy to understand will help to avoid confusion. You should avoid asking multiple questions, as these may be difficult for the individual to answer. Open and closed questions can be used. It is vital that the answers are listened to though to ensure understanding.

Using language appropriate to the individual's understanding

It is important to avoid using language that individuals do not understand, for example using adult language when working with a child would be inappropriate. Likewise, using sophisticated language when communicating with an adult with learning difficulties is unsuitable. If acronyms or technical terminology are used these should always be explained, to ensure that the person understands what has been said. You should always assess the individual you are communicating with before progressing with your communication, so that the interaction is as effective as possible.

Repetition and paraphrasing

Saying points again, respectfully, may help individuals to understand. It may be that occasionally there are times when key points need to be paraphrased. This entails rewording or rephrasing something to express the meaning in another way, which may be better understood.

Using non verbal communication

Use written formats

It may be the case that some individuals understand more if key points are written down, not only to ensure understanding there and then, but for future clarification or to act as a reminder.

Using gestures

Gestures are expressive movements of the body, mainly hands, arms, shoulders and neck to communicate a message. Using a simple 'sshhh' gestures (i.e. fingers to the lips) to help an individual with learning difficulties to understand that it is 'quiet time'.

Observing the individual

Ask any teacher, the best way to check understanding is to watch an individual's body language. Facial expressions, lowering the eyes, fidgeting, may well be indicators of confusion.

Evidence activity
SHC 21 · SHC 31

SHC 21 3.3 · **SHC 31** 3.4

Strategies to ensure communication is understood and clarify misunderstandings

Possibly in a care setting you are familiar with, think of two occasions over the next few weeks where you will have to communicate with a service user. Describe any methods you could use to clarify understanding.

3.4 · **SHC 21** · 3.5 · **SHC 31**

Identify sources of information and support or services to enable more effective communication

See section in LO2 for other information on translation services and interpreting services.

▮ Research and investigate 🔍

SHC 21 3.4 · **SHC 31** 3.5

Support available

Using the following websites, research two other support systems to enable more effective communication.

Speech and language services
www.rcslt.org

Advocacy services
www.bild.org.uk/04advocacy.htm

Services will need a referral for assistance to begin. Self-referral from an individual with learning difficulties may of course happen, but it may be more likely to be a professional or third party referral which requests the use of services. It may be that a simple phone call is made, and the services could arrive in a short period of time to assist with communication. But for longer term care, the use of a service may be embedded into the care plan of an individual.

Evidence activity
SHC 21 · SHC 31

SHC 21 3.4 · **SHC 31** 3.5

Sources of support

L2 3.4 Consider a work placement of your choice and identify the sources of information and support or services to enable more effective communication.

L3 3.5 Explain how the services indentified in LV 2 Evidence Activity 3.4 can be accessed.

LO4 Be able to apply principles and practices relating to confidentiality, especially at work

4.1 Explain the term 'confidentiality'

What is confidentiality?

Confidentiality means that personal and private information obtained from or about an individual must only be shared with others on a 'need-to-know' basis. Information given to a worker should not be disclosed without the person's informed permission. Confidentiality is an important principle in health and social care because it provides guidance on the amount of personal information and data that can be disclosed without consent. A person disclosing personal information in a relationship of trust reasonably expects his or her privacy to be protected, that is they expect the information to remain confidential. The relationship between health and social care professionals and their patients/clients centres on trust, and trust is dependent on the patient/client being confident that personal information they disclose is treated confidentially. However, confidentiality can be countered when there is a public interest in others being protected from harm.

Case study

    Ms X

Ms X lives with her two children in a small market town. One of the children has a learning disability which requires extra care. She is to have a minor operation and arrangements need to be made for the care of her children while she is in hospital and convalescing.

Arrangements for the care of the children are being discussed at a case conference by Ms X and the family's GP, social worker and health visitor. The elder child's school will be informed of the final arrangements.

Various pieces of information are known to the four people at the case conference, although not every piece of information is known by each individual. The privacy of interests of Ms X, her children and their absent father may be different.

Here are some criteria that can influence whether or not information is disclosed or shared:

* confidence that the recipient of the data will handle it responsibly
* the need for consent to disclosure and respect for refusals to consent

* the accuracy, relevance, and pertinence of the data.

1) Can you think of any other considerations?

It is not always easy to decide which pieces of information should be shared. Consider the following:

The GP knows that the absent father is HIV positive. To the best of the GP's knowledge, neither the social worker nor the health visitor are aware of this. It is also possible that Ms X is unaware.

2) In these particular circumstances, should the GP share this information with the following people, and why?

   (a) Ms X

   (b) the health visitor

   (c) the social worker

3) As a health or social care professional it is vital that you apply the principles of confidentiality. Inappropriate disclosure of information can have a significant negative impact on people's lives. What could be the impact of disclosure in this situation?

Evidence activity SHC 21 SHC 31

(4.1) Confidentiality

Explain what is meant by the term confidentiality.

3.7 Safe and secure

(4.2) Demonstrate ways to maintain confidentiality in day to day communication, especially in line with agreed ways of working

Maintaining confidentiality is a very important aspect of building trust between a client and a worker. Without trust, communication is less likely to progress between two or more people. This involves honouring commitments and declaring conflicts of interest. It also means making sure that the policy which relates to ways of communicating with people is followed.

The right to confidentiality is paramount in care.

There are occasions when a worker may have to break confidentiality. Such situations arise when:

- a person is likely to harm themselves
- a person is likely to harm others
- a child or vulnerable adult has suffered, or is at risk of suffering, significant harm
- a person has been, or is likely to be, involved in a serious crime

It must also be remembered that other professional workers will need to have specific information on a need-to-know basis and, in these circumstances, information may have to be passed to others.

Ways to maintain confidentiality

- Safe storage of information so that people who should not see the information cannot gain access to it.
- The use of passwords for computer logon.
- Only giving information on a need-to-know basis.
- Not passing on information without the relevant permission.
- Only using the information for the intended and agreed purpose.
- Adhering to relevant legislation relating to data protection and accessing personal files.

The most common ways in which confidentiality can be breached

- Notes left in an unattended area.
- Failure to ask whether information may be disclosed to others.
- Discussions in public areas about service users.
- Failure to log off the computer system.
- Allowing others to know and use your password.
- Leaving information on a VDU screen which can be seen by the public.
- Failure to establish a person's identity before giving them information.
- Holding conversations, including on the telephone, in a public area.
- Leaving personal and private information in a car.

Legal requirements

The approach of the courts of law to record keeping tends to be that 'if it is not recorded, it has not been done'. Workers across the sectors have both a professional and a legal duty of care to their clients, so their record keeping should be able to demonstrate:

- a full account of their assessment and the care that has been planned and provided
- relevant information about the condition of the patient/client at any given time
- the measures taken by the worker to respond to their needs
- evidence that the worker has understood and honoured their duty of care, that all reasonable steps have been taken to care for the patient/client and that any actions or omissions on the part of the worker have not compromised their safety in any way
- a record of any arrangements that have been made for the continuing care of a patient/client.

Organisational policies

All organisations have their own policies and procedures regarding recording and reporting of information to make sure that all practitioners observe the regulations that apply to them. Some users of services bring issues with them and provide personal details in order for practitioners to help them. By being assured that their information is going to be recorded, stored and shared appropriately, individuals feel more able to disclose information that they may not have been previously happy to discuss. Some people feel intimidated by, or reluctant to talk about, their issues. Young people, refugees and offenders, for example, may feel especially vulnerable. Users of services need reassurance that they will not be judged, and that anything they tell workers will not be shared with others without the client's knowledge and consent.

Many different organisational policies refer to responsibility in relation to recording and reporting of information, including:

- confidentiality policies
- health and well being policies
- information governance policies
- health and safety policies
- child protection policies
- assessment, recording and reporting policies
- codes of conduct and national standards frameworks relating to practitioners across the sectors, which also apply within organisations.

Meet the needs of individuals

Only information required to meet the individual's specific needs should be recorded and reported. Information that is not relevant should not be recorded at all. For example financial information would not be relevant to a patient who has been admitted to hospital for an operation; however, it may be needed to determine an individual's ability to pay for adult social care services. Information describing personal characteristics such as age, gender, disability, ethnicity, religion and sexual orientation should only be used to support the provision of high-quality care to meet individual needs.

The Caldicott Principles were developed for the NHS in relation to the recording and sharing of personal information. These principles can easily be applied to any organisation or setting. The Caldicott Standards are based on the Data Protection Act 1998 principles.

The Caldicott Principles

1. *Justify the purpose(s) of using confidential information*

   Every proposed use or transfer of patient-identifiable information within or from an organisation should be clearly defined and scrutinised, with continuing uses regularly reviewed by an appropriate guardian.

2. *Do not use patient-identifiable information unless it is absolutely necessary*

   Patient-identifiable information items should not be included unless it is essential for the specified purpose(s) of that flow. The need for patients to be identified should be considered at each stage of satisfying the purpose(s).

3. *Use the minimum necessary patient-identifiable information that is required*

   Where use of the patient-identifiable information is considered to be essential, the inclusion of each individual item of information should be considered and justified so that the minimum amount of identifiable information is transferred or accessible as is necessary for a given function to be carried out.

4. *Access to patient-identifiable information should be on a strict need-to-know basis*

   Only those individuals who need access to patient-identifiable information should have access to it, and they should only have access to the information items that they need to see. This may mean introducing access controls or splitting information flows where one information flow is used for several purposes.

5. *Everyone with access to patient-identifiable information should be aware of their responsibilities*

   Action should be taken to ensure that those handling patient-identifiable information – both clinical and non-clinical staff – are made fully aware of their responsibilities and obligations to respect patient confidentiality.

6. *Understand and comply with the law*

   Every use of patient-identifiable information must be lawful. Someone in each organisation handling patient information should be responsible for ensuring that the organisation complies with the legal requirements.

Procedures and practices

Across the sectors there are different procedures and practices that may be expected to be followed within each organisation.

Every organisation must have a policy that explains the procedures to be followed for sharing information. The policy should clearly state:

- which senior managers have the responsibility to decide about disclosing information
- what to do when action is required urgently
- how to make sure that information will only be used for the purpose for which it is required
- procedures to be followed to obtain manual records
- procedures to be followed to access computer records
- arrangements for reviewing the procedures.

Relevant legislation relating to data protection, accessing personal files and medical records

Data Protection Act 1998

The Data Protection Act 1998 governs access to the health records of living people. It became effective on 1 March 2000, and superseded the Data Protection Act 1984 and the Access to Health Records Act 1990, though the Access to Health Records Act 1990 still governs access to the health records of deceased people. The Data Protection Act 1998 gives every living person the right to apply for access to their health records. The Data Protection Act protects people's rights to confidentiality and covers both paper and electronic records. The act provides individuals with a range of rights, including:

- the right to know what information is held on them and to see and correct this information
- the right to refuse to provide information
- the right that data held should be accurate and up to date
- the right that data held should not be kept for longer than is necessary
- the right to confidentiality – information should not be accessible to unauthorised people.

The Data Protection Act 1998 is not confined to health records held for the purposes of the National Health Service (NHS). It applies equally to the private health sector and to health professionals' private practice records. It also applies to the records of employers who hold information relating to the physical or mental health of their employees, if the record has been made by or on behalf of a health professional in connection with the care of the employee.

Access to Medical Reports Act 1988

This Act gives guidelines covering requests from employers or insurance companies wanting medical reports on individuals. For example, the individual's specific consent has to be given before a medical report can be written for employment or insurance purposes. The individual also has the right to see the report before it is passed to the employer or insurance company; they can then request alterations to be made and refuse permission for the report to be sent. For example, a GP could not give information about an individual's medical history to an insurance company without a consent form signed by the individual stating that they agree to their personal information being given. The consent form would include a statement saying that the individual did or did not want to see the report before it was sent to the insurance company.

Other legislation

Other appropriate legislation may include:

- Crime and Disorder Act 1998
- Criminal Procedures and Investigations Act
- Human Rights Act 1998
- Freedom of Information Act 2000
- Children Act 2004

Evidence activity SHC 21 SHC 31

 4.2 Maintaining confidentiality

At a residential setting for adults with learning disabilities, a client's cousin has telephoned from Australia asking for an update on their family member's health. They say that due to the distance, they will not be able to get over to visit for a long time so they should be given the information.

1. What action do you take and why?
2. What policies and procedures would you need to follow?
3. What legislation would you need to adhere to?

3.8 Records must be kept securely

4.3 **Describe situations where information normally considered to be confidential might need to be passed on**

English common law makes provision for a confidential relationship and the duty of confidence. The Data Protection Act 1998 and Human Rights Act 1998 have introduced enforceable rights for service users about how the information they provide is used. The Data Protection Act has restrictions on storing personal data in all formats, written and electronic. The Human Rights

Act 1998 emphasises respect for private life and strengthens the hand of those advocating increased privacy for the individual. Due to these Acts and the duty of confidentiality there is a potential conflict between protecting the privacy and confidentiality of individuals and protecting the public, and a duty of care to the service user.

Confidentiality can be breached:

- To protect children at risk of significant harm as defined by the Children Act 1989.
- To protect the public from acts of terrorism as defined in the Prevention of Terrorism Act 1971.
- As a duty to the courts.
- Under the Drug Trafficking Offences Act 1986.
- Section 115 of the Crime and Disorder Act 1998 gives public bodies the power, but not a duty, to disclose information for the prevention or detection of crime.
- To ensure the service provides a duty of care in a life-threatening situation, for example serious illness or injury, suicide and self-harming behaviour. This includes when a service user continues to drive against medical advice when unfit to do so. In such circumstances relevant information should be disclosed to the medical advisor of the Driver and Vehicle Licensing Agency, without delay.
- To protect the service provider in a life-threatening situation, for example calls to police regarding a violent service user. There is government guidance about the issue of violence against staff, which can be accessed via the Department of Health website.

   www.doh.gov.uk/violencetaskforce

When to disclose confidential information, what to disclose and who to

When information is shared, the full details surrounding the collection of the information may not be explicit. Practitioners receiving the information may not fully understand the individual's circumstances. There could be confusion over when it is appropriate to share confidential information, how much of the information can be shared and who the information should be shared with. Ethical dilemmas can create issues in this way, for example when a 15 year old goes to see her GP because she is pregnant, should the girl's parents be informed? Services should include guidance on this in their confidentiality policy to ensure that all workers are following the same procedures and are absolutely clear about these issues.

Risks involved in information sharing

Whenever and wherever information is shared there are always going to be **risks** involved, whether the information is shared verbally or in written format.

Key terms

Risks, in this context, are things that may cause loss of or damage to information.

Risks to individuals

Information could be passed on to people who should not have access to it. If unauthorised people gained access to personal details, medical or financial information this could be used fraudulently by others. The identity of the individual could be used by someone else to take money from them or to pretend they are the individual for a variety of reasons. The individual could be put at risk themselves. The information may not be passed on accurately and this could result in their welfare or care needs not being met. Clearly those with learning difficulties may be more vulnerable to risk.

Risks to practitioners

Practitioners may not understand the information that has been shared and could make mistakes. The accuracy of the information shared may lead to misinterpretation by the practitioner which could mean they cannot carry out their role effectively, such as when and where to provide the care required. Practitioners may, inadvertently, break confidentiality without realising what they have done by including too much detail in the information they share or, when receiving information, sharing it with others who did not need to know.

Importance of accuracy of records

All records that are kept must be accurate, as others may need to use them and mistakes can be made as a result of the wrong information being recorded. Workers should always read through the information they have recorded to check that it is accurate. There are a number of reasons why accuracy is particularly important:

- It may be a legal document: A legal document may be required to be used as evidence in a court of law. If the information is not accurate the evidence recorded could cause many issues. For example, if it were to be used for criminal proceedings, the person may not be able to be prosecuted or, if there was a claim that malpractice had been carried out in the care provided to an individual, the records may not support the evidence given and a worker could be sued, when in fact they had not done anything wrong.

- If it is a medical record: Medical records have to be accurate to ensure that the needs of the individual are met. When an individual sees a care professional regarding their medical care, the records of their previous treatment and care may need to be referred to, to ensure that any changes or progression of their care meets their needs. This may not be possible if there are any inaccuracies in the records that have been made. It is also important to remember that individuals have the right to see their medical records under the Access to Medical Records Act and may be annoyed if the information is not accurate or points have been made that are insensitive or judgemental.

- Misinterpretation of illegible drug dosage could be fatal: On drugs charts used in hospitals and nursing homes the dosage the individual is prescribed must be accurate and legible. If this is not the case, individuals could easily be given too much of the medication which could have fatal consequences. Too little of the medication could result in their health deteriorating and their needs not being met.

Currency, accuracy, validity and reliability

All records that are kept should be current (up to date), accurate, valid and reliable.

Accuracy of information is essential to ensure that mistakes are not made and the needs of individuals are met. In health, up-to-date information about a patient's condition is crucial. In children and young people's care settings, accurate details of children's allergies might be essential. In adult social care, accurate contact information for next of kin may be necessary, and any care plan changes must be recorded clearly.

Evidence activity SHC 21 SHC 31

4.3 Disclosure

Produce a report describing situations in a care setting you are familiar with where you may need to break confidentiality or disclose concerns. If you use any specific individuals as examples, ensure you keep them anonymous.

4.4 SHC 21 **Explain how and when to seek advice about confidentiality**

The decision to break confidentiality can be a difficult one and hence guidance may be sought. An individual may be at risk, but, at the same time, the trust with an individual can be broken. Plus, there may be many strong moral and ethical reasons for and against. Therefore, you should never make this decision on your own. You must seek assistance.

Where can you go to seek advice?

→ Refer to legal requirements – What does the law say should happen?

→ Refer to organisational policies and procedures – What does your care setting advise?

→ Refer to Codes of Conduct and National Standards Frameworks relating to practitioners across the sectors. What do Professional Council and National services advise?

→ Refer to the needs of the individuals – what is right for them and their situation?

→ Consult with your supervisor or line manager – what is their advice?

3.9 Where can you go to seek advice?

In many circumstances, a discussion with a practitioner with a position of more responsibility can be enough, and indeed, it may be therefore that it is them themselves who make the decision whether to breach confidentiality or not.

Evidence activity SHC 21

4.4 Seeking advice about confidentiality

Consider a care setting you are familiar with. Speak to your supervisor, read the organisational policies and so on and explain how and when you would need to seek advice about confidentiality. It may be useful to use some examples.

Your reading of this chapter and completion of the activities will have prepared you to be able to engage in personal development in health, social care or children's and young people's settings.

Assessment Summary for Unit SHC 21

To achieve the unit, your assessor will require you to:

Learning outcomes	Assessment criteria
1 Understand why communication is important in the work setting by:	**1.1** Identifying the different reasons people communicate See Evidence activity 1.1, p. 50.
	1.2 Explaining how effective communication affects all aspects of the learner's work See Evidence activity 1.2, p. 51.
	1.3 Explaining why it is important to observe an individual's reactions when communicating with them. See Evidence activity 1.3, p. 52.
2 Be able to meet the communication and language needs, wishes and preferences of individuals by:	**2.1** Showing how to find out an individual's communication and language needs, wishes and preferences See Evidence activity 2.1, p. 53.
	2.2 Demonstrating communication methods that meet an individual's communication needs, wishes and preferences See Evidence activity 2.2, p. 54.
	2.3 Showing how and when to seek advice about communication. See Evidence activity 2.3, p. 58.
3 Be able to overcome barriers to communication by:	**3.1** Identifying barriers to effective communication See Evidence activity 3.1, p. 61.
	3.2 Demonstrating ways to overcome barriers to effective communication See Evidence activity 3.2, p. 63.
	3.3 Demonstrating ways to ensure that communication has been understood See Evidence activity 3.3, p. 64.
	3.4 Identifying sources of information and support or services to enable more effective communication. See Evidence activity 3.4, p. 64.

Learning outcomes	Assessment criteria
4 Be able to apply principles and practices relating to confidentiality at work by:	**(4.1)** Explaining the term confidentiality See Evidence activity 4.1, p. 65.
	(4.2) Demonstrating confidentiality in day-to-day communication See Evidence activity 4.2, p. 68.
	(4.3) Describing situations where information normally considered to be confidential might need to be passed on See Evidence activity 4.3, p. 70.
	(4.4) Explaining how and when to seek advice about confidentiality. See Evidence activity 4.4, p. 70.

Assessment Summary for Unit SHC 31

To achieve the unit, your assessor will require you to:

Learning outcomes	Assessment criteria
1 Show that you understand why effective communication is important in the work setting by:	**(1.1)** Identifying the different reasons people communicate See Evidence activity 1.1, p. 50.
	(1.2) Explaining how communication affects relationships in the work setting See Evidence activity 1.2, p. 51.
2 Be able to meet the communication and language needs, wishes and preferences of individuals by:	**(2.1)** Demonstrating how to establish the communication and language needs, wishes and preferences of individuals See Evidence activity 2.1, p. 53.
	(2.2) Describing the factors to consider when promoting effective communication See Evidence activity 2.2, p. 54.
	(2.3) Demonstrating a range of communication methods and styles to meet individual needs See Evidence activity 2.3, p. 57.
	(2.4) Demonstrating how to respond to an individual's reactions when communicating See Evidence activity 2.4, p. 57.

3 Be able to overcome barriers to communication by:	Explaining how people from different backgrounds may use and/or interpret communication methods in different ways See Evidence activity 3.1, p. 59.
	Identifying barriers to effective communication See Evidence activity 3.2, p. 61.
	Demonstrating ways to overcome barriers to communication See Evidence activity 3.3, p. 63.
	Demonstrating strategies that can be used to clarify misunderstandings See Evidence activity 3.4, p. 64.
	Explaining how to access extra support or services to enable individuals to communicate effectively See Evidence activity 3.5, p. 58 and Evidence activity 3.5, p. 64.
4 Be able to apply principles and practices relating to confidentiality by:	Explain the meaning of the term confidentiality See Evidence activity 4.1, p. 65.
	Demonstrating ways to maintain confidentiality in day-to-day communication See Evidence activity 4.2, p. 68.
	Describing the potential tension between maintaining an individual's confidentiality and disclosing concerns See Evidence activity 4.3, p. 70.

Web links

Community Care	**www.community-care.co.uk**
Royal National Institute for the Deaf	**www.rnid.org.uk**
Royal National Institute of the Blind	**www.rnib.org.uk**
Social Care Sector Skills Council	**www.skillsforcare.org.uk**
Health Care Sector Skills Council	**www.skillsforhealth.org.uk**
Skills for Justice Sector Skills Council	**www.skillsforjusticce.com**

4 Provide and promote active support

Unit LD 203 Provide active support
Unit LD 303 Promote active support

What are you finding out?

We will look at what active support is and why and how it will benefit people we work with. To explore this we need to examine the models that are used and the importance of the correct introduction of active support. Active support follows the person-centred approach to social care and was developed from legislation in Valuing People Now: The delivery plan 2010–2011 (Department of Health 2010). We all sometimes want to do nothing, but as individuals we get bored and depressed if we are inactive for even a short period of time, and we can become isolated and develop low self-esteem. Active support is not about making someone do excessive physical activity but is about engaging individuals in daily activities to allow them to be involved and gain purpose.

The reading and activities in this chapter will help you to:

- Understand how active support translates values into person-centred practical action with an individual

- Be able to interact positively with individuals to promote participation

- Be able to implement person-centred daily plans to promote participation

- Be able to maintain person-centred records of participation

Key terms

Active support means to support individuals to take part in meaningful, everyday activities regardless of their disabilities.

The hotel model is waiting-on individuals and attending to their needs during transition from institutions to community care.

4.1 The name 'hotel model' suggests the kind of care that used to be given

LO1 Understand how active support translates values into person-centred practical action with an individual

Most people find that if they do nothing they fall asleep because they are bored and this helps to pass the time. You find that you have no energy even though you have done nothing all day. Imagine if you were unable to do anything for a period of time, how would you feel? Initially you might enjoy the rest but after a while you would become frustrated and bored. When you are a guest you offer to help out, partly to be polite but mainly to feel useful. Research has shown that with increased activity we become less frustrated and increase our sense of worth. We have a purpose.

Active support is not about teaching new skills, although this may occur during the process. Active support is about engaging individuals, irrespective of their disability, in meaningful activity. As the supporter your role is enabling the individual to achieve goals and ensuring they are not inactive for long periods of time. Active support can be the simple tasks of laying the table for dinner, making a cup of tea and so on, not tasks that are beyond the individual's capabilities.

1.1   LD 203   Explain how the key characteristics of active support differ from the hotel model

The hotel model meant that the carer treated the individual as if they were in a hotel; making their tea, cleaning and providing all their meals. The name describes the model well and it can sometimes be helpful, though care should always be taken to not disempower the individual by taking over. But the model also means the individual has long periods of inactivity while the carer is busy. The rationale behind the model was that the carer could complete tasks faster than the individual could, but this denied the individual the rights or choice of preparing anything for themselves. One of the reasons this model was designed was to justify the costs of care.

Evidence activity   LD 203

1.1   Compare and contrast

In the box below identify what the differences are in the hotel model compared to the active support model:

Hotel model	Active support model
Washing up by carer	Washing up done by individual with support

1.1   LD 303   Compare the characteristics associated with active support and the hotel model in relation to an individual's support

When looking at the hotel model of care we need to explore what it means to the individual involved. With the hotel model the individual is assisted with washing and dressing prior to breakfast being served. After breakfast the carer needs to ensure the bedroom and washing area are cleaned and left tidy. During this time the individual is left waiting for the next interaction. This might come when tea / coffee is made and served. Another period of inactivity for the individual follows. The next step might be preparing the individual for lunch, a task that the carer is involved in but not necessarily the individual, who would again be waiting for interaction.

With active support this morning routine is reversed for the individual and the carer. With active support, the individual would identify the way they would like to be assisted to wake up in the morning. The carer would be there to support them through the process. The main difference is that the individual is in control, and inactive periods are greatly reduced. The carer is much more actively involved in listening and supporting the individual in their daily tasks. Communication is more active and involves frequent discussions with the individual over what support they require.

Evidence activity LD 303

1.1 Compare and contrast

Identify in your workplace a daily routine and clarify what model it takes, either hotel or active. Describe the difference if it were to be changed to the alternative model.

1.2 LD 203 **Define the terms:**

- **Promoting independence**
- **Informed choices**
- **Valued life**

4.2 Independent choice is crucial; any individual should be able to choose when they would like a hot drink

By using active support we are encouraging the individual to take control and make decisions for themselves, decisions we make daily without thinking. Individuals with learning disabilities require support and planning. An example of this would be the process of making a cup of tea. As an individual we decide when we want a hot drink and set about making this; it is an automatic process. Consider the difference it would make to your life if you could not have a hot drink when you wanted and had to wait for someone to make a drink for you. Consider also the impact of waiting with no interaction whilst this process was occurring. With active support the individual can start the process, no matter what their disability, and the role of the support worker is to support this process. This may consist of communicating the process, offering assistance with pouring the hot water and so on. When supporting the individual communication is continuous and you are enabling them to feel a sense of achievement in completing the task and giving them a sense of normality. Society expects all adults to be able to make a hot drink for themselves.

Promoting independence means enabling someone to achieve something that makes them less dependent on others. Therefore by supporting the individual to make a hot drink for themselves you have reduced their dependency on staff/others to perform this task for them in the future.

Independent choice is the ability, in this instance, of the individual to state when they want the hot drink.

Time to reflect

LD 203 **1.2**

Think of a time when you have assisted someone to complete a task for themselves. Describe what the activity was, explain how this task helped the individual to be independent, allowed them to have free choice and made them feel valued.

1.2 LD 303 **Identify practical changes that could be made within a service setting to:**

- **Promote an individual's independence**
- **Support informed choices**
- **Improve quality of life**

In a home setting enabling active support can sometimes be difficult due to environmental restrictions. If a shared kitchen is used and all residents wish to make a hot drink at the same time then restrictions might include the number of support workers available and the completion of any risk assessments prior to a task. Planning is of the greatest importance to identify any obstacles prior to the activity to ensure successful achievement of active support. Prior planning ensures obstacles are removed. If we take the example of making a hot drink, we need to identify the level of support required depending on the individual's present ability. We need to ensure that the equipment for making a drink is suitable for the individual to use, for example the work surfaces are at the correct height. A golden rule of active support is the need for clear communication, not only with the individual but also with all staff members, thus ensuring awareness of the daily activities where extra support may be needed.

when it is completed to give a sense of achievement. As previously discussed, the hotel model required no input from the individual, food and drink was supplied at regular intervals. There was no need to plan the task of dressing as this was also organised for the individual. In all respects the individual had no input and had limited choices and self-value. They spent most of their time inactive and isolated and completely reliant on the carer. The change in caring role to a supportive role for the carer not only required a name change but a complete review of attitude to the role. It required a clear identification of expectations as they were no longer glorified domestics but enablers for individuals to live their lives as independently as possible.

Evidence activity

 Practical changes to support independence

Within your workplace setting identify a daily task you could support an individual with and the changes you would need to make to the environment to enable the activity. By doing this activity, how have you promoted the individual's independence? How has this supported the individual's choices? And how has this improved the quality of their lives?

 Explain how use of active support can promote independence, informed choice and a valued life

In our own lives we don't keep a list of what we are doing each day; we may keep a diary to ensure we do not forget important events but as a rule we do not keep a detailed plan of our daily lives. We are able to mentally plan the activities we need to do daily. Unfortunately for persons with a learning disability, life is a bit more complex; therefore they require a plan to help them concentrate and to allow them to mark off a task

Case study

 LD 203 **1.3** **Jennifer**

Jennifer has autism and has lived in institutionalised care for the majority of her life. She is 20 years old and has recently moved into supported housing. Jennifer has never been taught or encouraged to wash up and previous attempts to encourage Jennifer in any activity resulted in challenging behaviour. Her angry outbursts required high staffing levels. Staff that looked after Jennifer said they felt that doing the daily tasks for Jennifer made the shift go quicker and they believed they were demonstrating their caring role. During the time the staff were doing the 'caring' Jennifer had quiet time. On moving to the new supported housing, the support worker for Jennifer has arranged with her and all involved in her person-centred planning to engage Jennifer in active support, starting with washing breakfast dishes.

Explain how the support worker can promote Jennifer's informed choice and independence and give value to her life by using active support.

4.3 Active support gives value to an individual's life

LO2 Be able to interact positively with individuals to promote participation

 LD 203 Explain the three elements in positive interaction that promote an individual's participation in activity

Active support enables the individual to participate in their own life and not be a spectator as in the hotel model. To be an active support worker, there are three identified elements to ensure positive interaction:

- levels of assistance
- task analysis
- positive reinforcement.

Levels of assistance will vary depending on the task and on the individual's abilities. An example might be buttering toast: some individuals who have completed this before may need verbal guidance, whilst someone doing this for the first time may require a demonstration, pictorial instructions and so on.

Task analysis refers to the need to break the task down into small achievable steps. To use the buttering of toast example, you may need to break the process into stages, e.g. take bread out of bread bin, take two slices out. Place into toaster and pull toaster slider down. Wait for toast to pop up. Place toast onto a plate, obtain butter and knife and so on.

Positive reinforcement refers to the encouragement the support worker needs to give to the individual to encourage participation and development.

2.1 LD 303 Assess the levels of help an individual would need to participate in a range of new activities

We have discussed the fact that active support requires us to use a person-centred approach. We need to look at each individual and assess their abilities and explore their capabilities and support needs. The first stage is identifying the level of assistance the individual requires.

Evidence activity LD 203

2.1 Promoting participation

In the table below are three tasks. Using the idea of active support and thinking of individuals you work with, place your actions against the headings to promote positive interaction for the individual.

Positive interaction	Washing up	Getting dressed	Emptying the bins
Levels of assistance			
Task analysis			
Positive reinforcement			

Time to reflect

LD 303 **2.1** Assessing help levels

Identify an individual you work with, and identify a new task for them. Clarify their ability to do the task and the skill areas they will need to develop. Write down your findings; were you surprised by the skills they already had? Can you see what would work well and can you identify where you would need to give support?

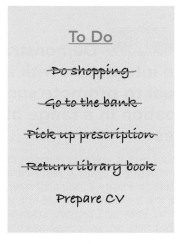

To Do

~~Do shopping~~

~~Go to the bank~~

~~Pick up prescription~~

~~Return library book~~

Prepare CV

4.4 Routine tasks need to be broken down into manageable steps

2.2 **LD 203** Break a routine task into manageable steps for an individual

Identifying a task in which to involve the individual is not necessarily going to make them independent. If this occurs following completion of the task it is a bonus. Remember that active support is all about participation to improve quality of life. To support individuals in completing new tasks, manageable steps are required. These can be set out in many ways. Once a new task is identified, knowledge of the individual will help you break down the task into manageable steps for them, through verbal instructions, pictorial cues or by demonstration.

These steps may need to be carried out several times depending on the individual's learning levels. Time is the most effective tool. All new tasks require expert planning with every person involved in the individual's needs.

Evidence activity LD 203

2.2 Breaking a task into steps

Write down the steps for a task. Describe how you would actively support an individual through each stage of the task.

2.2 **LD 303** Use task analysis to break a range of new activities into manageable steps for an individual

Task analysis is exactly what it says. The aim of task analysis is to observe someone doing a task such as washing up. Because we are so used to doing this on a regular basis the steps we take to complete this task are made unconsciously. But individuals who have never washed up before may not know what steps to take first. A task analysis of washing up would be to observe someone washing up and make detailed notes of each step the person takes to successfully wash up, such as obtaining a bowl and placing it in the sink. Turn the hot tap on. Put washing up liquid into a bowl, two small squirts of washing up liquid. When water has reached half way up the bowl, turn the tap off and so on.

Evidence activity LD 303

2.2 Using task analysis

Identify a new task. Observe someone completing the task and then write the detailed steps needed to complete the task.

2.3 | LD 203 | Provide different levels of help to support an individual to participate in a task or activity

The individual's abilities guide the level of support required. In active support the level of support should be sufficient to enable the individual to participate, with a gradual reduction in support as their abilities increase. The different levels of support are defined as:

- Ask / tell/ suggest
- Instruct
- Prompt
- Show
- Guide
- **Ask** would be to give a verbal prompt so the individual is aware that the task or activity needs to commence.
- **Instruct** is to give verbal prompts on each step, reminding the individual of the process of the task.
- **Prompt** is to give verbal direction but could involve visual clues for each step.
- **Show** is demonstrating the next steps.
- **Guide** might be physical support, for example when cutting bread you may need to place your hand above the individual's to demonstrate the action of slicing bread.

Time to reflect

LD 203 **2.3** Different levels of support

Write down a task you completed while supporting an individual. Write the levels of support you gave from the list above. Write about what went well, what did not go so well and what you would do differently next time.

2.3 | LD 303 | Evaluate different ways of positively reinforcing an individual's participation in a range of new activities

Evidence activity | LD 303

2.3 Participation in new activities

An individual you are looking after wishes to try picture bingo. She has never been enabled to participate before but would like learn how. Her learning disability is classed as profound and she has multiple learning difficulties (PMLD). How will you support her to fully participate in the game? Identify the levels of support and how you would positively reinforce these actions.

2.4 | LD 303 | Demonstrate positive interaction with an individual to promote successful participation in a range of new activities

To meet this criteria you will need to demonstrate positive interaction during a planned observation by your assessor. Positive interaction will only have occurred if the individual feels able and confident to participate. They will require acknowledgement from you that they are progressing and are able to complete the tasks. Some tasks are reinforced by their outcomes, for example buttering toast is a positive interaction with the positive reinforcement of eating the toast, buttered in the way they like. Other forms of positive reinforcement may need to come from the support worker through praise at correct times or reinforcing the outcomes.

Time to reflect

LD 303 **2.4** Positive interaction

Write about an experience of positive reinforcement you have been involved with, identify what went well, what you could have done differently and what you have learnt from the experience.

2.4 | LD 203 Positively reinforce an individual's participation in an activity

Sometimes when we try to do something new, we can get frustrated if we do not get it right first time. If we looked at this experience negatively we might not attempt the task again. Fortunately we can reason that we are learning and therefore lower our expectations of achievement first time and continually try to achieve until we master the skill. As support workers we need to adapt our role as teachers / enablers through giving support, advice and guidance to those learning the new task. We must give encouragement for each attempt. By encouraging continual participation we also provide positive reinforcement.

To involve the individual we first need to identify what they wish to do, the level of support needed and how / what type of positive reinforcement is effective for the individual.

Time to reflect
LD 203 | 2.4 Positive reinforcement

Write about a time you have used positive reinforcement, the type of reinforcement you used, what went well, what did not go so well and what you would do differently next time.

4.5 Promoting participation and communication are vital

LO3 LD 203 Be able to implement person-centred daily plans to promote participation

LO3 LD 303 Be able to develop and implement person-centred daily plans to promote participation

Active support can only be given in conjunction with person-centred planning. In these plans should be a clear identification of the active support to be given; who will support the individual and how to support them will be detailed in step by step actions. Any plans that are written should not be so inflexible as to stop progression. An example of this would be involving the individual in a daily task and due to an unexpected problem, such as the individual needing to see a doctor, the task cannot be completed. The plan would need to be amended to accommodate the change and possibly rearranged for another time. Plans are effective in communicating to all involved the actions prepared and agreed upon. In a residential setting the plan ensures the task being performed is free of conflict with any other activity. An example of this would be making lunch and using the kitchen equipment, ensuring no one else was using the equipment at the time you have arranged to support the individual.

3.1 | LD 203 Provide opportunities for an individual to participate in activity throughout the day avoiding lengthy periods of disengagement

Disengagement, as with the hotel model, can lead to isolation, boredom, lack of self-worth, disempowerment and depression. As a support worker in person-centred care you need to ensure individuals are involved and are participating at all times. Lengthy periods of inactivity have a negative impact. Planning daily tasks and activities ensures this will not occur.

We all have preferences over when we like to do something. An example of this would be having a bath; some people enjoy them most in the morning whilst others enjoy them in the evening. We need to write out a basic plan that is flexible enough to allow the preferences of individuals. Some tasks/

Evidence activity LD 203

3.1 Avoiding disengagement

List the activities / tasks that need to be completed in one day in your workplace. Divide the list into three categories: self-care, household and leisure/ social. In the template provided, list the participation for the individuals in your workplace (remember confidentiality and do not use their real names) listing the times, activities and support worker.

Monday	Morning	Afternoon	Evening

activities need to be done at certain times. An example of this would be putting out household rubbish for collection by the recycling team. They only provide this service on certain days so house-holders need to ensure the rubbish is put out on the correct day. Plans need to be written, especially in residential supported housing, to clearly communicate all of the activities arranged and who is supporting who. The plans should also reflect activities that have been completed or need to be rearranged. Another purpose of plans is that they allow managers to identify how to effectively manage staff, ensuring the staffing levels reflect the amount of resources needed and delivered. Plans also let the individual see how they have progressed and what they will be involved in, while also demonstrating the contribution that their task/ activity makes for the household.

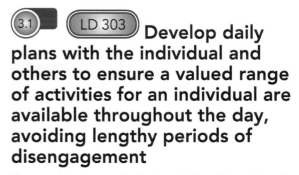

3.1 LD 303 **Develop daily plans with the individual and others to ensure a valued range of activities for an individual are available throughout the day, avoiding lengthy periods of disengagement**

The need to ensure limited periods of inactivity for the individual is paramount. Variation is important. We are all aware of tedious tasks we need to do, such as ironing, and when the task is completed we tend to ensure we have an enjoyable treat afterwards. Some people find ironing satisfying due to having an end product to show for the work. But if we continually did ironing and no other activity we would quickly become bored and reluctant to do the task. Having a variety of activities enables us to cope with more mundane tasks.

 Evidence activity LD 303

3.1 Ensuring a range of activities

Identify an activity plan in your workplace and look at the mundane tasks it includes. See what variety is in the activity plan. Discuss with your colleagues their thoughts on the activity plan. Rewrite an activity plan that enables a variety of activities and ensures the whole day is filled to reduce periods of inactivity. Remember that to be effective in a person-centred process the involvement of the individual is paramount.

 **Use a structured person-centred format to ensure that a valued range of activities for an individual is available**

 LD 303 Support the implementation of daily plans that promote an individual's participation in a range of activities

Person-centred planning identifies tools to assist participation. Person-centred planning requires the ability to listen to the individual's wishes, choices and dreams. You need to make these a reality with small achievable steps, exactly the same as with active support. It is important to listen to the individual, and help them to achieve with varying levels of support. Active support involves finding everyday tasks for the individual to participate in while we observe the activity and support them to achieve.

Person-centred tools include: MAPs, What's working and what's not, PATH, Essential life planning and Personal Futures Planning.

Evidence activity LD 203

3.2 Using a person-centred format

Write an account of what person-centred tools you would use to assist you in preparing an active support plan.

3.2 LD 303 Support the implementation of daily plans that promote an individual's participation in a range of activities

To ensure a plan is effective it needs to be agreed. You need to ensure everyone understands the plan and agrees the actions, that everyone is aware of when the plan commences and finishes and that everyone knows who will be involved and the equipment / resources needed. The plan needs to be written and available for all to see so this information is communicated effectively. The individual also needs to contribute to the planning. In sheltered supported housing, regular verbal communication sessions to check the plan ensure that all are aware of actions and needs. Each workplace will have their own format for writing activity plans. They should include the staff on duty, the day of the week (which should be broken down further by hours of the day), and there should be details of the person allocated to support the individual. The plan should also include optional leisure / social choices, household tasks and pre-arranged appointments, for example to the dentist.

3.3 LD 203 Use a structured format to plan support for an individual to participate in activities

As previously discussed it is necessary to formalise a plan in an agreed format for all to be able to understand and contribute to it. This encourages person-centred thinking. You need to review these plans on a regular basis to see what is working and what is not. Plans should not be rigid and inflexible as they need to respond to the individual's needs and any changes that may occur during the day. Remember that these tasks are to make the individual feel valued and are not about getting the housework done. The tasks need to be varied

---

Evidence activity LD 303

3.2 Supporting the implementation of daily plans

Read your policies regarding activity plans and review your workplace's templates for daily plans. Write up a daily plan for your own activities in an average day; look at how varied the tasks are and then compare this to an activity plan for someone you support. Identify how active your plan is compared to theirs. Once you have done this, review their activity plan and create the same amount of variety of tasks as your personal daily plan.

Evidence activity LD 203

 Using a structures format

In everyday life we make plans for ourselves, whether this is looking after our own personal care and hygiene, doing the housework or leisure activities. We don't normally plan these but to understand the process of activity plans, complete the table below as an activity plan for yourself to help identify why this format can be useful.

Self-care	Household tasks	Leisure

and include household tasks, leisure/ social tasks and self-care. They should be designed to make the individual feel part of the community and a valued member of the household.

As a support worker you need to ensure that the individual can manage the tasks and support them to do so. The level of support necessary will vary with each individual and with each task. Therefore person-centred planning is paramount to identify their abilities and what they can do. The sorting plan is useful for identifying what's working and what is not working. From this person-centred tool you can identify what the individual is able to do and which activities they

need support with. Remember the different levels of support you can offer and include them in the plan: ask, show, instruct, prompt and guide.

A good activity plan needs to start with the individual and all involved in their care. The tasks for the individual should be transferred into a weekly activity plan. This plan then needs to be communicated to all involved in the support, the individual, staff members, family and so on. In residential settings the plan should be reviewed at regular intervals throughout the day with staff and management to ensure it is working for the individual. Most workplaces have their own template for completing an activity plan as this ensures consistency.

Evidence activity LD 303

 Review and revise

In the table below, write down the participation you have completed with the individual you support, noting any changes that could be made to make things easier or if any of the tasks need reviewing.

	Morning	Afternoon	Evening
Monday			
Tuesday			
Wednesday			
Thursday			
Friday			
Saturday			
Sunday			

3.3 **LD 303** **Review and revise an individual's daily plan with the individual and others to increase the opportunities for participation**

Starting activity plans and following them through each day quickly becomes natural. If the individual's abilities or needs change then the activity plan will need to be reviewed to reflect this. As previously stated frequent meetings with colleagues during the day to ensure the activities are working well and all are aware of the events of the day are an excellent way of achieving flexibility. Include the individual in any discussion of how well they are doing or extra support they may need. Always remember that these meetings cannot inform any staff that are not on duty that day. Nor can they inform anyone of progress or the activity the individual has completed. To monitor whether an activity is working or not requires review on a formal basis. Records are needed to demonstrate this, ideally written records.

LO4 **LD 203** Be able to maintain person-centred records of participation

LO4 **LD 303** Be able to use person-centred records to evaluate an individual's participation in activities

As with all records, the need for accuracy and factual information is paramount. Records of any description are legal documents and could be used in a court of law. Records need to be kept in accordance with the Confidentiality Act / Data Protection Act 1998. This requires you to ensure the information is correct and in agreement with the individual concerned. Precautions as to where these records are written and who has access to them will be laid out in your workplace setting.

4.1 **LD 203** **Record an individual's participation in activities**

To monitor both the plan's effectiveness plus any problems that occur during its implementation requires recordkeeping. Person-centred planning is about recording achievements, goals/dreams with the involvement of all.

The main reasons we need to record activities are to demonstrate achievement, clarify tasks the individual has achieved as well as those they found difficult and required more support with, and to identify what makes the person happy and contented and what upsets them. In other words, for person-centred planning tools, what is working and what is not.

The records that are kept need to be factual, and should contain no personal interpretations.

Time to reflect

LD 203 **4.1** **Recording participation**

Recall a typical day at work and its record-keeping. How did you record information? Was it factual? Who had access to this record and where was it stored? Could you have written it differently, did this account accurately represent the day and what could you have done differently?

4.1 **LD 303** **Develop a person-centred record to monitor an individual's participation in activities**

Records must be informative to ensure all involved are aware of changes and any difficulties / progressions. The format in which they are written requires an agreed and acceptable template that all involved can access and understand. In your own workplace you will have an agreed template for recording information. To ensure the record is person-centred we need to include certain criteria.

Person-centred planning is about the individual and what they have learned, learning logs and review programmes that highlight what is working for them and what is not. There should be action plans to achieve their goals and clear communication charts that identify the preferences of the individual as regards communication skills.

Reviews should be completed at least once every six months but daily events and activities need to be recorded at the time to influence the process of daily planning.

Evidence activity LD 303

 Monitoring participation

Marie is new to the day setting and to the role of support worker. You have been given the task of mentoring her. Marie has been given an individual to support; write how you would assist her in developing the records required for their needs.

4.2 LD 203 **Describe changes in an individual's participation over time**

4.2 LD 303 **Review an individual's participation in activities to assess changes over time**

The aim of active support is to make the person feel valued, to increase their self-confidence and self-esteem. The desired outcome of the planning is the individual achieving their personal goals. As they master their activities (or find them too challenging) we need to amend their plan of action with them. This is a bit like making a New Year's resolution. If the task we set ourselves is unrealistic we are unlikely to achieve it and this has a negative effect on how we perceive ourselves. When setting such a task we frequently anticipate achieving certain milestones. This enables us to measure how well we are doing. This is the same principle behind person-centred planning.

If an individual has mastered their activity they will require less support from the carer, whereas if they find the task too challenging they may require a change in support or a new way of learning the task. Reviewing and recording these changes ensures anyone taking over the role of support or engagement understands the individual's development or difficulties and ensures any previous achievements are recognised.

Time to reflect
LD 203 **4.2** **Describing change and progress**

Identify someone you have supported in your workplace. Write about the initial steps to enable them to achieve a task, how they progressed and how you supported them to achieve their outcome. Would you do anything different next time and what have you learnt from the experience?

■ **Research and investigate**
LD 303 **4.2** **The review process**

Identify your workplace policies and procedures regarding the review process. Identify the tools needed for person-centred reviewing and those who need to be involved in the review process. Think of the last review process you were involved in and describe the process.

4.3 LD 203 **Report the extent to which an individual's participation represents the balance of activity associated with a valued lifestyle**

When commencing any activity plan we need to ensure a balance for the individual is maintained. None of us would like to just work and have no social life and it is no different for an individual with learning disabilities. Active support is not just supporting the individual with tasks such as washing up. A range of activities are required to ensure a balanced involvement and increased self-esteem is achieved for the individual; from shopping to socialising.

Evidence activity LD 203

 4.3 Balancing activities

In the table below insert the activities an individual might do and in the last column identify the balance between enjoyable tasks and household duties. In the second chart do the same for your activities during a normal day. How does this differ, or are they equal?

Activity	Chore	Social	Balance

Your activity	Chore	Social	Balance

4.3 **LD 303** **Evaluate the extent to which an individual's participation over time represents the balance of activity associated with a valued lifestyle**

When creating a plan of activities over a week we can usually ensure an equal balance and variety of activities. As previously stated, plans are not written in stone and can be adapted at very short notice due to changes in circumstances or environmental factors. When writing a plan it may be more difficult to review the long-term goals. The Care Quality Commission states that good practice is to have reviews of care at least once every six months.

Evidence activity LD 303

 4.3 Ensuring variety

Using your experience describe the benefits of regular reviews and the importance of ensuring a variety and balance of activities.

4.4 **LD 303** **Explain the changes required to improve the quality of an individual's participation to promote independence, informed choice and a valued life**

With every plan and activity we have identified the importance of reviewing and ensuring a correct balance of activities. To make sure good ideas come to fruition we need to ensure that everyone involved in the care is aware of what the individual wishes to achieve. Some individuals with learning disabilities may not find it easy to make their wishes known and may require support to enable themselves to be heard. Sometimes the relatives or carers are not the best person to achieve this and the individual may require the services of an independent advocate. Your role is to ensure this occurs. As a supporter and champion of person-centred planning, the need to promote the individual to the centre of the planning process is your responsibility. Any difficulties in doing this need to be reported to your line manager. Anyone working in this role needs to focus on the individual and ensure they feel valued, have a purpose in life, and are fully engaged in their planning with the use of person-centred planning. Everyone the individual wants to be involved must be encouraged to participate in this planning.

Research and investigate

  Improving quality of participation

Look at three person-centred plans within your work setting. Identify the reviewing process and the individuals invited to attend and participate. How could you improve participation of others involved in the process? Identify how you would assess whether the balance of activities is sufficiently addressed and recorded in the plans. Reflect on this process and identify any changes you could make to improve independence, choice and value for the individual.

Assessment Summary for Unit LD 203

To achieve the unit, your assessor will require you to:

Learning outcomes	Assessment criteria
1 Understand how active support translates values into person-centred practical action with an individual	Explain how the key characteristics of active support differ from the hotel model See Evidence activity 1.1, p. 75.
	Define the terms: • promoting independence • informed choice • valued life See Time to reflect 1.2, p. 76.
	Explain how use of active support can promote independence, informed choice and a valued life See Case study 1.3, p. 77.
2 Be able to interact positively with individuals to promote participation	Explain the three elements in positive interaction that promote an individual's participation in activity See Evidence activity 2.1, p. 78.
	Break a routine task into manageable steps for an individual See Evidence activity 2.2, p. 79.
	Provide different levels of help to support an individual to participate in a task or activity See Evidence activity 2.3, p. 80.
	Positively reinforce an individual's participation in an activity See Time to reflect 2.4, p. 80.
3 Be able to implement person-centred daily plans to promote participation	Provide opportunities for an individual to participate in activity throughout the day avoiding lengthy periods of disengagement See Evidence activity 3.1, p. 82.
	Use a structured person-centred format to ensure that a valued range of activities for an individual is available See Evidence activity 3.2, p. 83.
	Use a structured format to plan support for an individual to participate in activities See Evidence activity 3.3, p. 84.

Learning outcomes	Assessment criteria
4 Be able to maintain person-centred records of participation	**(4.1)** Record an individual's participation in activities See Time to reflect 4.1, p. 85.
	(4.2) Describe changes in an individual's participation over time See Time to reflect 4.2, p. 86.
	(4.3) Report the extent to which an individual's participation represents the balance of activity associated with a valued lifestyle See Evidence activity 4.3, p. 87.

Assessment Summary for Unit LD 303

To achieve the unit, your assessor will require you to:

Learning outcomes	Assessment criteria
1 Understand how active support translates values into person-centred practical action with an individual	**(1.1)** Compare the characteristics associated with active support and the hotel model in relation to an individual's support See Evidence activity 1.1, p. 76.
	(1.1) Identify practical changes that could be made within a service setting to: • promote an individual's independence • support informed choices • improve quality of life See Evidence activity 1.2, p. 77.
2 Be able to interact positively with individuals to promote participation	**(2.1)** Assess the levels of help an individual would need to participate in a range of new activities See Time to reflect 2.1, p. 79.
	(2.2) Use task analysis to break a range of new activities into manageable steps for an individual See Evidence activity 2.2, p. 79.
	(2.3) Evaluate different ways of positively reinforcing an individual's participation in a range of new activities See Evidence activity 2.3, p. 80.
	(2.4) Demonstrate positive interaction with an individual to promote successful participation in a range of new activities See Time to reflect 2.4, p. 80.

3 Be able to develop and implement person-centred daily plans to promote participation	**3.1**	Develop daily plans with the individual and others to ensure a valued range of activities for an individual are available throughout the day, avoiding lengthy periods of disengagement See Evidence activity 3.1, p. 82.
	3.2	Support the implementation of daily plans that promote an individual's participation in a range of activities See Evidence activity 3.2, p. 83.
	3.3	Review and revise an individual's daily plan with the individual and others to increase the opportunities for participation See Evidence activity 3.3, p. 84.
4 Be able to use person-centred records to evaluate an individual's participation in activities	**4.1**	Develop a person-centred record to monitor an individual's participation in activities See Evidence activity 4.1, p. 86.
	4.2	Review an individual's participation in activities to assess changes over time See Research and investigate 4.2, p. 86.
	4.3	Evaluate the extent to which an individual's participation over time represents the balance of activity associated with a valued lifestyle See Evidence activity 4.3, p. 87.
	4.4	Explain the changes required to improve the quality of an individual's participation to promote independence, informed choice and a valued life See Research and investigate 4.4, p. 88.

Further resources

Department of Health (1970), *Chronically Sick and Disabled Persons Act*, Department of Health.

Department of Health, (2001), *Valuing People: A New Strategy for Learning Disability for the 21st Century*, The Stationery Office.

Department of Health, (2002), *Fair Access to Care Services: Policy Guidelines, Department of Health*.

Emerson, E, Malam, S., Davies, I. and Spencer, K.(2005), *Adults with Learning Disabilities in England 2003/2004*. www.ic.nhs.uk/pubs/learndiff2004

5 Positive risk taking for individuals with disabilities

Unit LD 205 Principles of positive risk taking for individuals with disabilities
Unit LD 305 Understand positive risk taking for individuals with disabilities

What are you finding out?

We are going to explore what risk is and how to approach risk taking in a person-centred way. We will identify the legislation regarding risk taking, and the history of risk taking. We will explore what risk taking means to you as the carer, to the individual, relatives and outside agencies. We will explore methods of risk taking to empower the individual to take risks and therefore be included in everyday society.

The reading and activities in this chapter will help you to:

- Know the importance of risk taking in everyday life for individuals with disabilities

- Understand the importance of positive person-centred risk assessment

- Know how legislation and policies are relevant to positive risk taking

- Understand how to support individuals with disabilities in decisions about risk taking

- Understand how to support individuals with disabilities to manage identified risks

Key terms

Risk is identified as a probability of injury, harm, loss or danger.

Empowerment is identified as enabling the individual to have more control/ power over their lives /choices.

5.1 Risk can be a burden on our capacity to enjoy or ability to live life

It is important to explore the history of risk taking for individuals with disabilities to understand the changes that have occurred and the importance of these changes.

Individuals with learning disabilities were classed in the Mental Deficiency Act 1913 as idiots, imbeciles, the feeble minded and morally defective. With these labels they were then placed into institutional care where they were excluded from society and had no rights. Institutional care controlled any signs of individualism displayed through restraint and control methods. Risk was not an issue as these individuals were not accepted by society; the law had clearly defined the social status of any individuals with any form of disability. To put this into perspective, women were also seen as lesser people with no rights.

In 1927 an amendment to the Mental Deficiency Act occurred with the replacement of *moral defective* with *moral imbecile* thus allowing the condition to be identified later in life and not just from birth. In 1946 Mencap was formed, previously known as National Association of Parents of Backward Children. In 1948 mental health officers were established to work in the community. Not until 1995, when the Disability Discrimination Act came into force, did the labelling change and opportunities for individualism start, and attitudes to the disabled began to change too. In 2001 the Department of Health published its policy Valuing People with an emphasis on talking to the relatives.

LO1 (LD 205) Know the importance of risk taking in everyday life for individuals with disabilities

LO1 (LD 305) Understand that individuals with disabilities have the same right as everyone else to take risks

1.1 (LD 205) Identify aspects of everyday life in which risk plays a part

1.1 (LD 305) Explain ways in which risk is an integral part of everyday life

We all take risks everyday and don't even think about their implications. We all walk near roads and never contemplate the dangers around us, e.g. if a car skids off the road and hits us, or if we fall into the road and a car is coming at the same time. Do we consider the risks of cooking, the possibilities of a fire or food poisoning? In the back of our minds we do think and consider these risks in small detail; we are generally careful when crossing the road and look out for traffic, when we are cooking we keep an eye on the heat and check things are cooked thoroughly, but in everyday activity this is not detailed and is not written down. The reason for this is we would not have time to do the activities we want to do and we accept that sometimes we may be in danger but this is an acceptable risk. We want to be in control of our lives and able to do the things we enjoy. We can see from the history of disabilities this was not a luxury everyone had.

> ## Time to reflect
>
> ### 1.1 Risk taking
>
> Recall an incident when you have taken a risk. This might be when you were younger and were told you were not old enough to do an activity, such as go on the big slide by yourself. Write down what the risk was, how you felt because you were not allowed to do the activity and, when you could do the activity, how this made you feel.

1.2 (LD 205) Identify aspects of everyday life in which, traditionally, individuals with disabilities were not encouraged to take risks

1.2 **LD 305** Explain why, traditionally, people with disabilities have been discouraged or prevented from taking risks

History shows us that persons with learning disabilities would have been very restricted in their everyday life. They would not have been allowed to hold any money, be able or encouraged to feed themselves, wash themselves or even dress themselves in items of clothing of their own choice. The reasons for not choosing their own clothes would have been a risk of ridicule, the reasons for not washing themselves could have been due to risk of drowning or flooding of the building. Really extreme risks were identified. Remember: a risk is identified by an individual and may not be perceived as a risk by others.

Evidence activity **LD 205** **LD 305**

1.2 Everyday risks

The Disability Discrimination Act in 1995 identified the need to treat people as equal no matter what their disabilities are. Prior to this people with disabilities were not seen as equal, they had limited rights and so everyday activities like shopping would not have been allowed for those with disabilities as the risk would have been too high.

Think of the individuals you support. Write a list of the daily activities they take part in during any one day and identify the activities they would not have been able to do prior to the Disability Discrimination Act 1995, and why they would have been seen as a risk.

1.3 **LD 205** Outline the consequences for individuals with disabilities of being prevented or discouraged from taking risks

1.4 **LD 205** Explain how supporting individuals to take risks can enable them to gain in self-confidence, develop skills and take an active part in their community

1.3 **LD 305** Describe the links between risk taking and responsibility, empowerment and social inclusion

As previously stated we all take risks in everyday life, we protect children from any risky situation we have identified. Measurement of that risk is made by the adult looking after them; some parents allow their children to use the internet, others feel this activity is too risky and do not allow it. Some parents may not let their children watch certain programmes and may be restrictive over the content of information they receive. Children frequently talk about television programmes they have watched, internet sites they have been on and so on in school. Those children who have had restrictions placed on them by parents may feel left out of conversations as they cannot contribute.

Evidence activity **LD 205** **LD 305**

1.3 Being excluded

Reflect on a situation where you were not able to participate and others were. Describe how this made you feel. Identify what could have been done differently to enable you to participate.

We understand that if children are never allowed to take risks they will never develop their own skills of judgement.

Evidence activity LD 205

1.4 Participation

Identify a skill and the risk related to that skill. Describe what you can do to encourage development of that skill and reduce the risk to the individual. Also explain how, by completing the skill, the individual is enabled to participate in their community. Why is this important?

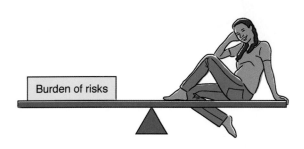

5.2 We need to balance the risk against the possible outcome

LO2 LD 205 Understand the importance of positive, person-centred risk assessment

LO2 LD 305 Understand the importance of a positive, person-centred approach to risk assessment

2.1 LD 205 Explain how a person-centred approach to risk assessment can have a more positive outcome than traditional approaches

2.1 LD 305 Explain the process of developing a positive person-centred approach to risk assessment

Prior to recent legislation the medical model was used for assessing risk taking. The traditional medical model identified the individual as an object not an individual; therefore a blanket statement concerning risks was easily made. Generalised statements were made that persons with disabilities were unable to live at home due to the risk of being a danger to themselves or others. Therefore they needed to be cared for in an institution. The majority of persons in institutions were not encouraged to think or act for themselves; if they did this was seen as negative and required restraint or medication (also known as chemical restraint).

Fortunately, with the introduction of legislation and person-centred approaches, we are now enabling the individual to take risks and support them through an individual approach. This is an inclusive approach to the individual.

An excellent film to watch is *Inside I Am Still Dancing*. This film highlights risks and the individuals in the film embrace them and the changes this makes to the individuals concerned are massive.

With person-centred risk taking the individual makes the decisions, identifies the risks and minimises them for short term and long term gain. The role of the carer in this scenario is to support, guide and promote opportunities.

Positive risk taking enables people to live, to grow and to learn skills of decision making. Traditional models of risk assessment had a negative impact on the individual. With the person-centred approach the aim is to identify people close to the individual that they choose to support and guide them making the risks. The tools for this are displayed in the diagram below (Figure 5.3) and are part of the person-centred thinking process.

5.3 Person-centred thinking tools

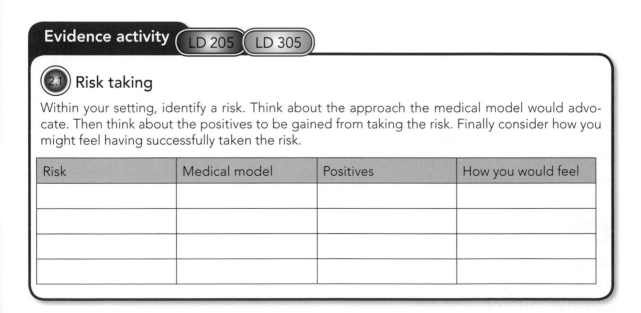

2.2 **LD 205** **Identify the features of a person-centred approach to risk assessment**

2.3 **LD 205** **Describe ways in which traditional risk assessments have tended to have a negative focus**

2.2 **LD 305** **Explain how to apply the principles and methods of a person-centred approach to each of the different stages of the process of risk assessment**

The person-centred approach to risk taking identifies seven steps:

1. Involvement of others. This includes the individual's circle of friends and key people to support them.
2. Positive and informed risk taking. This is about identifying the skills the individual has and what we admire about the individual. This encourages positive reinforcement of the individual.
3. Proportionality. This identifies the risks of not doing the activity and the effect of this on the individual. Depending on the severity of the risks it may take longer to obtain extra support to enable the individual.
4. Contextualising behaviour. Identifying what makes the individual happy, sad, frightened and angry. What works for the individual.
5. Defensible decision making. Through the process above, notes, drawings and so on will be made and recorded, demonstrating any legal issues or risks and the resolutions to these issues.
6. A learning culture. Clear identification of what is working and what is not, demonstrating learning from the process.
7. Tolerable risks identifying the balance of safety and risk. A clear process of identifying risk from that perceived and compromises to give the individual a positive outcome.

Person centred risk course book
(Allen et al 2008)

Case study

2.2 Joe

Joe is 15 years old and was involved in a car accident when he was 14 years old. His father blames himself as he was driving at the time. Joe was injured and lost the use of his legs due to the severity of the impact. Joe has not been able to go out by himself. His mother is reluctant for Joe to attend mainstream schools as she is concerned about how Joe will feel and be treated by his friends. His friends from school have not been welcomed to his home as his mother reinforces the idea that Joe is unwell. The school has been understanding and feels Joe should return to complete his exams. Joe has to attend a rehabilitation centre on a monthly basis; his mother always attends with him.

On talking to Joe, he is anxious about returning to school, believes his friends don't want to know him anymore and is angry about his disabilities, believing he will not be able to participate in school again.

Using person-centred thinking:

- Explain using the above case study who Joe is, his strengths and weaknesses and how best to support him.
- Where is he now, what are the risks, what does he want to happen?
- Where and what would Joe like?
- What is working and what is not?
- What happens next?

Evidence activity LD 205

 Looking at the negatives

Using the medical model for care, what would the risk assessment process be for the above case study?

LO3 (LD 205) Know how legislation and policies are relevant to positive risk taking

LO3 (LD 305) Understand the legal and policy framework underpinning an individual with disabilities' rights to make decisions and take risks

(3.1) (LD 205) Identify legislation and policies which promote the human rights of individuals with disabilities

(3.1) (LD 305) Explain how legislation, national and local policies and guidance provide a framework for decision making which can support an individual to have control over their own lives

We have already identified some relevant legislation regarding disabilities, we now need to identify how they influence our practice and relate to our employment policies.

- **The Equality Act** in 2010 highlighted the rights of disabled persons to education, health and employment and ensured no discrimination as regards to the above and rights of owning property, goods and licences, to name but a few. The act clearly defines the right not to be discriminated against due to disability.

- **The Human Rights Act** of 1998 identifies the right to be treated in agreement with European rights. Within these is the responsibility to respect other people's rights, and they must respect your rights.

- *Valuing People Now* was published in September 2010. It promotes a person-centred agenda and reports back on the partnership board's effectiveness.

- **Partnership boards** are a group of local people who meet on a regular basis to identify what needs to happen to improve the lives of persons with disabilities. The findings from local partnership boards are then fed to the Department of Health to effect changes in line with their *Valuing People Now* plan. An example of this might be that a carer identifies that an individual wishes to attend a social event and is restricted due to environment concerns. The partnership board will take this to the DoH to identify ways of enabling the person to attend. This is a very simple example.

Evidence activity LD 205 LD 305

(3.1) Understanding legislation

To check your understanding of the legislation and guidance listed below, identify polices and procedures from within your workplace and match them against the legislation. In the spaces provided list the policies and procedures relating to the relative legislation.

Human Rights		
Equality Act		
Valuing People Now		
Health and Safety Law		
Disability Discrimination Act 2005		
Mental Capacity Act 2007		
Safeguarding Children and Vulnerable Adults		
Putting People First 2007		

3.2 LD 205 **Describe how to use a human rights based approach to risk management**

We need to be aware of the relevant legislation and policies to protect and promote the ability of risk taking. Taking care of their own personal budgets used to be seen as impossible for an individual who was disabled. With new policies and person-centred thinking this is now a reality. We need to identify perceived risks but also look at the support the individual may need and ways of supporting them to achieve their goals.

Evidence activity LD 205

(3.2) Active support

Identify a person you support and describe how you could support the individual when taking a positive risk and the relevant legislation this relates to.

LO4 LD 205 **Understand how to support individuals with disabilities in decisions about risk taking**

LO4 LD 305 **Understand the importance of considering with an individual with disabilities the risks associated with the choices they make**

4.1 LD 205 **Explain the connection between an individual's right to take risks and their responsibilities towards themselves and others**

Changes in legislation and increased understanding of disabilities have increased the disabled individual's experiences and choices. A change of labelling enabled their transition from institutions to becoming part of a community. Although these changes took time and legislation, the positive outcome for the individual has been enormous. With any change, however positive, there are some risks which could be very serious, hence the development of safeguarding of vulnerable adults.

As carers, be it paid or voluntary, we also have to be aware of our duty of care. Living in a community holds risks for anyone, for individuals who are more vulnerable the risks increase. Unfortunately in communities today there are opportunists who seek vulnerable people. Our role in person-centred thinking is to promote the individual whilst recognising and minimising the risks.

Time to reflect

LD 205 **4.1** Perceiving risk

Think of an individual you work with, and a situation where a risk was involved, a perceived risk to themselves or others. Describe the situation and what occurred. What was the outcome, what went well, what did not? What could you have done differently and, finally, what did you learn from the situation?

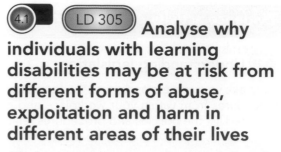

4.1 **LD 305** Analyse why individuals with learning disabilities may be at risk from different forms of abuse, exploitation and harm in different areas of their lives

All of us may come across abuse, verbal or physical, in our lives. We have skills to recognise abuse or exploitation or know the correct procedures to follow to report the situation. Persons with learning disabilities may not have this awareness and are seen as vulnerable in this area.

Abuse comes in many forms: financial, physical, sexual, verbal, emotional, religious and neglect. Abuse is defined as a negative, distressing to the individual. As carers and support workers our role is to identify if abuse is occurring and protect the individuals.

4.2 **LD 205** Outline how the principle of 'Duty of Care' can be maintained whilst supporting individuals to take risks

Evidence activity LD 205 LD 305

LD 205 **4.2** **LD 305** **4.1** **4.2** Duty of care

Fill in the table below by thinking of risks involved in living in the community, the risk to any individual, the risk to a person with a disability, and your duty of care towards that individual.

Identified risks living in the community	Risk to individuals	Risks to persons with disabilities	What is our duty of care

4.2 **LD 305** **Explain how to support individuals to recognise and manage potential risk in different areas of their lives**

Duty of care is an area we are all aware of, as paid carers the individual's safety is paramount. So how does this affect person centred risk taking? With person-centred risk taking we should have a clear idea of the individual's informed choices, the options explored, and the dangers/risks that may be apparent. As we do this assessment with the individuals and others the process will support their decisions.

The risk involved for some individuals with disabilities living on their own was highlighted in the published report *Get a Life* which looked at employment issues, with its main focus on full time employment. Using a person-centred approach a variety of individuals and agencies are involved, and targets have been set to obtain full time employment for all youngsters leaving the education system who have severe learning disabilities.

> ### Key terms
>
> **Duty of care** is a legal requirement that any action the carer performs must be in the best interest of the individual they care for. The individual must be at the centre.

4.3 **LD 205** **Describe ways of enabling individuals with disabilities to make informed choices about taking risks**

4.3 **LD 305** **Explain the importance of balancing the choices of the individual with their own and others' health and safety**

Individuals with disabilities frequently have problems identifying what a risk is and the consequences if they do not address the risks with plans.

Case study

4.3 **Jane**

Jane wants to go out for a meal in the local pub and wants to go tonight, but none of her family members can take her. Jane feels she can go on her own and is becoming insistent that she will go. Jane's disability means she can become very angry and aggressive and has major difficulties in calming herself when this occurs. Jane also has epilepsy. A paid carer has offered to go with her but Jane has decided she wants to go by herself. Jane has limited social skills and poor budget awareness.

LD 205 **4.3** How would you identify with Jane the risks involved in this trip?

LD 205 **4.3** How could you support Jane in a person-centred way to achieve her goals?

5.4 How could you best support an outing to a pub?

LD 305 **4.3** In Jane's scenario, how could we protect the community from any problems with aggression she may have?

4.4 **LD 205** Outline the particular challenges that may arise when supporting individuals to make decisions if they have had limited previous experience of making their own decisions

4.4 **LD 305** Describe how own values, belief systems and experiences may affect working practice when supporting individuals to take risks

Working in the care sector we may confront risks frequently and our employers will identify and aim to cover these risks, as required by law. Remember that risks are what the individual perceives as a risk. A parent might stop their children going into a garden shed because of the parent's fear of spiders. While it is true that garden sheds are likely to house spiders, it is also true that spiders are harmless and children may not be frightened of them. Can you reflect on a risk situation where you allowed your fear to influence your judgement when supporting an individual? Why do you need to be aware of your own values and beliefs?

Time to reflect

LD 205 **4.4** Unexpected challenges

Describe a situation where you have been involved in planning risk and identify some of the unexpected challenges this has involved and ways to deal with them. Would you do anything different next time?

4.5 **LD 205** Explain the potential positive and negative consequences of the choices made about taking risks

4.6 **LD 205** Describe what action to take if an individual decides to take an unplanned risk that places him/herself or others in immediate danger

It is a fact of life that we are frequently put in situations that we have not expected and have not planned for. Within a person-centred approach, tools are identified to manage a contingency plan. Even then we can be surprised by events that are not expected.

An individual with disabilities may not be used to making decisions about risks. Therefore our role is to clarify the consequences of risks. An example might be of a person who has lived in institutional care, or has recently become disabled. In these situations the individual needs to learn to look at risks in a different way in order to avoid unplanned risks that could put themselves or others in danger. It is important to identify within your work setting the policies that address this issue. Within these policies are the procedures that clarify the actions you need to take in these circumstances.

Research and investigate

LD 205 **4.5** **4.6** Policies for unplanned risk

Locate your workplace's policy and procedures and write what you must do if someone takes an unplanned risk that puts themselves or others in danger.

4.7 **LD 205** Explain why it is important to record and report all incidents, discussions and decisions concerning risk taking

4.5 **LD 305** Explain the importance of recording all discussions and decisions made

With any risk or process we need to record our actions not just for legal purposes, but also to clarify our plans of actions and to inform others, individuals, staff and outside agencies. (According to the Data Protection Act 1998 and the Confidentiality Guidance GMC 2009.) By recording our actions we can identify what has worked and what has not worked. The tools in person-centred thinking give guidelines on recording actions. All centres are inspected by the Care Quality Commission, looking for risks identified in standards 1–6, 7–10, 11–16, 17–21 and 22–27. These can all be easily identified in a person-centred approach.

■ Research and investigate 🔍

LD 205 **4.7** **LD 305** **4.5**

Within your workplace obtain a person-centred plan and identify the relevant standards from CQC.

LO5 (LD 205) Understand how to support individuals with disabilities to manage identified risks

LO5 (LD 305) Understand the importance of a partnership approach to risk taking

5.3 **LD 205** **Outline why it is important to communicate and work in a consistent way with all those supporting the individual**

5.1 **LD 305** **Explain the importance of a person-centred partnership approach**

With person-centred planning and risk taking we need to work in partnership. We need to listen to and hear the individual's dreams. It may not be possible within the setting to fulfil these; sometimes a compromise will need to be made and implemented through partnership working in order to find support from others. Identifying this circle of support and matching staff/carers can make this work. The manager of the setting's role is to identify ways of making the individual's dreams a reality and they need to report back to the partnership boards on any obstacles that need to be overcome.

Evidence activity (LD 205) (LD 305)

5.1 **Involving People**

Within your work setting identify a risk plan. Without breaking confidentiality list the persons involved in the process and identify the outcome. In the last column write what the outcome would have been had they not been involved in the plan.

Risk plan	Persons involved	Positive outcome	Negative outcome if person not involved

An example of not working in partnership would be the individual wishing to go to church every Sunday with their relatives. If we do not include the relative in this planning, this would not be achievable. If we do not explain to the relative and show them the communication plan they will not understand what frustrates the individual.

5.1 **LD 205** Explain the importance of including risks in the individual's support plan

When completing risk assessments we need to identify what the risks are, how severe they are and what actions are needed to reduce the level of risk. They form part of the support plan and require reviewing to see if the actions achieve the desired outcome, if more support is needed or if there has been any change in the perceived risk. This must always be done in a person-centred manner and the focus must constantly be on the individual.

5.2 **LD 205** Explain why it is important to review risks in the individual's support plan

5.4 **LD 205** Describe ways of supporting individuals with disabilities to test out the risk they wish to take

5.1 **LD 305** Describe ways of handling conflict when discussing and making decisions about risk

Sometimes we can see a potential risk, but until we test it we do not know its severity. An example would be of someone cooking for themselves for the first time. We know the health and safety risks of burns, possible fire and undercooked food. To enable a person to cook for themselves we could show them how and support them when they first cook. We would make this a gradual process by starting with a simple dish and then progressing. We would ensure the correct tools were available, such as oven gloves, and would explain to the individual how to use them and the reason for the gloves. Once we had done this we would need to review the risks to see if they had reduced.

5.5 The kitchen is somewhere that we need to make decisions about the level of risk

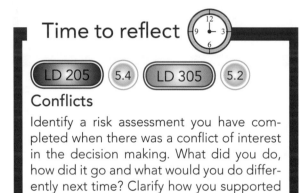

Time to reflect

LD 205 **5.4** **LD 305** **5.2**

Conflicts

Identify a risk assessment you have completed when there was a conflict of interest in the decision making. What did you do, how did it go and what would you do differently next time? Clarify how you supported the individual in this process.

Throughout this chapter we have looked at person-centred care, clarifying the importance that the focus is on the individual and their ability to live their lives in the manner they choose. We are all aware that this sometimes causes conflicts and frustration and can be an exhausting process. We have to keep in mind the results that can be achieved and the importance of empowerment. Individuals with disabilities have moved from the fringes of society to a positive position where we respect the individual and recognise their abilities.

Evidence activity **LD 205**

5.2 **5.3** The importance of risk taking

In your own words write an explanation of the importance of risk taking, the need to review the level of risk and communicate, and ways of supporting the individual.

Assessment Summary for Unit LD 205

To achieve the unit, your assessor will require you to:

Learning outcomes	Assessment criteria
1 Know the importance of risk taking in everyday life for individuals with disabilities	**1.1** Identify aspects of everyday life in which risk plays a part See Time to reflect 1.1, p. 93.
	1.2 Identify aspects of everyday life in which, traditionally, individuals with disabilities were not encouraged to take risks See Evidence activity 1.2, p. 94.
	1.3 Outline the consequences for individuals with disabilities of being prevented or discouraged from taking risks See Evidence activity 1.3, p. 94.
	1.4 Explain how supporting individuals to take risks can enable them to have choice over their lives to: • gain in self-confidence • develop skills • take an active part in their community See Evidence activity 1.4, p. 95.
2 Understand the importance of positive, person-centred risk assessment	**2.1** Explain how a person-centred approach to risk assessment can have a more positive outcome than traditional approaches See Evidence activity 2.1, p. 96.
	2.2 Identify the features of a person-centred approach to risk assessment See Case study 2.2, p. 97.
	2.3 Describe ways in which traditional risk assessments have tended to have a negative focus See Evidence activity 2.3, p. 97.
3 Know how legislation and policies are relevant to positive risk taking	**3.1** Identify legislation and policies which promote the human rights of individuals with disabilities See Evidence activity 3.1, p. 99.
	3.2 Describe how to use a human rights based approach to risk management See Evidence activity 3.2, p. 99.

Learning outcomes	Assessment criteria
4 Understand how to support individuals with disabilities in decisions about risk-taking	(4.1) Explain the connection between an individual's right to take risks and their responsibilities towards themselves and others See Time to reflect 4.1, p. 100.
	(4.2) Outline how the principle of 'Duty of Care' can be maintained whilst supporting individuals to take risks See Evidence activity 4.2, p. 100.
	(4.3) Describe ways of enabling individuals with disabilities to make informed choices about taking risks See Case study 4.3, p. 101.
	(4.4) Outline the particular challenges that may arise when supporting individuals to make decisions if they have had limited previous experience of making their own decisions See Time to reflect 4.4, p. 102.
	(4.5) Explain the potential positive and negative consequences of the choices made about taking risks See Research and investigate 4.5, p. 102.
	(4.6) Describe what action to take if an individual decides to take an unplanned risk that places him/herself or others in immediate or imminent danger See Research and ivestigate 4.6, p. 102.
	(4.7) Explain why it is important to record and report all incidents, discussions and decisions concerning risk taking See Research and investigate 4.7, p. 103.
5 Understand how to support individuals with disabilities to manage identified risks	(5.1) Explain the importance of including risks in the individual's support plan See Evidence activity 5.1, p. 103.
	(5.2) Explain why it is important to review risks in the individual's support plan See Evidence activity 5.2, p. 104.
	(5.3) Outline why it is important to communicate and work in a consistent way with all those supporting the individual See Evidence activity 5.3, p. 104.
	(5.4) Describe ways of supporting individuals with disabilities to test out the risk they wish to take See Time to reflect 5.4, p. 104.

Assessment Summary for Unit LD 305

To achieve the unit, your assessor will require you to:

Learning outcomes	Assessment criteria
1 Understand that individuals with disabilities have the same right as everyone else to take risks	Explain ways in which risk is an integral part of everyday life See Time to reflect 1.1, p. 93.
	Explain why, traditionally, people with disabilities have been discouraged or prevented from taking risks See Evidence activity 1.2, p. 94.
	Describe the links between risk-taking and responsibility, empowerment and social inclusion See Evidence activity 1.3, p. 94.
2 Understand the importance of positive, person-centred risk assessment	Explain the process of developing a positive person-centred approach to risk assessment See Evidence activity 2.1, p. 96.
	Explain how to apply the principles and methods of a person-centred approach to each of the different stages of the process of risk assessment See Case study 2.2, p. 97.
	Explain how a service focused approach to risk assessment would differ from a person-centred approach See Evidence activity 2.3, p. 97.
3 Understand the legal and policy framework underpinning an individual with disabilities right to make decisions and take risks	(3.1) Explain how legislation, national and local policies and guidance provide a framework for decision making which can support an individual to have control over their own lives See Evidence activity 3.1, p. 99.

Learning outcomes	Assessment criteria
4 Understand the importance of considering with an individual with disabilities the risks associated with the choices they make	**(4.1)** Analyse why individuals with disabilities may be at risk of different forms of abuse, exploitation and harm in different areas of their lives See Evidence activity 4.1, p. 100.
	(4.2) Explain how to support individuals to recognise and manage potential risk in different areas of their lives See Evidence activity 4.2, p. 100.
	(4.3) Explain the importance of balancing the choices of the individual with their own and others' health and safety See Case study 4.3, p. 101.
	(4.4) Describe how own values, belief systems and experiences may affect working practice when supporting individuals to take risks See Time to reflect 4.4, p. 102.
	(4.5) Explain the importance of recording all discussions and decisions made See Research and investigate 4.5, p. 102.
5 Understand the importance of a partnership approach to risk taking	**(5.1)** Explain the importance of a person-centred partnership approach See Evidence activity 5.1, p. 103.
	(5.2) Describe ways of handling conflict when discussing and making decisions about risk See Time to reflect 5.2, p. 104.

Further resources

Person centred risk course book (Allen et al 2008)

www.elfrida.com

www.learningdisabilities.org.uk

www.bild.org.uk

www.mencap.org.uk

www.valuingpeople.gov.uk

www.ico.gov.uk

www.gmc-uk.org

www.cqc.org.uk

www.directgov.uk

www.legislation.gov.uk

www.helensanderson.co.uk

Personal hygiene
Unit 206 Principles of supporting an individual to maintain personal hygiene
Unit 206C Support individuals to maintain personal hygiene

What are you finding out?

Personal hygiene is an important factor in our everyday life. Our personal hygiene demonstrates to others we look after ourselves, take pride in our appearance and enables us to be accepted in social circles. Poor hygiene results in a lack of opportunities for us. Good personal hygiene also improves our mental state: when we have freshened ourselves up we tend to feel more positive, revived and ready to take on the day. Personal hygiene is very personal to the individual. Dignity about our personal appearance is important for everyone. Most people do not like the idea of someone washing our private areas. Within this chapter we are going to explore the concept of personal care and how we can improve the care we deliver to maintain an individual's self respect. We will look at how, with the advent of person-centred thinking, we have progressed from institutional concepts of personal care that required the individuals to have a bath once a week with a bath book record and communal baths.

The reading and activities in this chapter will help you to:

- Understand the importance of good hygiene
- Know how to encourage an individual to maintain personal hygiene
- Know how to support an individual to maintain personal hygiene
- Understand when poor hygiene may be an indicator of other underlying personal issues

Key terms

Preferences relates to choices, allowing the individual to express how they would like things done, in what order and the process of events.

Dignity as defined by the RCN (2008) is 'To treat people as being of worth, in a way that is respectful of them as valued individuals'.

An **individual** is a single human being as distinct from a group or class, or family. (Wikipedia).

LO1 Understand the importance of good personal hygiene

 Explain why personal hygiene is important

When we get up in the mornings we all have a routine we follow: a wash, shower or bath, followed by cleaning our teeth and putting on deodorant before dressing. By following this ritual we reduce our chances of getting infections and spreading germs. The Department of Health promoted the importance of personal hygiene in their *Essence of Care Benchmarks* published in 2010. The outcome for personal care is listed as 'People's personal hygiene needs and preferences are met according to their individual and clinical needs'.

Good personal hygiene reduces infection and transition of germs; bad personal hygiene reduces self-esteem and increases health problems. Therefore promoting personal hygiene is paramount when supporting individuals. This was demonstrated when the swine flu epidemic was feared and the government advertised the importance of good personal hygiene to reduce the risk of infection and the importance of washing your hands.

- Influenza can be caused by poor hygiene but is also an airborne infection.
- Head lice are only passed in clean hair.
- Urinary tract infections may be caused by poor hygiene skills; washing your hands after using the toilet is the main preventative.
- Appendicitis is not believed to be caused by poor personal hygiene.
- Boils are due to an accumulation of bacteria which live on the skin, good hygiene skills reduce the chance of boils.
- Tapeworms are related to undercooked meats and poor personal hygiene.
- Ringworm is a parasite that can be prevented by good personal hygiene.

6.1 Tapeworms and nits can be transmitted between individuals

Evidence activity

1.1 Transmisson

In the table below identify the infections and germs that can be transmitted through poor personal hygiene.

Infection/disease	Transmitted due to poor personal hygiene	Not affected by poor personal hygiene skills
Influenza		
Head louse		
Urinary tract infections		
Appendicitis		
Boils		
Tapeworm		
Ringworm		

Describe the effects of poor personal hygiene on health and well being

We have identified some infections and parasites that are transmitted due to poor personal hygiene. We need to be aware of the physical complications that can occur due to poor personal hygiene skills and the need to promote and educate the individuals that we work with to improve these standards. Not only will we reduce possible infections for the individual, we will also improve their social interaction skills.

No one wants to sit next to another person who smells of perspiration. We all prefer to sit next to a person who smells nice.

Sometimes when people are physically unwell and have stayed in bed, they can get into the character of an 'ill person', yet when they have got up and washed and dressed they tend to feel better. One of the first signs of depression is a dishevelled appearance and lack of motivation to attend to general appearance.

 Time to reflect

1.2

Recall a period when you have been either physically or mentally not well. Describe how you felt, recall if your personal hygiene deteriorated. How did your behaviour change when you began to feel well again?

LO2 (LD 206C) LO3 (LD 206)
Be able to support individuals to maintain personal hygiene

We have explored the importance of maintaining our own personal hygiene. We are now going to put this into the context of our work setting and the individuals we support. When we are due to go to work, we may have to get up earlier and not spend as much time as we would like on our personal appearance. We may have to wear a form of uniform, and we may not be able to choose what we would like to wear. Most people who work say they do not like the limited time they have to prepare for work.

Therefore we should all be able to identify with those individuals who need support to get ready for the day and the importance of choice and time. In learning disability environments, time and routine enable this process to be more enjoyable and not a chore for the individual.

Before anyone is assisted with their personal needs, their consent must be gained. We would not like someone to come into our room and suddenly get us up out of our bed and begin washing us in a hurry.

When attending to anyone's personal needs, we need to identify what routine they like. It is important they have this choice in the same way as we have choices. We should recognise their preference of time to get up, how they like to be woken, whether they like to have breakfast before dressing and so on. By communicating and agreeing these aspects with the individual the process will become empowering.

Personal hygiene is not only to be promoted in the mornings upon waking; it also needs to be encouraged throughout the day. We can reinforce the positive message of good personal hygiene skills when planning with the individual their activities throughout the day.

2.1 (LD 206C) Support an individual to understand factors that contribute to good personal hygiene

When planning activities, good practice would be to highlight when it is important to wash hands, brush teeth and comb hair. As with all things that are good for us to do, we need to know why they are good for us and these reasons should be communicated clearly and in a format that will be understood. It is useful to use pictorial aids, such as images of hand washing on bathroom walls.

Case study

2.1 **LD 206C** **Paul**

Paul is a new resident within the home; he has Cerebral Palsy which is renowned for creating oral problems due to gastric reflux problems. Prior to moving in he was living at home with his parents who are elderly and were having difficulties with his personal care. Paul is 23 years of age, has not been used to communal living and has had limited support with personal hygiene. Unfortunately he has a gum infection and several appointments to attend at the dentist. Paul's parents had difficulty in assisting him to outside appointments, and Paul has a negative attitude towards the dentist as his mouth is very sore.

Describe how you would explain to Paul the importance of going to the dentist and the need to brush his teeth on a regular basis.

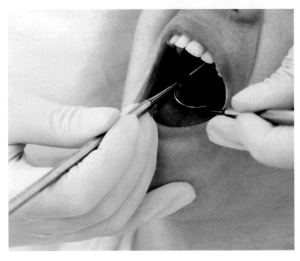

6.2 Good oral hygiene is crucial

LO2 (LD 206) Know how to encourage an individual to maintain personal hygiene

The need for good personal hygiene can be difficult for some people to understand. It is important to have the correct information and identify the individual's preferred ways of communication. If you were discussing how the lack of personal hygiene can lead to body odour and reduce or limit social interaction, you could explore this by talking about nice smells and smells that are not so nice in general day-to-day life, before relating the idea to hygiene.

2.1 **LD 206** **Explain how to address personal hygiene issues with an individual in a sensitive manner without imposing own values**

Most of us have come across someone who has a body odour problem or bad breath in our lifetime and we are aware of how this can damage a person emotionally if they are not tactfully alerted to the problem. Hopefully no one would approach them and say 'you smell and I don't want anything to do with you'. We have a tendency to avoid the person instead because we don't know how to approach the subject without causing them distress. We need to be aware of our manner in dealing with the people we support at the same level of integrity as we would with a work colleague. We must also be aware of individual standards. It may be that you as a person shower three times a day and wash your hands after everything you touch, but to instill these standards into everyone is not allowing choice and not allowing them to choose standards they feel are adequate to maintain personal hygiene.

As a support worker your role needs to be around the individual's needs and requirements as agreed in their personal planning. Your role is to promote personal hygiene to ensure well being, not to impose your own personal hygiene routine.

As previously stated we need consent and agreement, we must continually think of the individual through person-centred thinking. Choice, independence, value and dignity are paramount.

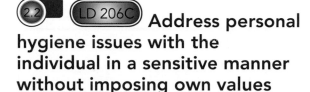 **Address personal hygiene issues with the individual in a sensitive manner without imposing own values**

When looking at an individual's personal hygiene problems we need to ensure we are not measuring them against our own standards. We need to identify if there is a reason for the issue not being addressed before, if this is a new problem or whether there is a history of poor personal hygiene. By exploring the reasons we may find the solution. The problem of body odour may be a new concept, they may not have had information promoting personal hygiene and its importance before. Body odour may occur due to illness, or excessive exercise. They may not have had the finances available to buy toiletries, or the ability to shop for these. They may require a different brand of deodorant as the one they have brought has not been effective. They may not have been informed that body odour can be an offensive smell to others.

A sensitive manner

Recall an individual who needed assistance with their personal hygiene. The first time they needed to address this sensitive issue, how did you inform them, how did you support them, what was their reaction and how has this been resolved? Thinking of this situation, what would you do differently next time?

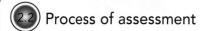 **Describe how to make an individual aware of the effects of poor hygiene on others**

Before any action to address personal hygiene issues, we need to identify the cause: education, finance or physical reasons. Once these have been identified, as a support worker you need to address the issue in a sensitive and empowering manner.

Evidence activity — LD 206

2.2 Process of assessment

Review your initial assessment forms in your workplace. Identify the process of finding out the cause for poor personal hygiene. Write the sequence you would follow to inform the individual of the effects of poor personal hygiene and the impact this would have on them.

2.3 LD 206C Support the individual to develop awareness of the effects of poor hygiene on others

In the majority of cases, individuals with learning disabilities learn the process of good personal hygiene as with any other task, in a sequential process using pictorial aids and positive reinforcement. When promoting good personal hygiene we as support workers need to demonstrate this. If a support worker turned up for work in a dishevelled state with bad body odour it would then be difficult to explain to an individual the importance of personal grooming. This is also a good time to reinforce with the individual the manner in which to speak to others who may have a problem with poor personal hygiene.

Evidence activity LD 206C

(2.3) Being aware

In the table below, list ways that you can support individuals to be aware of the effects of poor personal hygiene on others.

Personal hygiene problems	Pictorial	Sequential	Verbal
Bad breath			
Hair condition			
Body odour			
Nails			

(2.3) LD 206 **Describe how to support an individual to develop and improve personal hygiene routines**

If this is a new process for the individual it may take time to address. We have identified different mechanisms for this starting with personal individual planning. If body odour is an issue, after checking that there is no medical reason, we need to promote personal care in easy steps and encourage maintenance of these skills. You may wish to start by taking the individual out to the shops to purchase toiletries, with encouragement for them to choose what they like. As an individual we all have preferences as to what soap or cleansers we prefer, so the importance of the individual choosing their own toiletries is paramount. You also need to identify what routine they would prefer to attend to their personal needs, whether they prefer baths to showers, the time of day they prefer to wash and so on. We also need to identify their choice in clothing and when they prefer to dress.

When we have these details we can then help them to place this task, hopefully now an enjoyable task, into their individual activity plan. By doing this we can communicate to others when this procedure is going to occur and give information about the individual's preferences, including things like the water temperature they prefer. This plan should address their personal hygiene at a level that ensures well being, even if it is not as frequently or the process we would choose for ourselves.

Once this process has commenced we need to reinforce the message to the individual by communicating how well they have achieved and progressed. Hopefully they will feel for themselves the benefits of good personal hygiene on their emotional health and in the reflection from others wishing to engage with them. If you have done your job well, the individual will feel empowered and valued as a member of the community.

Evidence activity LD 206

 Promoting personal hygiene

Write out an activity plan for one of the individuals you support, identifying clearly the sequential steps to promote their personal hygiene and the action of reinforcing this positively.

LD 206C **Support the preferences and needs of the individual whilst maintaining their independence**

3.2 **LD 206** **Explain how to support the preferences and needs of the individual while maintaining their independence**

When working with individuals with learning disabilities, the people you support may come from a variety of different cultural backgrounds with different ethics and beliefs. Just as their disability is individual, so are their beliefs and preferences. That is why no plan can be the same for each individual you work with. Their individualism will also dictate the levels of support they require.

A key factor when supporting an individual is to give sufficient help but not to overtake. The main aim is to enable the individual to achieve the skills by themselves and become independent of support. Sometimes the individual will always require support in personal care. The support we give in these cases needs to be discreet and maintain the individual's dignity. We would never bathe someone with others watching. We need to ensure that when we discuss any personal issues we do this with confidentiality and privacy in mind. An example of this would be not asking the individual in front of others about their personal hygiene needs.

Case study

2.4 **LD 206C** Mohammed

Mohammed lives in the community with support. He has profound learning disabilities. Unfortunately no one has identified the need to address his personal hygiene needs. Mohammed is unable to inform you verbally of his choices. His friends are due to visit him this afternoon and he has no family members. How are you going to assess his personal needs?

Evidence activity **LD 206**

3.2 **Needs and preferences**

Write out an action plan using information from the individual you support and all others involved in their care, identifying how you can support their personal hygiene needs and preferences.

6.3 Enable the individual to choose their own toiletries

Describe how to maintain the dignity of an individual when supporting intimate personal hygiene

When attending to personal needs we need to ensure we promote the individual's dignity and encourage them to participate as much as they are able. When assisting with toileting, it is imperative we assist them when they wish to use the facilities, not when it fits into our work routines. Ensure you understand the individual's signals of when they wish to use the toilet; if you are unsure check with their personal plan about their preferred communication.

When assisting an individual, be discreet. Ensure the toilets you are about to use are private, free for use and are of sufficient size if you have a wheelchair to move around.

When washing and dressing ensure privacy is maintained by checking curtains are not open and that doors are shut. You can assist the individual's dignity and privacy through the manner in which you speak to them. Ask rather than demand, pay attention to your tone of voice and your use of terminology. It is so empowering to the individual if you use their terms of personal care and the terms they associate with personal hygiene.

 Identify risks to own health in supporting an individual with personal hygiene routines

 Describe risks to own health in supporting personal hygiene routines

When we are dealing with personal hygiene we are dealing with body waste, and there are risks associated with this. There are risks when moving individuals who cannot bear their own weight. There are risks identified with airborne infections.

Anyone receiving support must have a completed risk assessment. As a support worker it is your responsibility to read this, understand it and take the appropriate precautions.

Ensure you have the right equipment to move or handle an individual with minimum risk to you as the support worker. Ensure any open cuts you have are covered up so there is no possibility of infection. Ensure you follow the correct procedures for infection control, such as hand washing after attending to an individual's personal needs.

All risks can be minimised by following the correct procedural guidelines. As a support worker you need to be aware of the types of risk that can have an effect on you when dealing with personal care.

Evidence activity LD 206C LD 206

(2.5) LD 206C (3.3) LD 206 **Promoting dignity**

In the table below identify different ways you can promote an individual's dignity whilst attending to their personal needs.

Personal needs	Types of support	How this promotes dignity
Daily washing		
Brushing hair		
Brushing teeth		
Nail care		
Toilet		
Showering / bathing		

Evidence activity LD 206C LD 206

2.6 LD 206C **3.4** LD 206 **Identifying risks to self**

In the table below, you will see risks that have been identified for support workers whilst attending to the personal needs of individuals. Read your workplace policies and documents to identify the precautions put in place to reduce these risks, and complete the table below identifying the type of activity these risks may relate to and the precautions to reduce these risks in your workplace.

Risk	Activity	Precautions
Muscloskeletal		
Hepatitis		
Influenza		
Skin conditions		

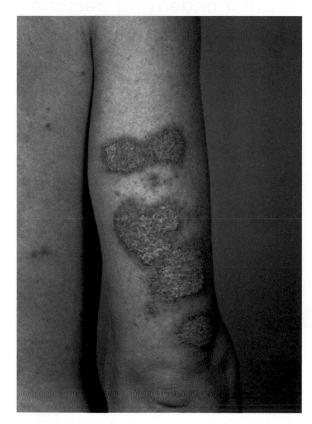

6.4 Developing eczema due to work related activity is a risk

2.7 LD 206C **Reduce risks to own health when supporting the individual with personal hygiene routines**

3.5 LD 206 **Describe how to reduce risks to own health**

By looking through your own policies and procedures you have identified ways of reducing the risk to your own health and others through simple procedures like thorough hand washing and wearing protective clothing.

It is important that health and safety rules and procedures are followed at all times to reduce injury to yourself and others. Manual handling regulations are designed to reduce injury when moving individuals. Infection control procedures reduce the chances of infections being transmitted from one person to another. If you identify a possible risk to yourself or others you have a duty of care to report this. The Care Quality Commission have standards that must be adhered to, these were designed not only to protect the service user but for carer/support worker's safety as well. The Department of Health has also issued legislation to reduce risk.

Research and investigate

Legislation and guidelines

Find legislation and guidelines on personal care relating to your working area.

6.5 Information about personal care items should be done with consent whilst maintaining confidentiality

Identify others who might be involved in supporting the individual to maintain personal hygiene

We have explored the risk to ourselves when addressing the personal hygiene needs of the individuals we support. We are now going to look at the risks to others that might occur when attending to personal hygiene. We have educated and promoted the importance of good personal hygiene to the individual we are supporting. Sometimes others are involved in attending to their personal needs. These may be family, friends, fellow carers and possibly other agencies such as hospital admissions. As we have already completed a risk assessment and analysed the risks involved in their care we need to share this information. This is important to reduce any injury to that person. As with any information we need to ensure confidentiality is maintained and there is consent for sharing the information.

Sharing of information must be in a factual manner and must not be influenced by personal opinion. Information must only be shared with the agreement of the individual.

LO3 [LD 206C] LO4 [LD 206]
Understand when poor hygiene may be an indicator of other underlying personal issues

Poor hygiene can be due to lack of skills or understanding of personal hygiene. Sometimes poor personal hygiene can be caused by other problems. Halitosis can be due to an infection in the mouth, or decaying teeth. Irritable bowel syndrome increases flatulence causing poor body odour. Some infections have a very unpleasant smell, such as an open ulcer. As previously discussed, when individuals are depressed they lose energy and cannot attend to their personal needs. Other mental health issues can lead to a lack of personal hygiene attention. An individual suffering a manic episode will sweat rapidly and will not have the time or patience to attend to their personal needs. Medications can cause drowsiness and lack of energy and therefore the individual's attention to personal hygiene may be reduced.

Case study

 **Ruth**

Ruth has a very supportive family who likes to take her out over the weekend to stay with them. In Ruth's family there are four sisters and two brothers. Ruth's grandmother also lives with her mum and dad. To transport Ruth to her home a local community voluntary service car is used and a support worker escorts her home. Ruth is incontinent and uses incontinence pads on journeys to reduce her embarrassment. During a recent doctor's appointment it was discovered that Ruth has herpes.

Write down the information that should be given to members of her family, identifying which members should be told and in what detail. Should the driver of the car be informed? What protection should go home with Ruth to help the family and who else should be notified?

Lack of physical agility due to mobility issues may reduce the individual's ability to tend to their own personal hygiene needs. Finance may be another issue, e.g. the lack of money to buy toiletries.

Repeated infections in an individual can be due to poor personal hygiene skills, and when individuals feel unwell it is even harder for them to attend to their personal hygiene needs, causing a viscous circle of events. This is why it is so important to review and reassess on a regular basis.

Identify underlying personal issues that may be a cause of poor personal hygiene

It is important to recognise any changes in a person's personal hygiene and ensure there are no other issues causing the personal hygiene problem. This reinforces the need to have a clear initial assessment of someone's abilities and medical conditions and emphasises the importance of ensuring information is relayed to the correct person.

Physical issues may include infections: gum disease can cause halitosis, urinary tract infections can cause an offensive discharge. Certain medications, vitamins and excessive use of coffee, tobacco and alcohol will also cause bad breath. Other physical causes include excessive sweating due to medical conditions like bromhidrosis and sweat gland secretion problems. We also know that excessive exercise makes us perspire more.

Psychological factors that can cause excessive sweating are anxiety, fear of washing, depression and lack of self-esteem; these may all be factors in poor personal hygiene skills. There are also cultural and environmental issues, such as a lack of clean water or role model.

Financial issues include lack of funds to obtain toiletries, or to clean clothes. In extreme cases they might result in no running water or no environment to attend to personal hygiene. There may be problems with the costs of paying for support to assist in attending to personal needs.

Evidence activity LD 206C LD 206

3.1 4.1 Identifying factors

Identify someone you support and complete a case study on their personal hygiene needs, identify what factors were involved in meeting their personal hygiene needs.

3.2 LD 206C 4.2 LD 206

Describe how underlying personal issues might be addressed

Once we have identified what the issues are that may have caused their personal hygiene problems, we then need to know how to assist the individual and promote good personal hygiene skills.

It is important to remember how sensitive an issue personal hygiene can be to the individual. The way that these issues are initially addressed can have a lasting effect on the outcome.

- If the issues are due to a physical problem like infection, we can give prescribed medication to clear the infection. We must also educate the individual on the effects of the infection and promote good personal hygiene skills.

- If the reason for poor personal hygiene is due to anxiety we need to address this and then re-educate the individual on the importance of good personal hygiene skills.

- If the problem is due to not having the monies or ability to purchase toiletries, we can support the individual to do this making it a positive and fulfilling experience.

Knowing the cause and being able to resolve it is the first step to promoting good personal hygiene skills. The Human Rights Act 1998, article three, states *freedom from inhumane and degrading treatment*. This makes it illegal not to care for the basic rights of individuals to be treated with respect and dignity in relation to their treatment and personal hygiene needs.

To address these issues we need to work with the individual, and others involved in their care, to design an agreed and acceptable plan of action. Person-centred thinking and planning needs to be introduced. Persons with learning disabilities may require a lot of support initially, and the plan will require regular reviewing to identify progress or any difficulties that may occur. Encouragement and positive reinforcement of their achievements is vital. Communication to all involved in their care will ensure a consistent approach for the individual.

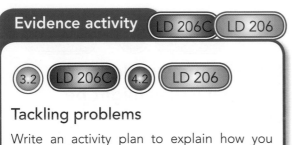

Evidence activity   LD 206C   LD 206

3.2 LD 206C   4.2   LD 206

Tackling problems

Write an activity plan to explain how you would promote good personal hygiene skills to an individual whose poor personal hygiene skills were due to a financial or physical or psychological cause.

LO3 LD 206 Know how to support an individual to maintain personal hygiene

Once we have commenced an activity plan to engage the individual in good personal hygiene skills we need to ensure the skills they have learnt are maintained and continued.

If the reason for poor personal hygiene skills was due to an identified cause and the problem has been resolved, it is important to maintain the standards they have achieved. It is important to educate the individual about the problems that can occur if personal hygiene is not maintained.

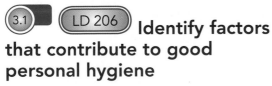

3.1   LD 206   Identify factors that contribute to good personal hygiene

Good personal hygiene requires regular cleaning to reduce the chances of infection and ensuring well being. When teaching these skills we need to ensure the individual is able to physically manage the task. We must also reinforce the achievement and ensure the task is an enjoyable experience for the individual. We can do this by promoting their independence, dignity and privacy.

Factors that contribute to good personal hygiene are:

- Regular washing with soap and drying of the body.
- Thorough brushing of the teeth at least twice a day.
- Regular washing of hair and ensuring it is combed at least once a day. If washing their hair is difficult for the individual, they may want to look at possibly having it styled shorter.
- Nails should be kept trimmed and regularly cleaned under the nails to ensure all dirt is removed.
- Regular baths and/or showers to wash the whole body should be taken. Always ensure all parts of the body are completely dry afterwards.
- An effective deodorant should be used.
- Clothes should be washed frequently, and individuals should have sufficient clothing to have a change.
- When using the toilet ensure the use of tissue to dry the region. Ensure that wiping this area is from front to back for females to prevent cross infection from bowel matter.
- Always wash and dry hands thoroughly afterwards.

To promote good personal hygiene skills in others you need to model this practice in yourself before assisting others.

Time to reflect

3.1   LD 206   Identify factors that contribute to good hygiene

Reflect on your own personal hygiene skills, identify your own routine, describe what works well and what you could do differently. Write what you would feel like if you needed support and how you would like that support to be given.

Assessment Summary for Unit LD 206

To achieve the unit, your assessor will require you to:

Learning outcomes	Assessment criteria
1 Understand the importance of good personal hygiene	Explain why personal hygiene is important See Evidence activity 1.1, p. 110.
	Describe the effects of poor personal hygiene on health and well-being See Time to reflect 1.2, p. 111.
2 Know how to encourage an individual to maintain personal hygiene	Explain how to address personal hygiene issues with an individual in a sensitive manner without imposing own values See Time to reflect 2.1, p. 113.
	Describe how to make an individual aware of the effects of poor hygiene on others See Evidence activity 2.2, p. 113.
	Describe how to support an individual to develop and improve personal hygiene routines See Evidence activity 2.3, p. 114.
3 Know how to support an individual to maintain personal hygiene	Identify factors that contribute to good personal hygiene See Time to reflect 3.1, p. 120.
	Explain how to support the preferences and needs of the individual while maintaining their independence See Evidence activity 3.2, p. 115.
	Describe how to maintain dignity of an individual when supporting intimate personal hygiene See Evidence activity 3.3, p. 116.
	Describe risks to own health in supporting personal hygiene routines See Evidence activity 3.4, p. 117.
	 Describe how to reduce risks to own health See Research and investigate 3.5, p. 118.
	Identify others that may be involved in supporting an individual to maintain personal hygiene See Case study 3.6, p. 118.

4 Understand when poor hygiene may be an indicator of other underlying personal issues	Identify underlying personal issues that may be a cause of poor personal hygiene See Evidence activity 4.1, p. 119.
	Describe how underlying personal issues might be addressed See Evidence activity 4.2, p. 120.

Assessment Summary for Unit LD 206C

To achieve the unit, your assessor will require you to:

Learning outcomes	Assessment criteria
1 Understand the importance of good personal hygiene	**1.1** Explain why personal hygiene is important See Evidence activity 1.1, p. 110.
	1.2 Describe the effects of poor personal hygiene on health and well-being See Time to reflect 1.2, p. 111.
2 Be able to support individuals to maintain personal hygiene	**2.1** Support an individual to understand factors that contribute to good personal hygiene See Case study 2.1, p. 112.
	2.2 Address personal hygiene issues with the individual in a sensitive manner without imposing own values See Time to reflect 2.2, p. 113.
	2.3 Support the individual to develop awareness of the effects of poor hygiene on others See Evidence activity 2.3, p. 114.
	2.4 Support the preferences and needs of the individual while maintaining their independence See Case study 2.4, p. 115.
	2.5 Describe how to maintain dignity of an individual when supporting intimate personal hygiene See Evidence activity 2.5, p. 116.
	2.6 Identify risks to own health in supporting an individual with personal hygiene routines See Evidence activity 2.6, p. 117.
	2.7 Reduce risks to own health when supporting the individual with personal hygiene routines See Research and investigate 2.7, p. 118.
	2.8 Identify others who may be involved in supporting the individual to maintain personal hygiene See Case study 2.8, p. 118.

Learning outcomes	Assessment criteria
3 Understand when poor hygiene may be an indicator of other underlying personal issues	(3.1) Identify underlying personal issues that may be a cause of poor personal hygiene See Evidence activity 3.1, p. 119.
	(3.2) Describe how underlying personal issues might be addressed See Evidence activity 3.2, p. 120.

Supporting Individuals with a Learning Disability to Access Health care

Unit LD 208c Contribute to supporting individuals with a learning disability to access healthcare

Unit LD 308 Support individuals with a learning disability to access healthcare

What are we finding out?

When we need to see a doctor or access any health care service, we know the procedure and carry out the task with little thought or consideration of any problems that may occur. Access to health care services is something we take for granted, and regard as a simple process. We don't need to consider the obstacles that people with learning disabilities may have to overcome, such as understanding the process of obtaining the correct service and organising treatment and follow up care. These can be very problematic for some individuals with learning difficulties as they may not understand the need or the process.

The reading and activities in this chapter will help you to:

- Understand legislation, policies and guidance relevant to individuals with a learning disability accessing health care services

- Understand the function of different healthcare services that an individual with a learning disability may need to access

- Understand how plans for health care and regular health checks underpin long-term health and well being for individuals with a learning disability

- Understand the role of professionals within different health care services that a person with learning disabilities may have to access

- Be able to contribute to plans for health care with individuals with a learning disability.

- Be able to support individuals to overcome barriers to accessing health care services

- Understand the issues that an individual with learning disabilities may face when accessing a variety of health care services

- Be able to support individuals with a learning disability to access a variety of health care services.

LO1 Understand legislation, policies and guidance relevant to individuals with a learning disability accessing healthcare

 **Outline what is meant by a rights-based approach to accessing health care**

7.1 Supporting access to health care services is crucial

Describe what is meant by a rights-based approach to accessing health care

With the changes in the culture and treatment of those with learning disabilities, the need to ensure that all are aware of the services available and have access to those services is crucial. Prior to changes in legislation, persons with learning disabilities were treated as second class citizens with no need for health promotion services. This was noted with dental services, for example, as due to lack of support many individuals in care were not encouraged to maintain good oral hygiene and if they encountered any problems with their teeth the solution was extraction. Sometimes teeth were extracted just in case the individual were to express their frustrations through biting.

This changed in January 2009 with the 'Valuing people now' strategy which identified that persons with learning disabilities were equal and had the same right to expect the same services and respect as anyone else.

The Human Rights Act explored how vulnerable people were being cared for and explored their access to health care services and noted that it was discriminatory. This problem has been tackled through the rights-based approach using person-centred thinking.

  **Identify legislation which supports a rights-based approach to accessing health care**

British human rights legislation sets out the requirement that everyone should be treated equally and should experience no difference in their care due to any form of disability. All health care services have a duty to provide an equal service demonstrating respect for the individual and ensuring equal status of care. To ensure this it is important that all staff are empowered and knowledgeable in this area. As support workers you need to have the knowledge to advocate for the individuals you support.

The House of Lords and the House of Commons have a joint strategy supporting the rights-based approach that was published in 2007 called 'A life like any other, human rights of adults with learning disabilities'.

■ Research and investigate

LD 208C 1.2 Legislation

Research the different legislation that aims at supporting and encouraging the use of a rights-based approach to health care services.

Time to reflect

Supporting access

Identify the last disabled person you supported to access health services. What were the difficulties, what went well, how was access addressed through a rights-based approach?

1.2 **LD 308** ## Outline the main points of legislation that exists to support a rights-based approach

Due to legislation, health care services and social services have agreed upon a protocol to ensure that their approach to individuals with learning disabilities reinforces equality of access and empowers the individual. Some disabilities may require us to look at different ways of communication to ensure understanding. An example of the relevant legislation in action supporting individuals with learning disabilities might be someone who needed support with their personal hygiene, who would have the right to dignity and to be respected as covered by the Human Rights Act. The four sections of the Human Rights Act that relate particularly to learning disabilities are:

- the right not to be tortured or treated in an inhuman or degrading way,
- the right to respect for private and family life, home and correspondence,
- the right to life and
- the right not to be discriminated against in relation to any of the rights in the European Convention.

Evidence activity **LD 308**

 1.2 #### Identifying legislation and guidelines

In your work setting, identify the relevant legislation and guidelines that support a rights-based approach for the individuals you are supporting.

1.3 **LD 208C** ## Describe ways that health care services should make 'reasonable adjustments' to ensure that they provide equal access to individuals with learning disabilities

In the recent past, individuals with learning disabilities were largely cared for within the institutionalised care system which meant others made decisions for them. This meant equal access

was not regarded as important. With the introduction of legislation, including the Human Rights Act, it has now become the priority. The main differences now for those with a learning disability, is the promotion of independence and person-centred planning and thinking. All public services need to be accessible and equal.

Case study

LD 208C **1.3** **Tracey**

Tracey has autism and difficulties with any changes in her routine. Tracey has become very distressed and appears to be in pain and she needs to see a doctor to establish what is wrong. The staff that support Tracey have contacted the local health care centre and tried to make an appointment for her to see a doctor. The health service say they can only offer an open surgery, which means waiting in the surgery on a first come first served basis.

Because of her autism, which is exacerbated by pain, this service does not meet Tracey's needs as she would be unable to sit and wait.

Thinking of Tracey's situation, what adjustments could the health centre make to ensure Tracey had equal opportunity to see the doctor?

1.3 **LD 308** ## Explain the requirements of legislation if an individual with learning disabilities is assessed to not have capacity to consent to a specific treatment

Due to their level of understanding and sometimes a fear of hospitals and medical care, individuals with learning disabilities may refuse treatment. With the changes in legislation, individuals with learning disabilities now have the right to say if they want the treatment or not in the same way as everyone else. If an individual with learning disabilities refuses treatment, no one can force them to have treatment against their will. If refusing the treatment puts themselves or others at risk, legislation is available to assess if they have the capacity to understand the consequences of not having the treatment. Capacity is defined as understanding the consequences of actions and being able to understand and assess the different options available. If an individual is believed to not have the capacity to understand or make the decision, this needs to be legally proved via a capacity test. If it is then proved that the individual does not have capacity, others can make decisions for them, generally through the Mental Capacity Act 2005.

Before assessing capacity it should be ensured that all the relevant information has been explained in a format that the individual understands. If the individual has assessed as lacking capacity and the decision has been taken for them that the treatment should proceed, staff need to be aware of how to support the individual and protect them. The Mental Capacity Act 2005 came into force to protect those who are unable to give informed consent due to lack of capacity to understand the procedure or treatment. It aims to ensure that the individual's rights are protected as much as possible.

Case study

LD 308 **1.3** **Rosemary**

Rosemary has profound learning disabilities and a fear of hospitals. She is suffering from acute abdominal pain and her GP immediately referred her to consultants at the hospital with suspected appendicitis. Rosemary is refusing to go because she is afraid. Rosemary does not want to go to the hospital but does not understand the possible consequences of this decision. Rosemary has stated she does not want to die but does not understand that her decision would put her at a high risk of dying.

Read your work policies and guidelines about your responsibility under the Mental Capacity Act and what you would need to do in this scenario.

1.4 **LD 208C** **Explain why it is important to ensure an individual is able to give informed consent to their treatment in line with legislation, policies or guidelines**

To be able to say that you understand the treatment you are being offered and agree to it helps in any procedure and aids recovery. If you do not understand or do not give consent then anxiety will inevitably increase.

Time to reflect

LD 208C **1.4** Giving consent

Identify a time when you were forced to do something that you did not agree to do. Write down how you felt, how this affected the outcome of the situation and what you could have done differently.

1.4 **LD 308** **Explain different ways to support an individual to give informed consent in line with legislation, policies or guidelines**

We have explored what informed consent is and why it is important for the individual to ensure their rights. If informed consent is not given then legislation comes into play, which can leave the individual disempowered. Therefore it is crucial to help the individual understand the procedures and decisions they need to make to try and enable informed consent whenever possible.

Evidence activity LD 308

(1.4) Promoting informed consent

In the table below list the different types of support you can give to promote consent from the individual.

Scenario	Support to understand
Hospital visit	
Dentist visit	
Doctors visit	
Taking medication	
Promoting personal hygiene	

(1.5) LD 208C Describe the actions to take if an individual cannot give informed consent to the treatment

The need for the individual to remain in control is paramount to improving their self esteem and confidence. Unfortunately sometimes they are unable to make decisions and we need to make those decisions for them in line with legislation, guidelines and procedures. To explore this further, look at the case study below and write down how you, as their support worker, could assist Sam through this process.

Case study

LD 208C (1.5) Sam

Sam has late onset diabetes; he needs to have regular injections of insulin to stop him from going into a diabetic coma and needs to eat sensibly following the diet the dietician has given him. Sam has been assessed under the Mental Capacity Act and it has been agreed he cannot give informed consent, due to his lack of understanding of the consequences of not having the injections. How are you going to support Sam?

(1.5) LD 308 Explain ways in which health care services should make reasonable adjustments to ensure that they provide equal access to individuals with learning disabilities

Legislation identifies how important it is that individuals with learning disabilities have the same access to services as those who do not have a learning disability. Legislation states that reasonable adjustments should be made to ensure equal access. An example of this would be that a dentist located on a second floor of a building should ensure that someone in a wheelchair can access the office. This may mean the installation of a lift to allow wheelchair access. The key word is 'reasonable' adjustments. So a reasonable adjustment may mean having a ramp instead of a step to enable someone in a wheelchair to have access.

Evidence activity LD 308

(1.5) Ensuring equal access

Make a survey of the area you work in and identify an area or tool that could be adjusted with minimum cost to improve equal access.

7.2 Services are obliged to make reasonable adjustments to ensure access for all

LO2 LD 208C LD 308
Understand the function of different health care services that an individual with a learning disability may need to access

We have discussed the need for equal access and the legislation relating to this. We now need to explore the different types of services available and what each service provides for the individual we work with. The person with disabilities is an individual, and as an individual their needs are personalised. Everyone needs registration and regular health checks from a local GP. In health care centres there are normally a variety of services provided, from advisory roles of promoting health to actual treatment centres. Dental services are also required to promote good oral health. Some individuals may require the services of a chiropodist, physiotherapist or occupational therapist. The range of services that an individual may require is vast, and their individual needs and health will dictate the frequency and intensity of health care access. Whenever we support an individual we must be aware of their health care needs and their preferred choices of services. We also need to know how often they need to attend to their health care needs and the different professionals they need to visit.

2.1 **LD 208C** **List a range of health care services that an individual with a learning disability may need to access**

People with learning disabilities need to ensure they remain healthy and regular check-ups are very important to maintaining health. When someone with learning disabilities becomes unwell they cannot always express their feelings or describe in enough detail the pain or discomfort they are feeling for the medical team to diagnose the illness; and of course any emergency intervention can increase anxieties and fears. Therefore prevention of illness is obviously the best course to follow.

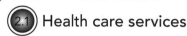

Evidence activity LD 208C

2.1 Health care services

Within your work practice, identify all the different health care services used.

2.1 **LD 308** **Explain the work of health care services that an individual with learning disabilities may need to access**

2.2 **LD 208C** **Describe the work of each type of health care service**

Within a learning disability environment the different types of health care needed can be vast. When supporting individuals to access these services it is important that we can clearly explain their different roles. An example of this could be someone visiting a speech therapist or an individual accessing a psychotherapist. Part of the support worker's role is to be able to inform the individual about the process that is about to occur and the treatment they should expect to receive. So in the example of the individual going to see the speech therapist, the support worker needs to communicate that the role of the speech therapist is to assist with their communications skills. The individual going to see the psychotherapist should expect them to help manage their emotional problems.

Evidence activity LD 308 LD 208C

(2.1) (2.2) Different professions

In the table below are the titles of some health care professionals that persons with learning disabilities may have to visit. In the column next to their title place a brief description of their role.

Title	Description
Psychiatrist	
Dermatologist	
Occupational therapist	
Dentist	
Orthopedist	
Ophthalmologist	

(2.2) LD 308 Explain how an individual can access each type of health care service

Most individuals will access specialist care through their GP's services. Health care services like the dentist and optician are arranged by calling the clinics and arranging an appointment. For someone with learning disabilities, the process of making appointments and waiting in busy waiting rooms can be too difficult because of communication and accessibility issues. The government has identified through several investigations that the access that individuals with learning disabilities get to health care services is not good. They have proposed enhanced health care services for individuals with learning disabilities.

Generally people with disabilities have more complex health care needs and their life expectancy is reduced. The government has identified barriers to access and are trying to improve the service. They identified that there was a lack of training in acute medical staff's understanding of communication issues and learning disabilities. The Michael Report (2008) was an independent inquiry into access to health care for people with learning disabilities. From this report the government made some changes to legislation, stating that all persons with a disability should have a yearly health check-up. They suggested that staff should be trained in special needs and communication issues, that information should be made available in different formats to improve communication, and that health care professionals should share information more effectively.

Time to reflect

(2.2) LD 308 Making it easier

Thinking of the individuals you support, write down the process for accessing health care services, any barriers you have encountered, and think about what you could do to make this process easier for the individual next time.

(2.3) LD 208C Outline the roles and responsibilities of professionals working in different types of health care services that an individual may need to access

We have explored the fact that there are a variety of health care services we may need to access for the individuals we support and that each professional has a specific role. It is important that we are able to identify for the individual what those different roles are.

Evidence activity LD 208C

 2.3 Health and care roles

Think of an individual you support and identify how many different health care services they use. List the roles of each service and describe how you would let the individual know the differences between these roles.

LO3 LD 208C LO4 LD 308
Understand how plans for health care and regular health checks underpin long-term health and wellbeing for individuals with a learning disability

Before legislative change and the introduction of a rights-based approach to health care, individuals in care did not have regular check-ups and were only seen when the carers thought it was necessary. This process could result in distress at the time of the meeting, which impacted on accurate accounts of symptoms being given, and gave limited time and information to make a diagnosis. We all know preventative measures are preferable, particularly because persons with learning disabilities are known to react to illnesses in a more intense way. Regular check-ups can help prevent acute illness.

LO3 LD 308 Understand the role of professionals within different health care services that a person with learning disabilities may have to access

Staff need to be aware of the variety of services available and the roles that each professional has. Communication with different professionals is vital in promoting the individual's health.

3.1 LD 208C **Explain how plans for health care can be of benefit to an individual with a learning disability**

4.1 LD 308 **Explain how plans for health care can be used to support the healthcare needs of an individual with learning disabilities**

With any health care procedure or appointment clear communication is important. To empower the individual we need to ensure they understand any treatment or procedure that they may need. Everyone who is prescribed medication is told when and how much to take. This is then recorded in their medical records. This is important to ensure the correct dose of medication is taken at the right time by the right person. By keeping a record in the medical notes, the doctor can identify past treatment and has knowledge of past health issues. If you move to another area the new doctor will also have access to these same notes.

For individuals with learning disabilities providing this information is paramount both for their treatment and to empower the individual. The person who is prescribed the treatment needs to consent, understand the frequency of the treatment and why they need to follow the instructions. Sometimes written and spoken formats are not enough for individuals with learning difficulties and they may require a different information format. As their support worker your role will be to identify the best ways of communicating this vital information.

Another reason records are needed are for legal reasons and good practice guidance. When more then one person is supporting an individual, communication is vital to ensure, for example, that medication has not been given twice.

Health care plans enable us to support the individual to maintain their health, while supporting their independence and respecting the individual.

Evidence activity LD 208C

3.1 Health plans

Within your work setting identify an individual's health plan. Describe the problems that would occur for that individual if the health plan was not available.

Time to reflect

LD 308 **4.1 Support through health plans**

Devise a health care plan for an individual within your work setting. Identify the support the health care plan gives to the individual. Think about what you could do differently to improve the support.

3.1 LD 308 ## Describe the role and responsibility of professionals working in different types of health care services

Individuals may come into contact with a variety of professional people. In health care services we have a range of specialists, from opticians to consultant psychiatrists, that an individual may be involved with at any one time. Therefore it is important to not only understand their specialism but also to be aware of the communication within the health care setting.

A professional nurse, dentist or general practitioner has the same aims as us: to make the individual well and to ensure their human rights are upheld. All professionals are aware of the importance of working together, as a holistic view is needed to treat the individual.

Every professional has a duty to record and work in partnership with all persons involved in their care. If more than one professional area is involved in the treatment a care coordinator is required to ensure that communication and understanding is freely shared with the individual's consent.

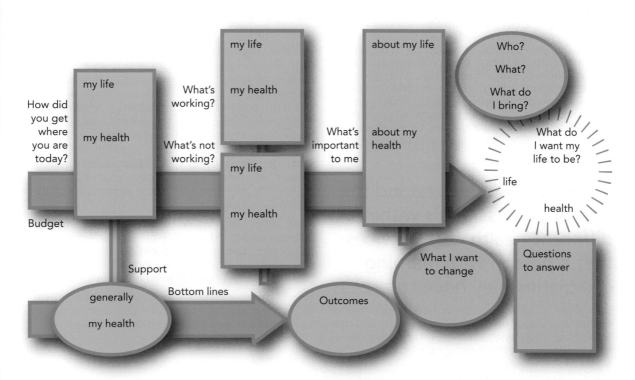

7.3 Health care plans are vital. Reproduced by permission of Helen Sanderson Associates.

Evidence activity LD 308

(3.1) Working together

Identify someone you support and list all the professional persons involved in their care. Identify how they ensure the support is consistent and how they communicate with other professionals involved in the care.

(3.2) LD 208C **Identify a range of regular health checks that an individual may have to support good health and wellbeing**

We have explored the need for regular health checks and the importance of these. It is vital that as a support worker we understand what the checks are for and their importance in order to support the individual to continually attend and understand their relevance themselves.

(3.3) LD 208C **Outline how missing regular health checks can impact on the individual's health and wellbeing**

  LD 308 **Explain the importance of routine health checks**

Routine health checks are aimed at promoting health and preventing illness. With an individual with learning disabilities it is sometimes difficult to establish what the problems are when the individual is in acute distress. Regular check-ups can prevent illness and distress and if the individual has a planned check-up you have time to prepare the individual. Ensure all communication tools are available for the visit. Plan the time of the visit, checking that all the information that may be required is available. This gives the professional time to spend with the individual.

Research and investigate

LD 208C (3.3) LD 308 (4.3)

Check-up frequency

Look up the Department of Health's 'Valuing people now' documentation and identify the guidelines for frequency of medical check-ups that individuals with learning disabilities should have and the different types of health care services.

Evidence activity LD 208C

(3.2) Risk taking

In the table below, the left column lists the types of health care checks that an individual may attend on a regular basis. In the column next to this list identify ways you can support and encourage them to attend these check-ups.

Regular check-ups	Support and encouragement
Optician	
Health check-up	
Chiropodist	
Dental check-up	

7.4 Check-ups are an important part of the health care service

food allergy, the family may be able to give a more precise information on the reaction the individual had when the allergy first became apparent.

LO4 (LD 208C) Be able to contribute to plans for health care with individuals with a learning disability

To ensure the individual is in agreement and understands the importance of access to health care, they need to be supported by person centred thinking and planning. It is important that everyone involved in the care, family and others, are also aware or involved in this planning. The individual needs to be involved in the whole process and it should be documented in a format that the individual can understand.

4.1 LD 208C Work with an individual and others to identify health care services the individual may require

Individual involvement is crucial to the success and effectiveness of the service. Sometimes the individual may not be aware of the services available or unaware of the assistance that may be needed. Person-centred planning and thinking is the most useful tool in this situation. An example of this might be the involvement of family members, who have known the individual for a longer time and are aware of problems they may have had in the past. For example, in the instance of a

4.2 LD 208C Agree with the individual and others the type and level of support the individual may require to access health care services

Cooperation is required to make any good plan effective. The easiest way to get cooperation is to involve everyone necessary. Sometimes health care can be frightening and daunting if, for example, you do not understand the terminology being used. To support individuals we need to identify what they want help with, how much help they require and if they actually want you to support them. Sometimes individuals may prefer family members/friends rather than a paid supporter.

4.2 **LD 308** **Explain the range of health checks available to individuals to support good health and wellbeing**

We have identified the importance of regular check-ups to prevent ill health. These check-ups need to be recorded and forward planning is needed to ensure future appointments are not missed. On completing a check-up it is useful to document what went well and what did not, so when the next check-up is due the person who supports the individual through this process will know what is effective and what needs to change. Although this is a regular occurrence it will need to be documented in their daily activity plan and should be made as enjoyable as possible. The more regularly the individual attends these sessions the less anxiety they should hopefully experience.

Time to reflect

4.2 **LD 308** **Your own health and wellbeing**

Think of your own health and wellbeing and identify the services you have used. Describe how you accessed these, the positive and the negative outcomes and list what you would do differently next time.

4.3 **LD 208C** **Demonstrate how the individual's needs, wishes and preferences are reflected in the health care plan**

5.1 **LD 308** **Identify who needs to be involved in the process of completing and reviewing plans for health care**

Documentation is important in any support we give for practical and legal reasons. As record-keeping is a legal requirement it is important that the documentation we use is in an acceptable format. Every individual who requires support

needs to have a health and wellbeing plan. This fulfils the legal requirements, but it is worth also making the plan an effective tool in your support of the individual. To make it effective as a working tool we need to engage everyone involved in writing the document and agreeing the process and steps identified within the plan rather than doing it in isolation. Person-centred thinking revolves around the individual you are supporting and the need for them to be fully involved in the process. Some individuals' communication skills may make this more difficult and this is why we need to ensure that the format we use is suitable for the individual involved.

Evidence activity

4.3 **Ensuring involvement**

Identify a health care plan you have assisted in. Describe the involvement of the individual in the process and clarify the format you used to develop their health care plan.

Evidence activity

5.1 **Individual contributions**

Identify a health care plan you have assisted in and list the people that were involved in the process. Describe the effect of each person involved on the health care plan.

4.4 **LD 208C** **Contribute to the review of plans for health care with the individual and others**

5.3 **LD 308** **Review plans for health care with an individual or significant others if appropriate**

Once a health care plan has been completed, it should then be used as an active tool.

It should be revisited at agreed times to ensure the information is still correct, any changes have been incorporated and that the plan is having the desired effect on the individual's health care and wellbeing needs. This process is known as a review. Reviews can be done when planned with the individual, normally every six months, or when any changes occur in the individual's health condition. The review process should be conducted in a person-centred manner with the involvement of the individual and others involved in their care with the agreement of the individual.

Time to reflect

LD 208C **(4.4)** Reviewing plans

Recall a health care plan review that you contributed to and write out the process of your involvement. Write what went well and what did not go as well. Write what you would do differently next time.

Research and investigate

LD 308 **(5.3)** Policies and requirements

Look at your workplace policies and procedures regarding reviewing health care plans and compare them to the Care Quality Commission's requirements. Then look at the government guidelines. Identify any differences and compare your role in developing the review process. Write an account of how you involve everyone in the process.

LO5 **LD 208C** Be able to support individuals to overcome barriers to accessing health care services

7.5 The care supporter's role is very varied

LO6 [LD 308] Understand the issues that an individual with learning disabilities may face when accessing a variety of health care services

Accessing the correct health care services at the right time can make all the difference to a positive outcome for the individual. All of us have had experiences of trying to get an urgent appointment with the dentist or doctors, generally because we didn't want to worry anyone or thought our problem was minor. Due to leaving the appointment until immediate attention was needed, we can end up having to wait to see the right professional. This can cause frustration and mean we are in pain for longer. For individuals with learning disabilities, who are not always able to verbalise their need for health care attention, a response from the health care team that they need to wait is not acceptable. This reinforces the need for regular check-ups.

Barriers to accessing health care services have been recognised and addressed by the government in their 'Valuing people now' agenda, and the need for access to good health care services was identified as one of their main targets. This legislation emphasises that regular check-ups should look at all their health care needs not just their disabilities. Health care professionals need better communication skills and there needs to be better communication between health care professionals about individuals. The Department of Health has incorporated these changes within the operation framework and their direct enhanced services.

5.1 [LD 208C] Identify barriers to accessing healthcare services that an individual with learning disability may experience

6.1 [LD 308] Describe barriers to accessing healthcare services that an individual with a learning disability may experience

Barriers for people with learning disabilities can be divided into three main categories.

- Environmental, which would include accessibility for wheelchair users.
- Communication, which would include the hearing loop.
- Process, which would include waiting times.

The majority of these issues have been investigated and changes in practice have happened. Feedback from previous users of the healthcare services has been sought and used to make these changes in cooperation with commissioning boards, the Care Quality Commission, local and national government.

As support worker, your role is to ensure that barriers are removed for the individuals you support. An example of this would be arranging suitable transport to take the individual to their health care appointment.

Evidence activity [LD 208C]

5.1 Identifying potential barriers

In the table below, identify barriers that people with learning disabilities may face when accessing health care services:

Barriers	
Physical	
Environmental	
Process	

Research and investigate

LD 308 **6.1** Local policies and procedures

Research your local policies and procedures. Identify the barriers individuals may experience in accessing health care services and clarify the relevant legislation, policies and procedures to assist you in overcoming these barriers for the individuals you support.

Time to reflect

5.2 **LD 208C** **6.3** **LD 308**

Understanding anxieties

Think of the first time you did something new, or had to go to an official appointment. Recall how you felt, what your anxieties were and what resolved the anxieties for you.

LO5 **LD 308** Be able to complete and review plans for health care

To ensure that the work that has been put into the planning is effective we need to regularly revisit and review the original plan. Person centred planning requires the individual and all involved in their support to be involved in the reviewing process. This promotes participation and increases the effectiveness of the planning.

5.2 **LD 208C** **Identify reasons why an individual may be reluctant to access health care services**

6.3 **LD 308** **Explain why an individual with learning disabilities may face additional barriers when accessing care**

Persons with learning disabilities may have had bad experiences with health care services; they may not have understood what was being said to them or just not been involved in the past with health care services. The individual may be frightened that they will need to stay in hospital, especially with their institutional connotations, they may be afraid of not coming out again or not being able to see family and friends whilst in there. They might fear the loud noises and bright lights. The reasons are varied and very similar to most people's initial anxieties about health care services.

5.2 **LD 308** **Complete plans for health care with an individual or significant others if appropriate**

To ensure the health care plan remains a working tool you need to involve the individual at all times. The important thing to remember when doing the plan is that it is for the individual and must be recorded in a format they can follow and understand. This may be an audio format, pictorial or written. The significant others are professionals, family, friends or unpaid carers. We need to engage everyone involved with the individual in the plan. This is an important role for the support worker and requires skill in creating enthusiasm and reinforcing the importance of everyone's involvement.

Case study

LD 308 **5.2** Jim

Jim has just returned from the dentist, who has said he has a decaying tooth that needs to be extracted. At present the tooth is badly infected and the gums are swollen. Jim needs to take antibiotics for seven days before the dentist can take the tooth out. Jim spends two days a week at the day centre and frequently goes out for trips with his brother. These day trips last on average six hours. The antibiotics need to be taken every four hours.

Write out a health care plan for Jim including who would be involved in this process and why.

5.3 **LD 208C** **Demonstrate ways to overcome barriers to accessing health care services**

6.2 **LD 308** **Explain ways to overcome barriers to accessing health care services**

We have already identified the types of barriers that people with learning disabilities may encounter when trying to access health care services. We are now going to explore ways of overcoming some of these barriers.

The government organised a review of access problems for those with learning disabilities. This was conducted by Professor J Mansell in 2010 (Raising our sights). Historically people with learning disabilities have not lived as long as others and part of the reason for this morbidity rate has been problems due to access. As the support worker for these individuals our role in removing barriers is key. An example of a barrier might be the lack of understanding of the professionals you are visiting about the needs of those with a learning disability. I am sure we have all come across a situation where a nurse or doctor talks to you as the support worker and not to the individual. It is very clear as support worker what to do in this situation: we clearly ask if they can talk to the individual.

Case study

LD 308 **6.2** Mary

Mary is due to have her eyes checked at the local opticians. To get to the optician a trip into town is required. The opticians are in a high street that has no vehicular access. Mary is nervous about going to the opticians because last time she visited they put drops into her eyes so they could clearly examine the lens. Mary found the drops cold and they stung her eyes. After they put the drops in they required Mary to wait whilst the drops worked. Mary has great difficulty in sitting still for any length of time and does not feel comfortable in busy places.

Explain how you could make this process easier for Mary by reducing the barriers she encounters.

5.4 **LD 208C** **Support the individual to access information about health care services in their preferred format**

7.2 **LD 308** **Provide accessible information related to health care to individuals**

When accessing health care services we also need to be aware of individuals' rights to access information in their health care records as part of the 1990 Act ensuring freedom of information. Sometimes when we visit the doctor's surgery they may use terminology we do not understand, or we may not understand the implications of a diagnosis. Information on medical conditions is available for individuals to be fully informed. However, it's important to take care when trying to access further information, especially when using the web. Make sure you only use accredited and accurate websites such as NHS Choices. Most information that we source will be in a written format, and for individuals with learning disabilities this may be a format they cannot

Time to reflect

LD 208C **5.3** Identifying barriers

Write about an occasion when you identified a barrier to accessing health care service for an individual, write what went well, what did not go so well and how you would do things differently next time.

understand. Most medical services have different formats available such as audio. As a support worker your role will include finding a format that the individual can understand. It is important to know where to get this information.

■ Research and investigate

LD 208C **5.4** Different formats

Explore the library and local health care services to identify the different formats that are available. Also look on the Internet for resources.

Case study

LD 308 **7.2** Freda

Freda has received a letter from the doctors informing her that she needs to go for a mammogram; but Freda cannot read. There were also some leaflets giving information about the procedure.

Write about how you would support Freda, identify different formats available to aid Freda's understanding of the process and where you could get these from.

LO6 **LD 208C** Be able to support individuals with a learning disability to access health care services

LO7 **LD 308** Be able to support an individual with learning disabilities when accessing a variety of health care services

As support worker/carer our role is to empower the individual and assist them to lead an independent life in the manner they wish. Part of living a normal life is the right to receive health care services when needed and the right to information on the services and treatments provided. Individuals also have the right to manage the treatment, deciding when they want to take the medication and how they wish to take it.

6.1 **LD 208C** Provide agreed support to enable the individual to use health care services

7.3 **LD 308** Work with others when supporting an individual to access health care services

With any health care service we will be dealing with personal and private information relating to the individual, so it is important that we obtain consent from the individual to give them support. Sometimes the support they want will not be from a support worker. It may be they would prefer the support from family members or others as health services are such a sensitive subject.

The level of support needed in these situations will vary depending on their abilities and understanding. Therefore it is vital that the first step is an agreed plan, this should clearly identify the level of support and the persons to be involved. Central to this plan will be the identification of a preferred communication style and format to provide information in. Planning is the most important factor to ensure the process works to support the individual. Planning needs to involve everyone, the professionals, the family and most importantly the individual themselves.

■ Time to reflect

LD 208C **6.1** Providing support

Write about the last process where you were involved in preparing to support an individual to access healthcare services. Identify the support you gave, what went well, what did not go so well and what you would do differently next time.

7.3 Working with others

Read your workplace policies and procedures regarding working with others. Describe a recent process of supporting an individual to access health care services with the full involvement of other relevant people. What went well, what could have gone better and what you would do next time?

6.2 LD 208C Support the individual to understand the reasons why they are being offered treatment

Sometimes a treatment will come with particular reasons and instructions. It may not be obvious why we have to change our routines to accommodate the treatment. An example of this would be taking tablets after eating four times a day. If you are not accustomed to eating four times a day, you will have to change your routine to accommodate this. It can be hard for someone with a learning disability to understand why they need to make changes to their routine and doing so can prove distressing to them. As support workers our role is to ensure that we can explain to the individual why the treatment is needed and why it needs to be administered in a specific way.

We then need to make these adjustments easier to manage for the individual to minimise the distress caused.

6.3 LD 208C Support the individual to understand the short and long-term effects of treatment

7.5 LD 308 Support the individual to make safe choices with regard to treatments and medication

Part of the role of support worker is to be an advocate for the individual, to support their wishes and ensure they are being heard. Sometimes this can be difficult when a treatment they have been prescribed is causing them problems. We need to understand the treatments being prescribed and their short and long term effects so the individual can give informed consent.

Anyone who is prescribed medication or treatment is informed of the effects and benefits and consequences of taking the treatment. If the treatment is over a period of time and comes with side effects we discuss this with the professional and weigh up the pros and cons. This is informed consent. We are given the information, good and bad, and make our own decision whether to take the treatment. Persons with learning disabilities are frequently unable to make this decision quickly,

6.2 Identifying potential barriers

In the table below, clarify how you could support an individual with their treatment.

Treatment	Support
Wearing glasses	
Medication	
Diet intake	
Brushing teeth correctly	

because they need more time to understand the concepts. Our role as carers is to assist in this process. We need to do this in a health care planning session with all relevant parties attending. During this process we need to support the individual as their advocate, ensuring they are heard and their wishes are listened to.

Part of our role is also to ensure medications are taken in the correct manner at the time as prescribed.

Case study

 **Mohammed**

Mohammed lives independently in the community. He is paralysed which means he is wheelchair bound and he has an autistic spectrum disorder. He has support workers who attend twice daily to support his personal needs of washing and dressing. Mohammed has recently been diagnosed with a chest infection. The treatment consists of rest, antibiotics three times a day after meals and plenty of fluids. Mohammed has two friends that visit him on a regular basis but no family contacts.

Describe the process of ensuring Mohammed understands and consents to the treatment, and identify how you would support him with the treatment prescribed.

Evidence activity

LD 308

 Supporting safe choices

Write up a case study of how to support an individual to make safe choices with regards their medication / treatment.

 LD 208C **Ensure the individual is able to give informed consent to their treatment in line with current legislation**

The definition of informed consent as given in a medical dictionary is 'a patient understanding the treatment and agreeing to the treatment' (*Mosby's Medical Dictionary*, 8th edition). Before we can say that a person has given informed consent we need to be sure they have understood the procedure or treatment. This includes the reasons they are being offered the treatment, possible side effects of the treatment and what happens if they refuse the treatment. The Department of Health clarifies informed consent further with its publication 'Seeking consent' (Department of Health 2001) and in their documentation, 'Reference guide to consent for examination or treatment' (July 2009) which highlights the need for consent to be made by the individual, not under pressure from others. If there is any concern a test can be performed to identify if they have capacity to consent; this is done via the Mental Health Capacity Act 2005.

Evidence activity

 Informed consent

Identify a situation where an individual has, in your opinion, been unable to give informed consent. Write up the process with regard to your policies and procedures and relevant legislation and what you as support worker can do to support the individual.

 and

7.6 **LD 308**

Record details of a health care visit in a format that an individual with learning disabilities can understand

We have explored the need to record all information, and for it to be an effective working tool we need to involve everyone in the process and to ensure it is in a format that all can understand. Records are legal documents and could be used in a court of law. Records need to be factual.

Evidence activity **LD 208C**

 6.5 Record keeping

Look through a health care plan that you have been involved with and identify who was involved in the process. Clarify the format used to record the information and state why it was recorded in that format. Give a clear explanation of the process and the reasons for its use.

Time to reflect

LD 308 **7.6** Recording information

Describe a health care visit you were involved with. Explain the process of recording the visit, clarify who was involved in the process and what formats were used. What went well, what did not go so well, what would you do differently next time? What other formats could you have used?

6.6 **LD 208C** Ensure that information is shared in line with agreed ways of working

Communication is vital when supporting an individual. Clear and accurate information needs to be shared with many people when accessing health care services. Part of the government's research into access to health care services for individuals with learning disabilities identified that communication was an issue. (The Independent Inquiry into access to Healthcare for People with a Learning Disability. Sir Jonathan Michael. July 2008).

Research and investigate

LD 208C **6.6** Sharing information

Read your workplace policies and agreements for shared communication.

7.1 **LD 308** Use a person centred approach to support an individual to access health care services

With intervention and support the individual is at the centre. Effective support can only be given if we work in agreement and with the involvement of everyone: the individual, family, friends, professionals and colleagues. This way of working is classed as person-centred thinking. People who have a learning disability can find changes and intervention threatening. Involving the individual in all aspects of planning empowers them and ensures the outcomes are more positive and less stressful.

Evidence activity LD 308

7.1 Using person-centred planning

Write up a health care plan of someone you support. Use a person-centred model. Afterwards reflect on what went well, what did not go so well and what you would do differently next time.

 LD 308 ## Support individuals in a range of practical health care situations

We have discussed throughout this chapter many health care situations where we can support the individual. A health care plan consists of appointments and medical interventions, and part of this process includes general wellbeing which comprises preventative measures. An example of this would be regular brushing of teeth to prevent tooth decay.

Case study

LD 308 7.4 **Adelajda**

Adelajda is relatively new to the supported house and has had some difficulties settling in due to communication issues and her personal hygiene. The medical records that came with her specified that Adelajda has severe eczema and requires regular bathing in a moisturising lotion as prescribed. Adelajda has a very caring family who are feeling guilty about not being able to care for her at home. Adelajda can be very confrontational and difficult to manage. Personal hygiene has been a major problem for Adelajda for some time.

Describe how you would commence the planning in a person-centred way. How you would communicate the necessary information to Adelajda and her family?

 7.7 LD 308 **Identify an individual's needs to health care professionals to ensure that the service can be accessed**

Sometimes a condition may occur that needs more urgent intervention from health care services. It has been reported that people with learning disabilities have difficulties explaining medical problems in a way that helps diagnosis and treatment (Mary Lindsey, 2012. Comprehensive health care services for people with learning disabilities.)

As a support worker your role includes identification, with the individual, of the need to access health care services, and the ability to access these effectively and in agreement with the individual. If the person you support requires assistance when communicating with health care professionals, you are required to give this.

Evidence activity LD 308

7.7 Ensuring access to services

Identify an individual you have assisted in accessing health care services. Write a case study on the process highlighting the identification of the need to access health care services, the process of accessing them and the outcome.

Assessment Summary for Unit LD 208C

To achieve the unit, your assessor will require you to:

Learning outcomes	Assessment criteria
1 Understand legislation, policies and guidance relevant to individuals with learning disabilities accessing healthcare	**1.1** Outline what is meant by a rights-based approach to accessing healthcare See Time to reflect 1.1, p. 125.
	1.2 Identify legislation which supports a rights-based approach to accessing healthcare See Research and investigate 1.2, p. 125.
	1.3 Describe ways that healthcare services should make 'reasonable adjustments' to ensure that they provide equal access to individuals with a learning disability See Case study 1.3, p. 126.
	1.4 Explain why it is important to ensure an individual is able to give informed consent to their treatment in line with legislation, policies or guidance See Time to reflect 1.4, p. 127.
	1.5 Describe the actions to take if an individual cannot give informed consent to treatment See Case study 1.5, p. 128.
2 Understand the function of different healthcare services that an individual with learning disabilities may need to access	**2.1** List a range of healthcare services that an individual with a learning disability may need to access See Evidence activity 2.1, p. 129.
	2.2 Describe the work of each type of healthcare service See Evidence activity 2.2, p. 130.
	2.3 Outline the roles and responsibilities of professionals working in the healthcare services that an individual may need to access See Evidence activity 2.3, p. 131.

Learning outcomes	Assessment criteria
3 Understand how plans for healthcare and regular health checks underpin long-term health and well-being for individuals with a learning disability	**3.1** Explain how plans for healthcare can be of benefit to an individual with a learning disability See Evidence activity 3.1, p. 132.
	3.2 Identify a range of regular healthcare checks that an individual may have to support good health and well-being See Evidence activity 3.3, p. 133.
	3.3 Outline how missing regular health checks can impact on the individual's health and well-being See Research and investigate 3.3, p. 133.
4 Be able to contribute to plans for healthcare with individuals with a learning disability	**4.1** Work with an individual and others to identify healthcare services the individual may require See Case study 4.1, p. 134.
	4.2 Agree with the individual and others the type and level of support the individual may require to access healthcare services See Evidence activity 4.2, p. 134.
	4.3 Demonstrate how the individual's needs, wishes and preferences are reflected in the healthcare plan See Evidence activity 4.3, p. 135.
	4.4 Contribute to the review of plans for healthcare with the individual and others See Time to reflect 4.4, p. 136.
5 Be able to support individuals to overcome barriers to accessing healthcare services	**5.1** Identify barriers to accessing healthcare services that an individual with a learning disability may experience See Evidence activity 5.1, p. 137.
	5.2 Identify reasons why an individual may be reluctant to access healthcare services See Time to reflect 5.2, p. 138.
	5.3 Demonstrate ways to overcome barriers to accessing healthcare services See Time to reflect 5.3, p. 139.
	5.4 Support the individual to access information about healthcare services in their preferred format See Research and investigate 5.4, p. 140.

6 Be able to support individuals with a learning disability to use healthcare services	**6.1**	Provide agreed support to enable the individual to use healthcare services See Time to reflect 6.1, p. 140.
	6.2	Support the individual to understand the reasons why they are being offered treatment See Evidence activity 6.2, p. 141.
	6.3	Support the individual to understand the short and long-term effects of treatment See Case study 6.3, p. 142.
	6.4	Ensure the individual is able to give informed consent to their treatment in line with current legislation See Evidence activity 6.4, p. 142.
	6.5	Record details of a healthcare visit in a format that the individual can understand See Evidence activity 6.5, p. 143.
	6.6	Ensure that information is shared in line with agreed ways of working See Research and investigate 6.6, p. 143.

Assessment Summary for Unit LD 308

To achieve the unit, your assessor will require you to:

Learning outcomes	Assessment criteria	
1 Understand legislation, policies and guidance relevant to individuals with learning disabilities accessing healthcare	**1.1**	Describe what is meant by a rights-based approach to accessing healthcare See Time to reflect 1.1, p. 125.
	1.2	Outline the main points of legislation that exists to support a rights-based approach See Evidence activity 1.2, p. 126.
	1.3	Explain the requirements of legislation if an individual with learning disabilities is assessed to not have capacity to consent to a specific treatment See Case study 1.3, p. 127.
	1.4	Explain different ways to support an individual to give informed consent in line with legislation, policies or guidance See Evidence activity 1.4, p. 128.
	1.5	Explain ways in which healthcare services should make 'reasonable adjustments' to ensure that they provide equal access to individuals with learning disabilities See Evidence activity 1.5, p. 128.

Learning outcomes	Assessment criteria
2 Understand the function of different healthcare services that an individual with learning disabilities may need to access	**2.1** Explain the work of healthcare services that an individual with learning disabilities may need to access See Evidence activity 2.1, p. 130.
	2.2 Explain how an individual can access each type of healthcare service See Time to reflect 2.2, p. 130.
3 Understand how plans for healthcare and regular health checks underpin long-term health and well-being for individuals with a learning disability	**3.1** Describe the role and responsibility of professionals working in different types of healthcare services See Evidence activity 3.1, p. 133.
4 Be able to contribute to plans for healthcare with individuals with a learning disability	**4.1** Explain how plans for healthcare can be used to support the healthcare needs of an individual with learning disabilities See Time to reflect 4.1, p. 132.
	4.2 Explain the range of health checks available to individuals to support good health and well being See Time to reflect 4.2, p. 135.
	4.3 Explain the importance of routine healthcare checks See Research and investigate 4.3, p. 133.
5 Be able to support individuals to overcome barriers to accessing healthcare services	**5.1** Identify who needs to be involved in the process of completing and reviewing plans for healthcare See Evidence activity 5.1, p. 135.
	5.2 Complete plans for healthcare with an individual or significant others if appropriate See Case study 5.2, p. 138.
	5.3 Review plans for healthcare with an individual or significant others if appropriate See Research and investigate 5.3, p. 136.

6 Be able to support individuals with a learning disability to use healthcare services	**6.1** Describe barriers to accessing healthcare services that an individual with learning disabilities may experience See Research and investigate 6.1, p. 138.
	6.2 Explain ways to overcome barriers to accessing healthcare services See Case study 6.2, p. 139.
	6.3 Explain why an individual with learning disabilities may face additional barriers when accessing healthcare services See Time to reflect 6.3, p. 138.
7 Understand how to maintain the primary focus on safeguarding and promoting the welfare of the child	**7.1** Use a person-centred approach to support an individual to access healthcare services See Evidence activity 7.1, p. 144.
	7.2 Provide accessible information related to healthcare to individuals See Case study 7.2, p. 140.
	7.3 Work with others when supporting an individual to access healthcare services See Evidence activity 7.3, p. 141.
	7.4 Support individuals in a range of practical healthcare situations See Case study 7.4, p. 144.
	7.5 Support the individual to make safe choices with regard to treatments and medication See Evidence activity 7.5, p. 142.
	7.6 Record details of a healthcare visit in a format that an individual with learning disabilities can understand See Time to reflect 7.6, p. 143.
	7.7 Identify an individual's needs to healthcare professionals to ensure that the service can be accessed See Evidence activity 7.7, p. 144.

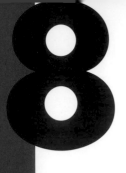

Autistic spectrum conditions
Unit LD 210 Introductory awareness of autistic spectrum conditions
Unit LD 310 Understand how to support individuals with autistic spectrum conditions

What are you finding out?

Autistic spectrum conditions are complex and not fully understood. They are lifelong conditions concerning the way the person's brain works, which affect an estimated 1 in 100 people in the UK. They are present from birth or very early life, but may not be diagnosed until later, especially in the case of Asperger Syndrome which is sometimes not formally identified until adulthood. Although more is being discovered all the time about these conditions, through research and by talking to people on the autistic spectrum and their families, there remain some areas of debate.

People with autistic spectrum conditions and their families can face many challenges, but with better understanding and the right support their quality of life can be enormously improved.

The reading and activities in this chapter will help you to:

- Understand the areas in which individuals with an autistic spectrum condition characteristically have difficulties

- Understand the concept of autism as a spectrum, and the implications for variation in the capacities and needs of individuals

- Understand the behaviours exhibited by some individuals with an autistic spectrum condition

- Understand how to contribute to the support of an individual who has an autistic spectrum disorder

- Understand how to communicate effectively with individuals on the autistic spectrum

- Understand the main characteristics of autism spectrum conditions

- Understand how autistic spectrum conditions can impact on the lives of individuals and those around them

- Understand different theories and concepts about autism

- Understand the legal and policy framework that underpins good practice in the support of individuals with an autistic spectrum condition

- Understand how to achieve effective communication with individuals with an autistic spectrum condition

- Understand how to support individuals with an autistic spectrum condition

LO1 (LD 210) Understand the areas in which individuals with an autistic spectrum condition characteristically have difficulties

LO2 (LD 210) Understand the concept of autism as a spectrum, and the implications for variation in the capacities and needs of individuals

LO1 (LD 310) Understand the main characteristics of autistic spectrum conditions

(LD 210) (2.1) (LD 310) (1.1)

Explain why it is important to recognise that each person on the autistic spectrum has their own individual abilities, needs, strengths, gifts and interests

One of the most important points to understand about autistic spectrum conditions is that each person on the autism spectrum is an individual with their own unique characteristics. People with autistic spectrum conditions vary enormously in their abilities, needs, strengths, gifts, preferences and interests. No two individuals with a diagnosis of an autistic spectrum condition are the same so it is essential not to make any assumptions about them.

■ Time to reflect

(LD 210) (2.1) (LD 310) (1.1)

Assumptions and generalisations

- Imagine you are going for a job interview. You had to put the name of your school on the application form. As soon as you go into the room, the interviewer says to you, 'Oh, I once met someone else who went to that school. She was really good at dancing, hated thunderstorms, was hopeless at cooking and loved bananas. As you went to that school, I expect you're good at dancing, hate thunderstorms, are hopeless at cooking and love bananas too'.
- How would you feel?

Evidence activity (LD 210) (LD 310)

(2.1) (1.1) **Importance of the individual**

- Think of two individuals with an autistic spectrum condition whom you work with.
- Make a list of all the ways in which they differ in terms of, for example, their abilities, their needs, their interests, their personalities and so on.

(1.2) (LD 310) **Analyse the main diagnostic features of autistic spectrum conditions, commonly known as the 'triad of impairments'**

(Note: material in (LD 210) 1.1, 1.2 and 1.3 is also relevant for this assessment criteria.)

So, how can we learn about people with autistic spectrum conditions if everyone is unique? Well, generalisations can be made about the types of difficulties that individuals tend to experience. These have been grouped into three main areas, commonly known as the '**triad of impairments**'. Typically individuals with an autistic spectrum condition have difficulties with:

1. language and communicating with others
2. social interaction and relationships
3. flexibility of thought

The triad is often illustrated as a triangle of over-lapping difficulties:

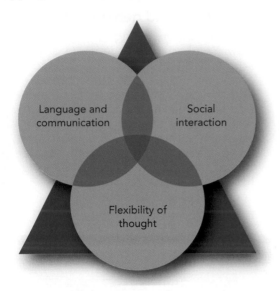

8.1 The triad of impairments

- not responding when spoken to; may act as if deaf although hearing is within normal range
- slow to understand spoken language (may take up to ten seconds to process a simple instruction)
- difficulty in understanding the give-and-take nature of conversations
- problems with appreciating jokes, puns and sarcasm
- problems in understanding non-specific instructions and inferences
- difficulty in working out metaphors.

Key terms

Inference means something that is implied from a statement, for example 'Your room's a mess!' implies 'Please tidy it up'.

Metaphor is a figure of speech in which an expression is used to refer to something that it does not literally denote in order to suggest a similarity, for example 'opening a can of worms'.

1.1 **LD 210** **Describe the types of difficulty that individuals with an autistic spectrum condition may have with language and other ways of communicating with others**

Normally communication is a two-way process in which each person expresses him/herself through verbal communication (speech) and non-verbal communication, and also interprets what the other person is saying. People on the autistic spectrum have varying degrees of difficulty in communicating effectively themselves and in understanding the language and communication of others.

Verbal communication difficulties may include:

- delay in learning to speak
- some people never develop meaningful spoken language
- repeating set words or phrases
- repeating what the other person has just said; this is known as echolalia

Case study

Meena

Meena has an autistic spectrum condition. Her mother is telling her off for going out in the rain without a raincoat:

'Come here you little monkey! Look, it's raining cats and dogs and you go out with nothing on! You'll catch your death! Next time I'll have to check your head's screwed on properly before I let you out. Your Dad will hit the roof when he comes home! Go and throw yourself into a hot shower before you freeze to death'.

Do you think Meena would find it easy to understand clearly everything that her mother is saying? If not, why not? Have a go at re-writing what the mother is trying to say in a way that Meena is more likely to understand.

Non verbal communication

People on the autistic spectrum typically find non verbal communication very difficult to use and understand. Indeed some experts in autistic spectrum conditions suggest that an impairment of non verbal communication is the most important characteristic that defines people on the autistic spectrum. As it is so important in face-to-face communication (it is estimated that as much as 90 percent of most people's face-to face-communication is non verbal), it is not surprising that people with autistic spectrum conditions have problems when trying to interact with others. Individuals vary in the type and degree of difficulties they experience, but typically they struggle to use and interpret:

- eye contact/gaze
- facial expressions
- body posture
- gestures
- volume, tone and pitch of the voice
- mirroring the other person's non verbal responses

 **Identify problems that individuals with an autistic spectrum condition may have in social interaction and relationships**

This area of difficulty is linked in some ways with problems with language and communication but also stands as a key issue in its own right. Indeed, Dr Lorna Wing, who first used the term 'triad of impairments' feels that the 'social interaction impairment' is the most important part of the triad. She argues that some people who are diagnosed as older children or adults may have learned to compensate for their disabilities in communication and restricted thought patterns, but their problems with social impairment are still evident, even though they may be shown in different, sometimes subtle ways.

Problems with social interaction and relationships may result in a real fear and avoidance of all social situations; come across as indifference and aloofness towards others; or lead to someone desperately trying to make friends but continually 'getting it wrong' through a lack of understanding of social rules and other people's feelings and behaviour.

Time to reflect

LD 210 **1.2** Social rules

- Think of a situation in which you have been recently where you had to interact with a number of other people – such as a party, work meeting, teaching session.

- Make a list of all the (unwritten) social rules that were influencing the way people behaved in that situation

- How do you think you would have coped if you did not understand any of those rules?

Most children learn how to get on with other children and adults intuitively, from a very early age, by watching and copying others. Their parents, teachers or other care-givers may have to tell or show them how to behave correctly when they do something wrong, but as they grow up most children learn how to behave in ways that enable them to make friends and be part of a social group. Children with an autistic spectrum condition, on the other hand, do not usually show a natural interest in others. Many parents report that as a baby their child with an autistic spectrum condition did not do the things that other children do to start to learn about social interaction, such as imitating their facial expressions and gestures; smiling when smiled at; responding to his or her name or to the sound of a familiar voice; or sharing interest and enjoyment through play with other people.

As children with an autistic spectrum condition get older, the gap between them and their peers in understanding and ability in social interaction tends to get wider. They may appear disinterested or unaware of other people or what is going on around them. They may not play 'pretend' or creative games or know how to engage in group games. As a result they may become socially isolated.

People with autistic spectrum conditions usually have trouble understanding or talking about their feelings and needs. As a result they express themselves in ways seen as 'strange' or 'inappropriate'. Commonly they struggle to see themselves and others as distinct individuals with their own thoughts, feelings, plans and points of view.

1.3 **LD 210** **Outline the problems of inflexibility and restrictiveness in activities and interests and how these may affect individuals on the autistic spectrum**

Difficulties with this typically lead to rigid and repetitive behaviour and restrictiveness in activities and interests.

2.2 **LD 210** **Describe why autism can be considered as a spectrum, encompassing individuals differing in the expression and severity of their symptoms**

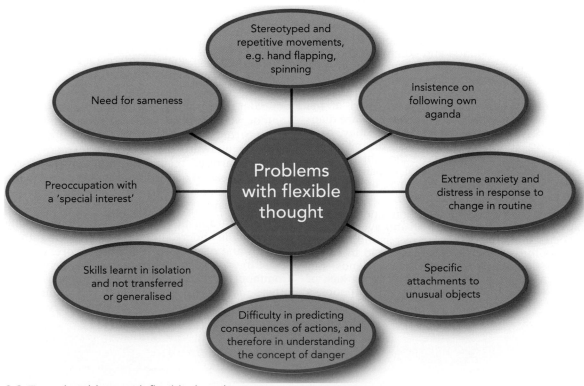

8.2 Typical problems with flexible thought

1.3 **LD 310** **Explain the meanings of the term 'spectrum' in relation to autism by reference to the notions of sub-conditions and individual variation within the autistic spectrum**

1.6 **LD 310** **Describe how language and intellectual abilities vary between individuals and sub-groups across the spectrum**

The term 'spectrum' was introduced to convey the fact that while all people with autism share certain areas of difficulty, their condition will affect them in different ways (as discussed at the beginning of this chapter). It was the research of Dr Lorna Wing and Dr Judith Gould in the late 1970s that was instrumental in defining autism as a spectrum, ranging from those severely affected to the – previously ignored – very high functioning. This is a helpful concept in that it reinforces the idea of individual variation and moves away from the old idea of autism as a single separate entity. However some people are now challenging the notion of a spectrum of severity of autism because it can be misleading to compare the severity of one person's autism to another. The effect of autism on an individual varies depending on their environment and many other factors, and some people labelled as having mild autism have more problems coping with everyday life than those diagnosed as more severely affected. Also, an individual described as being at the 'lower-functioning' end of the spectrum may have a remarkable ability in one particular area. Nevertheless, the term autistic 'spectrum' is still widely used and important to understand.

The autistic spectrum includes various 'sub-conditions', or types of autism which differ from classic autism. Classic autism is sometimes referred to as Kanner's autism, after Leo Kanner the child psychiatrist who first recognised children with 'autistic aloneness' in 1943, and typically describes those at the 'lower-functioning' end of the spectrum. Other types of autistic spectrum conditions include:

- **Asperger Syndrome**: This is the main 'sub group' of autistic spectrum conditions, named after Hans Asperger, an Austrian doctor who first recorded autistic tendencies in children with high IQs. Although Asperger's work was in the 1940s, it was not widely known about in the English speaking world until the 1980s and Asperger Syndrome only became an officially recognised diagnosis in 1994. While many of the typical features of classic autism and Asperger Syndrome are the same, individuals with the latter have average or above average intelligence and have no obvious delay in developing language. It is the lack of language delay that is seen as the key feature of Asperger Syndrome; people with autism who are of above average intelligence but were delayed in developing language are usually described as having 'high-functioning autism'.

But there is some controversy around the existence of Asperger Syndrome as a distinct condition on the autistic spectrum. Sometimes it can seem like diagnoses of Asperger Syndrome and high-functioning autism are given on an almost interchangeable basis. The lack of language delay in children with Asperger Syndrome may be questionable; the child may develop language but use it differently to other children. There are no sharp boundaries separating 'typical' autism from other autistic conditions, including Asperger Syndrome. It has been suggested that some people find a diagnosis of Asperger Syndrome more acceptable than autism because it has less social stigma attached to it. There has been interest in the media recently about famous people who, it is claimed, may have had Asperger Syndrome – such as Mozart, Einstein and even Michael Jackson – which may have given this label a certain amount of prestige, and misled the general public into thinking that everyone with Asperger Syndrome is a 'genius'.

Because of such issues Asperger Syndrome is being merged with autism into a single 'spectrum' category in the new DSM (The Diagnostic and Statistical Manual of Mental Disorders), the standard manual used by mental health professionals, due to be published in 2013, and therefore will not normally be used as a diagnosis after that date. Nevertheless, for some individuals, families and groups, the label Asperger Syndrome is an important part of their identity and this should be respected.

- **Atypical autism**: This term may be used when the person's behaviour pattern fits most but not all the criteria for 'classic' autism. Atypical autism usually differs from autism in terms either of age of onset or of not having aspects of all three of the triad of impairments. Atypical autism is likely to become noticeable only after 3 years of age and it is a type of autism that may go undiagnosed for years.

- **Pervasive developmental disorder (not otherwise specified)**: Commonly shortened to PDD-NOS, this refers to someone who has autistic characteristics but does not fully meet the criteria for a diagnosis of autism or Asperger Syndrome.

- **Semantic-pragmatic disorder**: With SPD (also known as Pragmatic language impairment – PLI), individuals experience difficulties with the semantic aspect of language (the meaning of what is being said) and the pragmatics of language (using language appropriately in social situations). Some people see this as part of the autism spectrum while others see it purely as a language disorder.

- **Pathological demand avoidance (PDA)**: This involves avoidance of the everyday demands made by other people, due to high anxiety levels when the individual feels that s/he is not in control. It can lead to extreme mood swings and socially inappropriate, in some cases aggressive, behaviour.

Evidence activity   LD 210   LD 310

The autistic spectrum

LD 210 **2.2** Explain what the term autistic spectrum means. You could use a drawing or image to illustrate your answer.

LD 310 **1.3** **1.6** Compare the abilities and needs of two individuals on the autistic spectrum, preferably diagnosed with two different conditions.

- How does your comparison relate to the idea of autism as a spectrum?
- How helpful do you think the concept of the autistic spectrum is?

8.3 Examples of sensory difficulties (see page 157)

LD 210 **Outline the sensory difficulties experienced by many individuals with an autistic spectrum condition**

1.4 **LD 310** **Describe the sensory and perceptual difficulties commonly experienced by individuals with an autistic spectrum disorder**

Everything we learn about and experience in the world comes through our senses – sight, hearing, touch, taste and smell. Although we may occasionally discuss a particular sensory experience – a beautiful sunset or piece of music, or some tasty food – we normally take our sensory world for granted and assume that it is the same as everyone else's (unless of course there is an obvious sensory loss, such as with deaf or blind people). However, that is not the case, particularly for people with autistic spectrum conditions. Although they live in the same physical world as other people and deal with the same 'raw material', the way they perceive the world through their senses turns out to be strikingly different. This can be described as having sensory integration difficulties, sensory processing disorder or sensory sensitivity.

Sensory perceptual issues are not part of the diagnostic criteria for autistic spectrum conditions. They are often overlooked and the difficulties they cause are attributed to other aspects of an individual's autism. However, sensory sensitivity is an integral part of the lives of most people on the autistic spectrum and can have a profound effect on the individual and on those around them. Because of this it is very important to try to understand the sensory world of each individual with an autistic spectrum condition, however difficult this may be for a 'neurotypical' person. Wherever possible, it is important to get a sensory assessment, ideally carried out by a specialist.

Key terms

Neurotypical (NT) is a term introduced by the autistic community as the opposite of 'autistic'. It refers to people who do not have an autistic spectrum condition and whose neurological development is therefore seen as 'normal' or 'typical'. An alternative term is predominant neurotype (PNT)

Many people with an autistic spectrum condition experience either hypersensitivity (heightened sensitivity) or hyposensitivity (reduced sensitivity) in at least one of the senses. Someone with heightened sensory sensitivity might find that looking at particular colours or patterns on clothing distresses them while others might find the noise of a hand-dryer or electric light intolerable. On the other hand, an individual with reduced sensory sensitivity might not respond to pain, for example continuing to walk on a broken leg thus causing it further damage.

Evidence activity **LD 210**

2.4 Sensory/perceptual issues

List the most common sensory difficulties experienced by people with autistic spectrum conditions.

■ Research and investigate

LD 310 **1.4 Impacts of sensory issues**

- Choose one of the statements from the speech bubbles in Figure 8.3 above.
- Research the type of sensory experience that the person may be talking about.
- Consider what you might be able to do to help with any negative effects arising from the issue raised.
- What impact might this kind of difficulty have on someone's everyday life?

2.3 **LD 210** **Identify other conditions which may be associated with an autistic spectrum condition**

1.5 **LD 310** **Describe other conditions that may be associated with the autistic spectrum**

The following are all conditions that can occur on their own, or in combination with each other, without an associated autistic spectrum condition. However, they often occur alongside an autistic spectrum condition. They are sometimes described as 'co-morbid' conditions, a rather unpleasant word used to indicate a condition existing simultaneously but independently with another condition. In the past some of the characteristics of these have been assumed to be part of an individual's autism, or vice versa, which may have prevented the person getting the right support. It is therefore important to get an accurate assessment of both the autistic spectrum condition and the co-existing condition. They include:

- **Learning disability**: Learning disability is the most common co-occurring condition with autistic spectrum conditions. Historically, autism was only recognised in individuals with severe learning disabilities and any provision for people with autism was through learning disability services, a situation which is still quite common today. It is very difficult to get a clear picture of the proportion of people with autistic spectrum conditions who have a co-existing learning disability, partly because definitions of both learning disability and autism vary between different studies. Some estimates put the figure as high as 70–80 percent of individuals with an autistic spectrum condition having a learning disability (using a definition of IQ less than 70). However more recently, and with a widening of the spectrum to include higher functioning individuals, figures of 40–50 percent have been quoted.

  Looking at the link from the other way round – in other words the percentage of those with a learning disability who also have an autistic spectrum condition – a recent study estimated a figure (for adults) of between 20 and 33 percent.

  Clearly, therefore, there is a significant association between autistic spectrum conditions and learning disabilities but they are two separate things.

- **Epilepsy**: Approximately 25 to 30 percent of people with an autistic spectrum condition have epilepsy, often starting either in early childhood or adolescence; this compares with less than 1 percent of the general population. Seizures, caused by abnormal electrical activity in the brain, can produce a temporary loss of consciousness, a body convulsion, unusual movements, or 'absences', in which the person appears to 'blank out' for a few seconds or minutes. Sometimes a contributing factor is a lack of sleep or a high fever.

- **Attention deficit/hyperactive disorder (ADHD)**: Poor attention span together with marked over-activity.

- **Attention deficit disorder (ADD)**: Poor attention span without marked over-activity.

- **Hyperkinetic disorder**: Marked over-activity without poor attention span.

- **Dyslexia**: Specific difficulty with reading, writing and spelling.

- **Dyspraxia (also known as Developmental co-ordination disorder)**: Specific difficulty with co-ordinating movements.

- **Disorder of attention, motor co-ordination and perception (DAMP)**: A term used when the person has a combination of these problems.

- **Tourette syndrome**: A neurological disorder characterised by tics – involuntary, rapid, sudden movements and vocal noises that occur repeatedly.

Evidence activity | LD 210 | LD 310

2.3 **1.5** **Other conditions that may be associated with the autistic spectrum**

Identify two conditions which may be associated with an autistic spectrum condition and write a short description of the main characteristics of each of them.

LO3 LD 210 Understand the behaviours exhibited by some individuals with an autistic spectrum condition

3.1 LD 210 **Describe behavioural characteristics associated with autistic spectrum conditions**

3.2 LD 210 **Identify reasons why individuals with an autistic spectrum condition may exhibit such behaviours**

5.1 **LD 310** **Give examples of how 'challenging behaviour' can be a way of expressing emotions where there are communication differences**

Just as everyone with an autistic spectrum is different, so is the way they behave and it is misleading to talk about 'typical' behaviours. On the other hand, each of the areas of difficulty described under the 'triad of impairments' may lead to certain types of behaviour; equally people experiencing particular sensory-perceptual issues may react in ways that are recognisable. Some of the behaviours listed as signs of autism are common among the general population – for example, 'temper tantrums' – while others tend to be more specific to people on the autistic spectrum, such as hand-flapping.

For people who do not have any knowledge of autistic spectrum conditions, the behaviour of individuals on the spectrum may appear strange, pointless, disturbing, fascinating, frightening and altogether impossible to understand. However, we all behave in particular ways for a reason and while it may sometimes be more difficult to work out why someone with an autistic spectrum condition is behaving in a certain way, it can be very important. For example, some repetitive behaviour, routines and special interests can be a source of great enjoyment for people with an autism spectrum condition, and a way to deal with anxiety, block out uncertainty and to cope with everyday life. Some behaviours which may appear odd to others serve as effective ways for an individual to control what is going on around them; this may reflect their lack of more usual methods of controlling their environment. People with sensory issues may go into 'meltdown' or total withdrawal when their senses are overloaded.

On the other hand, some behaviours are obviously problematic and are often labelled as 'challenging behaviour'. They include:

- physical aggression towards others
- self-injury (including head banging, hand or arm biting, eye gouging and skin picking)
- pica (putting inedible items in the mouth)
- smearing of faeces
- sexually explicit behaviour in public
- any behaviour which limits the individual's involvement in other activities
- any behaviour which causes significant disruption to other people, such parents, carers and family members

For some people, particularly those whose verbal communication skills are limited, their behaviour, although challenging to others, is their means of communicating their needs or emotions. Equally their behaviour may be a result of their difficulties in understanding information; for example when they are given too much language to process and can only understand the key words.

Evidence activity **LD 210** **LD 310**

LD 210 **3.1** **3.2**

Behaviour and the reasons for it

List, with examples, reasons why individuals may behave in ways typically associated with autistic spectrum conditions

LD 310 **5.1** Give examples from your work practice of how so-called 'challenging behaviour' is a way of expressing emotions, particularly for individuals who have difficulty with communicating in other ways.

3.3 **LD 210** **Describe what to do if an individual is highly anxious or stressed**

Anxiety is a constant problem for many, if not most, people with autistic spectrum conditions.

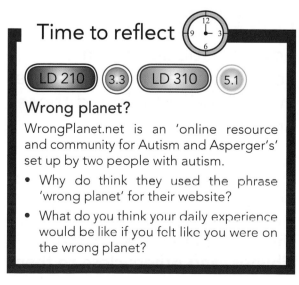

Time to reflect

LD 210 **3.3** **LD 310** **5.1**

Wrong planet?

WrongPlanet.net is an 'online resource and community for Autism and Asperger's' set up by two people with autism.

- Why do think they used the phrase 'wrong planet' for their website?
- What do you think your daily experience would be like if you felt like you were on the wrong planet?

Everyday life causes a certain level of anxiety for people on the autistic spectrum but then a particular event or situation – which may seem insignificant to an 'NT' person – may provoke a high level of anxiety and distress. As far as possible such situations should be prevented by altering the environment and/or by helping the individual to learn strategies to manage their anxiety levels. But once someone is highly anxious or stressed, it is important to know how to react. Of course the response will again depend on the individual and the situation concerned but some of the general principles include:

- Stay as calm as possible; otherwise the person may 'feed off' your reaction.
- Use positive language as much as possible.
- Be clear and consistent in what you say and do.
- Try to appear confident even if you do not feel it.
- Make sure the individual and others are not in immediate danger.
- Seek help if safe to do so.
- Record the details of what happened to trigger the episode, and how the person behaved during and after.

▶ Research and investigate

3.3 **LD 210** **Policies and procedures**

Find out the procedures to be followed in your workplace if someone becomes highly anxious or distressed.

LO2 LD 310 Understand how autistic spectrum conditions can impact on the lives of individuals and those around them

2.1 **LD 310** **Describe ways in which autism can impact on the everyday lives of individuals, their parents and carers and siblings, and others close to them**

First, it is important to return to the point that everyone is different and has their own individual experience. Some people may not receive a diagnosis until their 60s, having perhaps worked, got married, had a family, but always having felt a bit of an 'outsider'. Others are obviously very different to other children from a very early age and need a lot of specialist help and support – as do their families.

Second, the impact of the autistic spectrum condition is not primarily about the autism itself. It is more about how it affects the individual in a particular situation at a given time; this depends on the environment, the individual's mood, and the way other people treat him or her.

Key terms

Environment refers to a person's surroundings and all the things outside of themselves that influence their life and activities.

Many people with an autistic spectrum condition do find it hard to cope with everyday life in an everyday environment and this obviously affects their quality of life and that of their parents/carers, siblings and others close to them. Some families experience extreme stress through sleepless nights, difficult behaviour and a lack of support. On the other hand, a family member with an autistic spectrum condition can bring great joy and pride and a new perspective on life and what it means to be human.

2.3 **LD 310** **Explain how stereotyped views, discrimination and a lack of understanding of autistic spectrum conditions can compound the difficulties already experienced by individuals and families**

Understanding is the key to accepting and valuing all differences – whether it is about our race, culture, sexual orientation, religion, gender or whatever else makes up our individual identity. A lack of understanding can lead to stereotyped views, prejudice and discrimination, and sadly this is the experience of many individuals with autistic spectrum conditions and their families.

Case study

  Sami

Sami is 14 years old and lives with his Dad and two younger sisters. He has an autistic spectrum condition. Sami loves swimming and swims every week at the pool at his special school. The aim is for his class to start using the local pool next year.

Sami's sisters really want to learn to swim and when Sami's Dad suggests taking them to the local pool one weekend Sami is very keen to go too. Things start to go wrong when Sami hears the noise of the hundreds of children in the pool and lies down in the foot-bath kicking and screaming, blocking the entrance to the pool. Other people mutter rude things under their breath as they step over him. His Dad eventually manages to calm him down but has to stay with Sami while he swims to stop him from getting distressed, and Sami's sisters just sit at the side watching and getting very fed up as they have no chance even to get in the water. It is very difficult for Sami's Dad to persuade him to leave the pool even when Sami is shivering with cold.

The family go to use the communal showers between the men's and women's changing rooms, and before his Dad can stop him, Sami takes his swimming trunks off. When his Dad shouts at him to put them back on, Sami says 'That's what I do with school'. Sami insists on standing naked under the shower and giving himself a thorough wash.

As the family are leaving, the pool manager appears, together with a very angry woman who accuses Sami of indecent exposure. She wants the manager to call the police. The pool manager tells Sami's Dad that he realises that there is 'something wrong' with his son and that he won't call the police on this occasion. This concession, he says, is on the condition that neither Sami nor his family ever return to the swimming pool – and the ban includes Sami coming with his class from school.

- In what ways do you think Sami's autistic spectrum condition contributes to this situation?
- What do you think will be the impact on Sami?
- And what about the impact on his family?

2.2 **LD 310** **Explain how autistic spectrum conditions can impact on individuals differently according to factors such as their gender, ethnicity and social, cultural and religious environment**

Autistic spectrum conditions appear to be more common among boys and men than girls and women. It was widely believed that this is because of genetic differences between the sexes, but more recent research is highlighting the possibility that it is due to the gender bias in the criteria used to diagnose autism. For example, one of the diagnostic criteria is the presence of repetitive behaviour and special interests, which tends to be much more of a stereotypically male characteristic. There is growing evidence, both anecdotal and research-based, that autistic spectrum conditions present differently in girls and women. Society expects the female role to be a social one and some girls with autistic spectrum conditions learn to act in social settings by copying other people's behaviour. Any social and communication problems they may be having are therefore overlooked.

It could well be then that girls and women have in the past been significantly under-diagnosed with autistic spectrum conditions. Their difficulties may emerge in other ways, for example as a severe lack of self esteem, self-harm or an eating disorder. Fortunately, however, the National Autistic Society reports that referrals to its specialist diagnostic centre have seen a steady increase in the number of girls and women referred in recent years. It is important for everyone working in the field of autism to be alert to the issue of gender differences in its impact.

People with autistic spectrum conditions from **black and minority ethnic (BME) communities** experience discrimination on two fronts – their disability and their ethnicity. There has been a general neglect of BME families by researchers, professionals and service providers which,

Evidence activity　LD 310

Discrimination and prejudice

Ellie is 3. Her Mum tries to tell family and friends that Ellie has just been diagnosed with an autistic spectrum condition. Here are some of their responses:

- 'Oh, what a tragedy for you!'
- 'She can't have – only boys get that.'
- 'They can cure that in America you know – I could start up a charity for you to raise the money.'
- 'Must be on her Dad's side. We don't have things like that in our family.'
- 'Shame they don't have them hospitals any more where you could send them sort away to be looked after.'
- 'I was reading about that. Too much processed food, that's what does it!'
- 'Well, I don't want her mixing with my daughter anymore!'

Adam is 15. He has just been diagnosed with Asperger Syndrome and tries to explain to his friends. This is how they react:

- 'Cool! You must be a genius! What freaky things can you do like that guy in the film Rainman?'
- 'Well, you definitely won't get a girlfriend now.'
- 'So what drugs are you going to get put on for that?'
- 'That's just too weird. I'm off!'
- 'You'll have to go to that school for special needs kids.'
- 'At least you can always get a job with computers.'

1. What kinds of views about autistic spectrum conditions are reflected in the responses to Ellie's Mum and Adam?
2. How do you think they might feel as a result?
3. What might be more helpful to say to Ellie's Mum and to Adam in these situations?

according to a recent report by the National Autistic Society 'Missing out' (2007) is 'unacceptable' and 'must be addressed with urgency'. The authors found that evidence about the prevalence of autism in various communities and its impact on family life is inconsistent; communities may not be aware of autism, their rights and relevant services; and that services that are available do not always meet the needs of these families.

Evidence activity　LD 310

Different impacts

Prepare a presentation to give to your colleagues about the ways in which autistic spectrum conditions can impact on individuals differently according to either their gender or their ethnic, cultural and religious background.

2.4　LD 310　Describe ways of helping an individual and/or their parent/carer/siblings/ partner to understand their autistic spectrum condition

It is important for people with autistic spectrum conditions to understand their condition as much as they can. It can be helpful for someone to have an explanation as to why they find the world such a confusing and challenging place; why they feel they do not fit in, suffer constant anxiety and low self esteem. Equally, the parents, siblings, carer or partner of an individual with an autistic spectrum condition need support and information in order to understand the condition. Ways of explaining autistic spectrum conditions vary according to the individual and their level of understanding, but some general guidelines include:

- Do not try to tell the person everything at once; give small amounts of information and allow them to come back and ask questions at a later stage.

- Be honest and clear and check that they have understood what you are saying.
- Use tools suitable for the age and ability of the person; there are many books (fiction and non-fiction) and other types of information about autistic spectrum conditions.
- If appropriate, talk to the individual about famous people with autistic spectrum conditions, in history and currently.
- Offer to support the individual and/or their family to access support networks locally or on the Internet.

Evidence activity LD 310

2.4 How to help

Describe ways in which you have helped, or could help, an individual whom you support to understand their autistic spectrum condition.

LO3 LD 310 Understand different theories and concepts about autism

3.1 LD 310 Explain theories about autism related to brain function and genetics and psychology

Ever since autism was first recognised there has been a desire to understand and explain it. In the 1960s Bruno Bettelheim, an American psychoanalyst, suggested that autism was a reaction to 'cold' or unaffectionate mothering, an idea now completely disproved but not before some children were actually removed from their families and many parents were left feeling to blame for their child's condition. More recently, some researchers have approached the issue from a medical point of view, looking for a single cause of autistic spectrum conditions, with a view then to preventing and/or curing them. An infamous example of this was Andrew Wakefield's highly publicised theory that childhood immunisations were the cause; follow-up studies in a number of countries have shown no link.

Controversy remains, however, about the causes of autism, with debate between those who look at it from a psychological point of view and those who argue that it is biological in origin.

Key terms

Psychological means relating to the mind or mental processes.

Biological means relating to the structure of the body, including genetic make-up.

In reality there is beginning to be agreement that autistic spectrum conditions are biological in origin but that psychological theories are also necessary in order to explain the behaviour and psychological profile of people with autistic spectrum conditions.

Biomedical research has shown that there are some very significant differences in the autistic brain – in its structure and in the way it works. Evidence points towards the brains of children with autistic spectrum conditions developing differently both before birth and in the first few years of life. Most experts now accept that there are genetic factors in autistic spectrum conditions, but there are likely to be multiple genes involved rather than a single gene.

Professor Simon Baron-Cohen, a psychologist and expert in autism, has outlined five major psychological theories of autism and Asperger Syndrome:

- Executive Dysfunction theory – problems with planning, mental flexibility, impulse control, understanding 'what happens next'.
- Weak central coherence theory – difficulties with recognising the 'big picture' and knowing what is relevant and redundant; over-attention to detail.
- Mindblindness theory – or difficulty with 'Theory of Mind' – refers to problems in understanding that people may see things from a different point of view; difficulties in understanding and recognising emotional states in self and others, and with empathy and trust.
- Empathising-systematising theory – refers to delays or difficulties with empathy and, in contrast, average or above average ability to systematise (the drive to analyse or construct systems). This theory has been extended into the Extreme male brain theory, where autistic spectrum conditions are seen as extremes of the typical male profile.
- Magnocellular theory – a specific dysfunction in one visual pathway in the brain (the magnocellular pathway).

Research and investigate

 3.1 Theories about autism

Choose *either* the role of genes in autistic spectrum conditions *or* ONE of the above psychological theories.

Find out more about your chosen theory and write a short piece based on your research.

Key terms

Person-first language is a sentence structure that names the person first and the condition second, for example 'people with disabilities' rather than 'disabled people', in order to emphasise that they are 'people first'.

3.2 LD 310 Explain why there are alternative choices of terminology used to describe the autism spectrum

3.3 LD 310 Describe the strengths and limitations of different types of terminology

We looked earlier at the use of the word 'spectrum' with regard to autism and related conditions and this term has become widely adopted. However, as we have already seen, the complex nature of the autism spectrum gives rise to a range of personal and professional perspectives. The various viewpoints create a challenge in finding a common language.

- **Autistic spectrum condition** is the term chosen for this chapter and is the terminology used in the Department of Health's Autism Strategy. It is preferred by many (but not all) adults on the autistic spectrum, who often like to be referred to as people **with an autistic spectrum condition** as this is 'person-first' language.

- **Autism** is the more traditional term which is still widely used even though it does not reflect the concept of a spectrum. Some members of the autistic community reject 'person-first' language and choose to emphasise their autism as a positive part of their identity rather than a trait or a temporary condition. They may therefore call themselves **an autistic person** or **an autistic**.

- **Autistic spectrum disorder** is the 'official' terminology used in the 'Diagnostic and Statistical Manual of Mental Disorders', fourth edition (DSM IV). Many people object to the use of the word 'disorder', with its negative connotations, particularly given that cognitive processes in individuals with autism are typically highly 'ordered'. Others argue that the difficulties caused can be highly disabling and have a very significant impact on the person's quality of life. They feel that 'disorder' is therefore simply an honest reflection of this and an indication that help and support is needed.

- The autistic community has developed abbreviations for commonly used terms, such as **Aspie** – a person with Asperger syndrome – and **Autie** – an autistic person. The latter can be contrasted with 'aspie' to refer to those specifically diagnosed with classic autism.

Evidence activity LD 310

(3.2) (3.3) Terminology

Complete a table like the one below. The first line has been filled in as an example.

Term	When it might be used/ who might use it	Strengths of the term	Limitations of the term
Autistic spectrum disorder	As a diagnosis – doctors, psychiatrists, some families & individuals	Clear & honest about disabling effects; easier to access support	Negative connotations. Misleading as mind is highly 'ordered'

(3.4) LD 310 Explain the contributions of autism rights groups and the implications of their views for the support of individuals with an autistic spectrum condition

The autism rights movement (ARM) is a social movement which encourages autistic people to embrace their differences and wants society to accept 'autistics' as they are, including tolerance of harmless behaviours such as tics and 'stims'.

> ### Key terms
>
> **Stim, stims or stimming** is short for 'self stimulation'. Almost everyone does it – for example tapping feet, cracking knuckles or fiddling with hair – but in people with autistic spectrum conditions these behaviours are usually more pronounced. Autistic people often engage in stimming when they are stressed or to manage their sensory issues.

Common autistic stims are: rocking back and forth, finger flicking/rippling, spinning, humming, repeating words or sounds, and complex body contortions.

The movement aims to promote awareness of autistic spectrum conditions and the civil and human rights of autistic people. It advocates the creation of social networks and events that allow autistic persons to socialise on their own terms; and the recognition of the autistic community as a minority group. Any difficulties experienced by people with autistic spectrum conditions can be helped by teaching them coping skills rather than trying to teach them to be more 'neurotypical'.

Most autism rights groups are user-led and based on the principles of self-advocacy, whereby people with autistic spectrum conditions speak up for themselves. The first group was founded in America in the early 1990s and since then other autism rights organisations have been formed all over the world. The rise of the Internet has provided ideal opportunities for autistic individuals to connect, communicate and organise; for many people with communication and social difficulties the Internet is an invaluable tool.

The autism rights movement has been criticised for only including people with high functioning autism or Asperger Syndrome, and because some of its members write material which is insulting about neurotypical people.

Evidence activity LD 310

3.4 Messages from the autism rights movement

Think about the ways in which you support individuals with autistic spectrum conditions in your work.

If someone from an autistic rights group was observing you, what changes might they suggest you make in your practice?

 3.5 LD 310 **Outline controversies concerning the search for cures and interventions for autistic spectrum conditions and for pre-natal diagnosis**

COULD autistic spectrum conditions be cured, treated or prevented?

'Hope at last! - Defeat autism! Why suffer another day?'

'Autism breakthrough! Stem cell transplant to repair deficiencies - A miracle! (Results may significantly vary and positive results may not be achieved.)'

As we have seen, autistic spectrum conditions are very complex and life-long in that they affect the make-up of the brain and how it works. Most experts, such as the National Autistic Society, state clearly that 'there is no known cure for autism'. This has not stopped people seeking cures or ways of 'treating' autism as if it were a disease. Inflated claims such as the above are typical of those found on the Internet, where there are very many 'alternative' practitioners offering a variety of treatments from hormone injections to Electromagnetic Radiation. There are testimonials describing positive results, particularly from dietary changes, such as adopting a gluten-free diet. On the other hand, a lot of money is being made by people selling unproven and sometimes dangerous, even fatal treatments, for example:

Autistic boy dies during chelation therapy.
Pennsylvania, USA: A five-year-old autistic boy died on August 23 2006 while undergoing an increasingly popular - though controversial - medical treatment touted by some as a cure for autism.

(Looking up Autism, Volume 3, Number 12)

It should be noted that here we are talking about so-called treatments and cures FOR autistic spectrum conditions, rather than interventions and support aimed at helping individuals overcome some of the problems they may have in relation to their autism.

If it is not possible to cure autistic spectrum conditions, what about screening for them during pregnancy? Research has been taking place into ways of detecting autism prenatally and the introduction of a test similar to the one used to screen for Down's syndrome seems a distinct possibility.

That brings us to our next question:

SHOULD autistic spectrum conditions be cured, treated or prevented?

'I don't want to be cured because being autistic is who I am. There's nothing wrong with me, I'm just different. My main problem is other people's attitudes and that's not helped by those who say you should treat autism or get rid of us before we're even born. Hitler had those kinds of ideas about Jews and gay people.'

'I'd do anything to cure my son. He gets so distressed and it's so hard to understand what's wrong. I'd love him to be able to join in with other children and have fun. I just want us to be a normal family and be able to enjoy life again. It feels like autism has stolen that from us. If I ever get pregnant again I just hope there's a test for it. I love him but I couldn't cope with another one like him.'

 Evidence activity LD 310

3.5 SHOULD we search for cures, treatments and pre-natal diagnosis?

The two quotes above are just two viewpoints.

Write a list of the arguments for and against this search being pursued.

What do YOU think?

3.6 **LD 310** **Explain why it is important to take into account individual differences in views and ideas about what is important in life, and how this might be especially important when supporting individuals on the autistic spectrum**

This is another area in which we may need to challenge our assumptions.

Case study

LD 310 **3.6** Luke

Luke is moving into a council flat where he will receive support for a few hours twice a week. He has Asperger Syndrome and attended mainstream school where he was bullied. He has just left school and his social worker Kim has sorted out a place for him at the local college. She has also managed to get him a grant to help him buy things that he needs for his flat.

Kim makes a list of items that Luke needs and together they go shopping for a cooker, fridge, bed, table and chairs, chest of drawers and TV. One of Luke's support workers, Gary, helps him sort out the flat and decorate it so that it looks tidy and comfortable. Gary makes sure that Luke knows how to get to college as he starts the following day and helps him sort out what he will need.

Three days later, Gary calls round for his planned support session with Luke. He finds the curtains drawn in the middle of the afternoon. When Luke answers the door he is still in his pyjamas and has clearly not been to college. There is no sign of any of the items that Luke bought with his grant, apart from the TV. Instead there is a computer and a stack of games on the living room floor.

In response to Gary's shocked questions, Luke says: 'It's great here. I sold all those other things so I could buy the computer and loads of games and I get to play on it all day if I want. Why would I want to go college cos I don't like being with all those people and I'd just get bullied again! I don't need a cooker cos I'm living off takeaways which are much quicker and nicer than anything I could cook. And what's wrong with the floor for sleeping and sitting on?'.

- What do you think of Luke's actions and choices?

- What would you do if you were his support worker?

LO4 **LD 210** Understand how to contribute to the person-centred support of an individual who has an autistic spectrum condition

LO6 (LD 310) Understand how to support individuals with an autistic spectrum condition

4.1 **LD 210** **Explain why it is important to have in place structures and routines which match the wishes and needs of the individual**

6.1 **LD 310** **Explain why it is important to establish a person-centred plan catering to an individual's specific preferences and needs**

Key terms

A **person-centred** approach to supporting an individual involves a number of different aspects, including:

- the person being at the centre of all decisions about their lives, including what support they need; this means that the person has real choice and involvement, rather than having decisions made for and about them
- involving all the people who are important in an individual's life in helping to make plans with them
- developing support based on each person's individual wishes and needs rather than trying to fit the individual into existing services
- continually listening to the person so that their support can be adapted to their changing needs and/or preferences.

People with an autistic spectrum condition should be involved in their person-centred plan and support in ways that are meaningful to them. For example, the terminology used in some person-centred planning methods, such as 'circles', 'dreams'

and 'doughnuts' may be incomprehensible for someone with an autistic spectrum condition who understands language in a literal way.

The importance of tailoring the support of a person with an autistic spectrum condition to their individual wishes and needs relates to two points made earlier in the chapter. First, we noted how people with autistic spectrum conditions have hugely varied, diverse needs, and require services truly customised for each individual, with all of his/her personal needs and preferences taken into account; and second how, for many people with an autistic spectrum condition, it is particularly important to have their own specific structures and routines in place.

Evidence activity (LD 210) (LD 310)

4.1 **6.1** Importance of individual / person-centred plan and support

Look back at your response to Evidence activity: Importance of the individual (Level 2 2.1; Level 3 1.1).

- Compare the support provided to the two individuals you described.
- What might happen if their support was swapped around?

4.3 **LD 210** **Explain why it is important to involve families/ parents/carers in a person-centred approach to the support of individuals with an autistic spectrum condition**

6.2 **LD 310** **Explain why consultation with families/ parents/ carers is important in person-centred planning and support**

Until the middle of the twentieth century, autism was thought of as a variety of mental deficiency and many children with autistic spectrum conditions were sent to live in institutions. Now the vast majority are brought up within families.

Many continue to live with their family well into adulthood, as their parents move into old age. Other people with autistic spectrum conditions move into a variety of supported living situations, while others live independently; some get married or live with a partner and may have a family of their own. Once a young person reaches the age of 18, they are legally an adult and their parents can no longer make decisions on their behalf. But most parents, families and informal carers can still play an important role in person-centred planning and support for their son or daughter with an autistic spectrum condition.

Evidence activity LD 210   LD 310

 Involving others

Why is it important to involve parents and families in person-centred planning and support with individuals with an autistic spectrum condition?

6.6 **LD 310** **Explain how needs change for individuals and their families at different stages of their lives**

Clearly, as individuals with autistic spectrum conditions move through different stages of their lives, their needs change. The same applies to the needs of their families. It is impossible to make generalisations about this, apart from emphasising the fact that everyone with an autistic spectrum condition will go through the same life stages as everyone else. Each individual's experience of, for example, puberty and adolescence is unique, and indeed that can be a particularly challenging time for many young people with an autistic spectrum condition and their families (and neurotypical young people and their families!).

Research and investigate

LD 310 **6.6** **Changing needs**

Choose an individual who you support. With their permission, find out about their life history and their changing support needs at different stages of their life. Draw a time line to illustrate this. Also investigate their family's changing lives and support needs and add these to your time line in different colours.

4.2 **LD 210** **Identify formal and informal support networks for an individual with an autistic spectrum condition**

Support networks can be 'formal' (for example, support workers, college tutors, health professionals and care managers) or informal (family, friends, shop-keepers, church members and so on). The person with an autistic spectrum condition should be helped to identify their own support network and the roles the different people play. In some approaches to person-centred planning and support, 'Circles of Support' meetings are held, involving the people identified as part of the individual's support network. Such meetings may not be appropriate if the person with an autistic spectrum condition finds large groups of people stressful.

Evidence activity LD 210

4.2 **Support networks**

Identify the formal and informal support networks for an individual with an autistic spectrum condition whom you support.

4.4 **LD 210** **Describe ways of ensuring that support provided is consistent, both within own approach and with that of others**

For most individuals with autistic spectrum conditions the world is a confusing, chaotic and unpredictable place. In order to feel safe they need those who support them to be as consistent as possible. Consistency should be aimed for both within one's own approach and across different people's approaches, and should include the following areas:

1. communication
2. support routines and structures
3. expectations of the individual which are realistic and achievable whilst stretching and supporting them towards their maximum potential
4. responding to challenging or inappropriate behaviour.

Case study

LD 210 **4.4** Pedro

Pedro lives in a flat on his own. He has an autistic spectrum condition and needs support with some practical tasks and in organising himself. He gets very anxious with any change in his daily life and this can lead to deliberate self-injury. He receives support every day from a rota of three different workers (including you), with his cousin also providing informal support.

You become aware from Pedro's increasing episodes of self-harm that the other two workers, his cousin and you are all supporting him in different ways. What could be done to achieve greater consistency in your approaches?

4.5 **LD 210** Describe how to contribute towards the learning of an individual with an autistic spectrum condition

6.3 **LD 310** Describe different techniques and approaches to support individuals with an autistic spectrum condition to learn and develop new skills

People with autistic spectrum conditions normally have the capacity to learn and develop new skills throughout their lives. There are some specific techniques, approaches and interventions available, the choice of which depends on a number of factors, including the needs, age, abilities, preferences and communication skills of the individual, and the training, skills and experience of the person working with them. A note of caution: not all approaches have been properly tested; there is often a financial cost attached to them; and a few may actually have a detrimental effect on the individual.

Some of the more widely used interventions designed to develop, maintain or support skills include Social Stories (to help individuals develop greater social understanding); visual supports such as PECS (Picture Exchange Communication System); and TEACCH (a structured approach to people with autism to live or work more effectively at home, at school and in the community).

When planning or contributing to a programme of learning for someone with an autistic spectrum condition, it is important to think about the specific factors that will help that individual to learn. Everyone will have different needs, but here are some of the possibilities:

Please use clear and unambiguous language!

I need you to teach me things about every different situation – I can't 'generalise' my learning

I need you to repeat what you tell me lots of times and keep checking whether or not I understand

I need a clear structure and set routine to be able to learn and to be warned of any changes

You need to work out my learning style(s) to give me the best chance to learn

I need to do some hand-flapping and rocking after I've been concentrating for a while

8.4 Listen to what the individual is telling you

Evidence activity LD 210

(4.5) Contributing towards an individual's learning

Think of a situation in which you have contributed, or could contribute, towards the learning of an individual with an autistic spectrum condition. Describe how you did or would do this.

■ Research and investigate

LD 310 (6.3) Developing new skills

Find out more about two different techniques, approaches or interventions that could be or are used in your work to support individuals with an autistic spectrum condition to learn and develop new skills.

Compare what they claim to achieve; the credentials of the people who developed them; their cost; the supporting evidence for their effectiveness; any possible negative effects; and their suitability for individuals you support.

(6.4) LD 310 Explain how to reduce sensory overload, or increase sensory stimulation, by making adaptations to the physical and sensory environment

We saw above that the lives of many people with an autistic spectrum condition are affected by sensory issues – either heightened or reduced sensitivity in at least one of the senses. Much can be done to minimise the impact by adapting the individual's environment to reduce sensory overload or increase sensory stimulation. Modifications can be made to clothing, lighting, decor, food, utensils, routines, recreational activities and any other area of the person's life which is creating challenges. It is important for a sensory assessment to be carried out first.

Case study

LD 310 (6.4) Iqra

Iqra has a number of sensory issues: she becomes very agitated by electronic visual displays and the colour black; she is terrified of showers and hates even the sound of them (this extends somewhat to any running water); she also gets upset by strong smells. Iqra has a limited awareness of herself and the space around her and to counteract this does a lot of energetic jumping and rocking, often damaging furniture around her. She loves to listen to music at top volume and will switch on any source of music very loudly wherever she is.

- How could you adapt the environment to better suit Iqra's needs?
- What other adjustments might you make to help Iqra with her sensory issues?
- Who could you consult for advice?

(6.5) LD 310 Explain ways of helping an individual with an autistic spectrum condition to protect themselves from harm

A person with an autistic spectrum condition can be very vulnerable to harm, as a victim of crime, abuse and exploitation; or through violating the law without realising they were doing something wrong. Their difficulties with communication, social interaction and flexibility of thought may lead to situations where they misunderstand what is happening or their own actions and behaviour can be misinterpreted.

> 'A gang of killers have been jailed for life for the 'callous and cruel' torture and murder of a vulnerable man... Sentencing all three to life, (the) Judge ... said: "This was a particularly heartless and cruel murder. Your victim was extremely vulnerable with a very low IQ, autistic, disadvantaged and thought anyone who spoke to him was his friend."'
>
> (*Oxford Mail*, 19 April 2007)

'A man who posted abusive messages on memorial websites dedicated to dead children was jailed for 18 weeks... (His defence) said D. had been diagnosed with Asperger's syndrome at an early age. He said one of the characteristics was an inability to judge the reaction of others. He had struggled with alcohol problems and lived "a miserable existence".'

(*The Independent*, 14 September 2011)

'AN autistic man was abused by one of his carers who told him to keep it secret or face being told off, a court heard yesterday. Mr R is said to have warned his alleged victim that he would have his toys taken from him if he told anyone of his ordeal... The jury heard that Mr R repeatedly requested to do night shifts, which would have meant he was alone with the alleged victim. He is also said to have asked a manager if his family was very involved and if the man had ever made an allegation about a carer.'

(*The Northern Echo*, 17 March 2011)

Evidence activity

 Protecting individuals

The three cases above are perhaps extreme illustrations of the harm that can happen in relation to people with autistic conditions. They are nevertheless all true and, perhaps, preventable.

Bearing these examples in mind, provide suggestions of how to help an individual with an autistic spectrum condition to protect themselves from harm.

6.7 **LD 310** **Describe the role that advocacy can play in the support of individuals with an autistic spectrum condition**

The National Autistic Society defines advocacy, on its website, as 'a process of supporting and enabling people to express their views, to access information and services, to find out about options and make decisions, and to secure their rights'. As discussed earlier, some people with an autistic spectrum condition have joined together in groups such as the Autism Rights Movement to advocate for themselves. However, because of the difficulties in social communication and interaction associated with their autism, access to advocacy services and support is crucial for individuals with autism spectrum conditions. Although parents and carers can, in some circumstances, support the individual to advocate for him or herself or advocate on their behalf, in others an independent advocate is needed. It is important that the advocate has an awareness and understanding of autistic spectrum conditions and the willingness and capacity to get to know the individual concerned.

Evidence activity

 Advocacy

Give examples of situations in which advocacy can play a role in the support of individuals with an autistic spectrum condition.

LO5 [LD 210] Understand how to communicate effectively with individuals on the autistic spectrum)

LO5 [LD 310] Understand how to achieve effective communication with individuals with an autistic spectrum condition

5.1 [LD 210] Explain why it is important to be aware of the impact of own verbal and non verbal communication on an individual with an autistic spectrum condition

5.3 [LD 310] Explain how to maximise the effectiveness of communication by making adaptations to own verbal and non-verbal communication style

Because communication is a two-way process, its effectiveness is influenced by both people involved. Most people with autistic spectrum conditions have difficulties with communication, but these difficulties can either be exacerbated or minimised by the way the other person communicates with them. As has been emphasised throughout this chapter, every person with an autistic spectrum is an individual, so there can be no hard-and-fast rules.

But here are some guidelines that may help to achieve effective communication:

- Take time to observe the person and how they communicate and interact with others. If possible, study how someone who knows them well (for example, a parent) communicates with them.

- Start by engaging in activities with the individual. There are many forms of communication, including doing an activity together. It shows that you have an interest in the individual and may be less threatening than talking.

- Use language that is clear, specific and accurate. Avoid metaphors and inferences (see 'Key Terms', page 152), irony and sarcasm, and being careless in what you say. For example, do not say 'I'll be back in a minute', unless it will be precisely a minute!

- Demonstrate active listening skills. If you can engage the person in a conversation, listen to what (s)he is saying, and feed back to show that you have understood.

- Allow the person time to process what you have said, and do not repeat it, or say something else, too quickly.

- Use closed questions more than you might normally do.

- Sit to someone's side if they are uncomfortable with eye contact.

- Use the person's name often.

- Be calm and still, with no large gestures.

- Do not talk down to or patronise them.

- Be aware of aspects of your non verbal communication that the individual with an autistic spectrum condition may find difficult. For example, do not stand close to, touch or speak loudly to the person unless you know these are things they are happy with.

- Choose the right time to communicate. Do not expect to achieve effective communication with the individual when they are tired and/or stressed; social communication may take a lot of effort for people with an autistic spectrum condition.

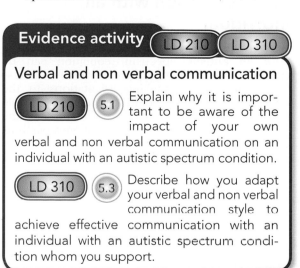

Evidence activity [LD 210] [LD 310]

Verbal and non verbal communication

[LD 210] 5.1 Explain why it is important to be aware of the impact of your own verbal and non verbal communication on an individual with an autistic spectrum condition.

[LD 310] 5.3 Describe how you adapt your verbal and non verbal communication style to achieve effective communication with an individual with an autistic spectrum condition whom you support.

5.2 LD 210 Identify aspects of the environment that affect communication with an individual

There are three main types of factors that can have an effect on communication:

1. Visual – for example lighting or visual distractions.
2. Auditory – such as noise or echo.
3. Individual – for example attitude; state of physical or mental health.

Time to reflect

LD 210 5.2 'I can't understand you!'

Think of a situation you have been in where, because of certain aspects of the environment, you were unable to communicate effectively.

Describe what aspects of the environment made effective communication difficult.

5.3 LD 210 Describe how to reduce barriers to communication with an individual

Barriers to communication with an individual with an autistic spectrum condition can be reduced both by changing your own communication style and by making adaptations to the environment. These could range from simple measures like turning off the TV or moving the seats around to more far-reaching ones, such as changing the lighting or introducing visual symbols throughout the living space.

Evidence activity LD 210

5.3 Identifying barriers to communication

Consider an individual with an autistic spectrum condition whom you know:

- Identify barriers to communication with him/her.
- Describe how these barriers could be reduced.

5.4 LD 210 Outline the use of visual communication systems for individuals who have an autistic spectrum condition

5.2 LD 310 Describe methods and systems used to develop and support an individual's communication

Visual supports present information in a visual way, alongside verbal language, enabling the person to have a better understanding of everyday life and to be able to communicate his or her needs. We all use visual prompts in our daily lives, such as road signs, logos for brand-names and computer icons. But people with autistic spectrum conditions are especially likely to benefit from visual supports because their visual skills tend to be stronger than their verbal ability. Visual supports allow them to use this visual strength to process, remember and respond to information. Improved understanding makes the world seem a more predictable, less stressful place; presenting information in a visual way can therefore reduce anxiety and promote confidence, self-esteem and independence.

Anything can be used as a visual support, provided that it is meaningful for the individual and the people supporting him or her. Examples include real objects (such as an apple to indicate snack time); 'objects of reference' (e.g. a swimming costume to represent a trip to the pool); photographs; picture symbols; miniatures of real objects; and written words.

As well as the informal use of visual supports designed around the individual's needs, there are more formalised approaches and communication systems, some of which were mentioned in the

'Supporting Learning' section above. These include PECS (the Picture Exchange Communication System), which encourages the person to communicate what they want or need by exchanging a picture card for a desired item or activity; TEACCH, which uses visual supports such as timetables to help provide routine and structure and develop understanding; 'Comic Strip Conversations', developed by Carol Gray, which combine stick-figures with conversation symbols to show what people say and think during conversations; and Makaton, a language programme which uses signs and symbols to help people with learning disabilities and/or communication difficulties make themselves understood – and to understand others.

Evidence activity `LD 210` `LD 310`

Use of visual support and communication systems

`LD 210` `5.4`

List everyday situations or particular events in your workplace in which visual supports and/or communication systems are being used or could be used.

`LD 310` `5.2` Identify an individual with whom you have used a particular approach to develop and support his/her communication. Explain why you chose that approach and how you used it, and describe how effective it has been.

`5.5` `LD 210`  **Identify who could provide advice about effective communication with an individual**

🔍 Research and investigate

`5.5` `LD 210` Where to find advice

Identify who could provide advice about effective communication with an individual.

LO4 `LD 310` Understand the legal and policy framework that underpins good practice in the support of individuals with autistic spectrum conditions

`4.1` `LD 310`  **Identify what legislation and national and local policy and guidance exists**

`4.2` `LD 310` **Explain what individuals or situations the legislation, national and local policy and guidance applies to**

`4.3` `LD 310` **Explain how the ways in which legislation and national and local policy and guidance apply to individuals on the autistic spectrum may differ according to their particular needs**

This depends on which of the UK countries you live in.

In **England**, the Autism Act was passed in 2009, 'to make provision about meeting the needs of adults with autistic spectrum conditions'. It was the first ever piece of legislation concerning people with a specific condition. It is important to emphasise that it applies to England only.

The Act committed the government to produce a strategy for adults with autism; this was published in March 2010. The Strategy is called 'Fulfilling and rewarding lives' and its key aims are:

- increasing awareness and understanding of autism;
- making it easier for adults to get a diagnosis;
- developing services for people to live independently with the right support;

- helping people with autistic spectrum conditions into work;
- supporting local councils and health authorities to plan and develop services to meet the needs of the people in their area

In order to make sure that local councils and health bodies implement the Autism Strategy, the government issued statutory guidance in December 2010.

Key terms

Statutory guidance means that it is laid down by the law; there is a legal duty to implement it.

The guidance specifies certain things that local authorities and the NHS must do, including:

1. Provide autism awareness training for all health and social care staff and specialist training for key staff, such as GPs.
2. Offer a community care assessment for all adults diagnosed with an autistic spectrum condition.
3. Develop a clear pathway to diagnosis and assessment for adults with autism.
4. Take the views of people with autistic spectrum conditions and their carers into account when developing services.
5. Identify a lead professional to take responsibility for the development of services.

Local councils and local NHS Trusts should be demonstrating that they are taking measures to implement the statutory guidance, although no additional money was provided for them to do so.

In **Scotland**, a Strategy for Autism was launched in November 2011. It sets out a 10 year plan with 26 recommendations. Unlike the English strategy, it covers children as well as adults and has extra funding attached.

Wales produced an Autistic Spectrum Disorder (ASD) Strategic Action Plan in 2008. As with the Scottish Strategy this sets out a 10 year all-age plan and some additional funding has been allocated.

Northern Ireland – The Autism Act (Northern Ireland) 2011 calls for an autism strategy setting out 'how the needs of people with an autistic spectrum condition are to be addressed throughout their lives'.

Research and investigate

   LD 310 Legislation

This activity enables you to find out about how the legal and policy framework influences the support of people with autistic spectrum conditions in your local area.

- In what ways is legislation and national policy being implemented in your local area?
- What local policy and guidance is there regarding people with autistic spectrum conditions?
- Which individuals and situations do the legislation, national and local policy and guidance apply to?
- What impact does the legal and policy framework have on:
  (a) the lives of the individuals with autistic spectrum conditions you support?
  (b) the way the support is provided?

Further reading

Baron-Cohen, S. (2008) *Autism and Asperger Syndrome* (The Facts) Oxford: OUP

Department of Health (2010) *Fulfilling and rewarding lives: the strategy for adults with autism in England* London: Department of Health

Wing, L. (2003) *The Autistic Spectrum: A Guide for Parents and Professionals* London: Robinson Publishing

Weblinks

The National Autistic Society, www.autism.org.uk

Wrong Planet – 'the online community for Autism and Asperger's', www.wrongplanet.net

Assessment Summary for Unit LD 210

To achieve the unit, your assessor will require you to:

Learning outcomes	Assessment criteria
1 Understand the areas in which individuals with an autistic spectrum condition characteristically have difficulties	Describing the types of difficulty that individuals with an autistic spectrum condition may have with language and other ways of communicating with others See Evidence activity 1.1, p. 154 and Case study, p. 152.
	Identifying problems that individuals with an autistic spectrum condition may have in social interaction and relationships See Time to reflect 1.2, p. 153 and Evidence activity, p. 154.
	Outlining the problems of inflexibility and restrictiveness in activities and interests and how these may affect individuals on the autistic spectrum See Evidence activity 1.3, p. 154.
2 Understand the concept of autism as a spectrum, and the implications for variation in the capacities and needs of individuals	Explaining why it is important to recognise that each individual on the autistic spectrum has their own individual abilities, needs, strengths, preferences and interests See Time to reflect 2.1, p. 151 and Evidence activity 2.1, p. 151.
	Describing why autism can be considered as a spectrum, encompassing individuals differing in the expression and severity of their symptoms See Evidence activity 2.2, p. 156.
	Identifying other conditions which may be associated with an autistic spectrum condition See Evidence activity 2.3, p. 158.
	Outlining the sensory difficulties experienced by many individuals with an autistic spectrum condition See Evidence activity 2.4, p. 157.
3 Understand the behaviours exhibited by some individuals with an autistic spectrum condition	Describing behavioural characteristics associated with autistic spectrum conditions See Evidence activity 3.1, p. 159.
	Identifying reasons why individuals with an autistic spectrum condition may exhibit such behaviours See Evidence activity 3.2, p. 159.
	Describing what to do if an individual is highly anxious or stressed See Research and investigate 3.3, p. 160 and Time to Reflect 3.3, p. 159.

Learning outcomes	Assessment criteria
4 Understand how to contribute to the person-centred support of an individual who has an autistic spectrum condition	**4.1** Explaining why it is important to have in place structures and routines which match the wishes and needs of the individual See Evidence activity 4.1, p. 168.
	4.2 Identifying formal and informal support networks for an individual with an autistic spectrum condition See Evidence activity 4.2, p. 169.
	4.3 Explaining why it is important to involve families/parents/carers in a person-centred approach to the support of individuals with an autistic spectrum condition See Evidence activity 4.3, p. 169.
	4.4 Describing ways of ensuring that support provided is consistent, both within own approach and with that of others See Case study 4.4, p. 170.
	4.5 Describing how to contribute towards the learning of an individual with an autistic spectrum condition See Evidence activity 4.5, p. 171.
5 Understand how to communicate effectively with individuals on the autistic spectrum	**5.1** Explaining why it is important to be aware of the impact of own verbal and non-verbal communication on an individual with an autistic spectrum condition See Evidence activity 5.1, p. 173.
	5.2 Identifying aspects of the environment that affect communication with an individual See Time to reflect 5.2, p. 174.
	5.3 Describing how to reduce barriers to communication with an individual See Evidence activity 5.3, p. 174.
	5.4 Outlining the use of visual communication systems for individuals who have an autistic spectrum condition See Evidence activity 5.4, p. 175.
	5.5 Identifying who could provide advice about effective communication with an individual See Research and investigate 5.5, p. 175.

Assessment Summary for Unit LD 310

To achieve the unit, your assessor will require you to:

Learning outcomes	Assessment criteria
1 Understand the main characteristics of autistic spectrum conditions	**1.1** Explaining why it is important to recognise that each person on the autistic spectrum has their own individual abilities, needs, strengths, gifts and interests See Time to reflect 1.1, p. 151 and Evidence activity 1.1, p. 151.
	1.2 Analysing the main diagnostic features of autistic spectrum conditions, commonly known as the 'triad of impairments' See Evidence activity 1.2, p. 154.
	1.3 Explaining the meanings of the term 'spectrum' in relation to autism by reference to the notions of sub-conditions and individual variation within the autistic spectrum See Evidence activity 1.3, p. 156.
	1.4 Describing the sensory and perceptual difficulties commonly experienced by individuals with an autistic spectrum condition See Research and investigate 1.4, p. 157.
	1.5 Describing other conditions that may be associated with the autistic spectrum See Evidence activity 1.5, p. 158.
	1.6 Describing how language and intellectual abilities vary between individuals and sub-groups across the spectrum See Evidence activity 1.6, p. 156.
2 Understand how autistic spectrum conditions can impact on the lives of individuals and those around them	**2.1** Describing ways in which autism can impact on the everyday lives of individuals, their parents/carers and siblings, and others close to them See Case study 2.1, p. 161.
	2.2 Explaining how autistic spectrum conditions can impact on individuals differently according to factors such as their gender, ethnicity and social, cultural and religious environment See Evidence activity 2.2, p. 162.
	2.3 Explaining how stereotyped views, discrimination and a lack of understanding of autistic spectrum conditions can compound the difficulties already experienced by individuals and their families See Evidence activity 2.3, p. 162.
	2.4 Describing ways of helping an individual and/or their parent/carer/siblings/partner to understand their autistic spectrum condition See Evidence activity 2.4, p. 163.

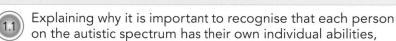

Learning outcomes	Assessment criteria
3 Understand different theories and concepts about autism	**3.1** Explaining theories about autism related to • brain function and genetics • psychology See Research and investigate 3.1, p. 164.
	3.2 Explaining why there are alternative choices of terminology used to describe the autism spectrum See Evidence activity 3.2, p. 165.
	3.3 Describing the strengths and limitations of different types of terminology See Evidence activity 3.3, p. 165.
	3.4 Explaining the contributions of autism rights groups and the implications of their views for the support of individuals with an autistic spectrum condition See Evidence activity 3.4, p. 166.
	3.5 Outlining controversies concerning the search for cures and interventions for autistic spectrum conditions and for pre-natal diagnosis See Evidence activity 3.5, p. 166.
	3.6 Explaining why it is important to take into account individual differences in views of what is important in life, and how this might be especially important when supporting individuals on the autistic spectrum See Case study 3.6, p. 167.
4 Understand the legal and policy framework that underpins good practice in the support of individuals with autistic spectrum conditions	**4.1** Identifying what legislation and national and local policy and guidance exists See Research and investigate 4.1, p. 176.
	4.2 Explaining what individuals or situations the legislation, national and local policy and guidance applies to See Research and investigate 4.2, p. 176.
	4.3 Explaining how the ways in which legislation and national and local policy and guidance apply to individuals on the autistic spectrum may differ according to their particular needs See Research and investigate 4.3, p. 176.

5 Understand how to achieve effective communication with individuals with an autistic spectrum condition	(5.1) Giving examples of how 'challenging behaviour' can be a way of expressing emotions where there are communication differences See Evidence activity and Time to reflect 5.1, p. 159.
	(5.2) Describing methods and systems used to develop and support an individual's communication See Evidence activity 5.2, p. 175.
	(5.3) Explaining how to maximise the effectiveness of communication by making adaptations to own verbal and non-verbal communication style See Evidence activity 5.3, p. 173.
6 Understand how to support individuals with an autistic spectrum condition	(6.1) Explaining why it is important to establish a person-centred plan catering to an individual's specific preferences and needs See Evidence activity 6.1, p. 168.
	(6.2) Explaining why consultation with families/parents/carers is important in person-centred planning and support See Evidence activity 6.2, p. 169.
	(6.3) Describing different techniques and approaches to support individuals with an autistic spectrum condition to learn and develop new skills See Research and investigate 6.3, p. 171.
	(6.4) Explaining how to reduce sensory overload, or increase sensory stimulation, by making adaptations to the physical and sensory environment See Case study 6.4, p. 171.
	(6.5) Explaining ways of helping an individual with an autistic spectrum condition to protect themselves from harm See Evidence activity 6.5, p. 172.
	(6.6) Explaining how needs change for individuals and their families at different stages of their lives See Research and investigate 6.6, p. 169.
	(6.7) Describing the role that advocacy can play in the support of individuals with an autistic spectrum condition See Evidence activity 6.7, p. 172.

Sexuality and sexual health
Unit LD 307 Principles of supporting individuals with a learning disability regarding sexuality and sexual health

What are you finding out?

The chapter introduces many of the issues and principles needed when supporting individuals with a learning disability regarding sex. It gives a broad summary of sexuality, sexual development and sexual health. The chapter also discusses relevant legislation which relates to the development of sexuality for an individual with a learning disability.

This chapter hopes to unlock some issues around sexuality and sexual health to ensure that individuals with a learning disability have the same rights to sex, which is as enjoyable, safe and consensual as other people's experience of it.

The reading and activities in this chapter will help you to:

• Understand the development of human sexuality

• Understand how the sexual development of individuals with a learning disability can differ

• Understand the issues of sexual health and how these can be supported

• Understand the relevant legislation influencing the support of sexuality and sexual health for individuals with learning disabilities

• Know how to support the sexual expression of an individual with a learning disability

LO1 Understand the development of human sexuality

1.1 Define the terms sexuality, sexual health, sexual orientation and sexual expression

Human sexuality is a complex issue; there are rarely any straightforward answers – maybe that it what makes it so interesting. Sexuality is a significant part of society; the morals of it, the legalities, the mystery of it. It is a major feature of movies, soap plots and so on. It is written about by great authors, artists, poets, philosophers and composers and many have worked to explore sexuality from the earliest times without coming up with any enduring answers and yet, ironically, it is still an area which is clouded in secrecy, whispered about and linked to embarrassment.

Terms in human sexuality are often interchangeable, and many would argue that 'sexuality' can be used for 'sexual orientation', and indeed 'sexual orientation' for 'sexual expression', but below is an attempt at defining the terms.

Sexuality describes how an individual expresses themselves as a sexual being, and how they value sexual behaviour. It can encompass both sexual orientation and sexual expression.

Sexual orientation is often referred to as the sexual preference one has for another. Simplistically, there are four broad categories of sexuality.

- Homosexual – when there is a preference for an individual of the same biological sex.
- Heterosexual – when there is a preference for an individual of the opposite biological sex.
- Bisexual – when there is a preference for an individual of either the same or opposite biological sex.
- Asexuality (or non-sexuality) is the lack of sexual attraction for any other individual.

Sexual expression is often how one expresses one's sexuality. This could be through the medium of our 'outer appearance', such as clothes, make up and so on, or through our behaviour, such as 'flirting' which is the language, both verbal and non verbal, we use when we are expressing our interest to another. It could also be through more specific sexual behaviour such as fantasies, the use of pornography, masturbation and so on. Sexual expression may often be linked to gender roles as there may be cultural norms about what are 'normal' masculine or feminine sexual behaviours.

Sexual health is the act of ensuring that any sexual behaviour or activity is safe for the individuals involved and others. Safety here is both physical and emotional. Good physical sexual health requires the consideration of contraception, regular health checks and so on and emotionally requires consent, being comfortable and at no point feeling degraded or humiliated.

9.1 What would I like to do tonight?

Evidence activity · LD 307

1.1 Terms

Define the terms sexuality, sexual health, sexual orientation and sexual expression.

1.2 Explain main sexual development milestones throughout an individual's lifespan

When we are born we all have primary sexual characteristics; these are often referred to as our sexual organs. The first question new parents ask is 'is it a boy or a girl'? The biological being of a boy or a girl affects how we are treated straight away from the clothes chosen for us, to the colours of our room, the toys we have, and even the behaviour expected from us.

Female primary sexual characteristics include:

- cervix
- clitoris
- fallopian tubes
- ovaries
- uterus
- vagina
- vulva.

Male primary sexual characteristics include:

- penis
- prostate
- scrotum
- seminal vesicles
- testicles.

In puberty during adolescence, secondary sex characteristics develop. Although some characteristics happen to boys and girls (e.g. growth of underarm and pubic hair), the majority occur in boys or girls and hence these are features which help to distinguish the two sexes, but they are not directly part of the reproductive system. This period of growth and transition can be a particularly difficult time for any adolescent.

Secondary sexual characteristics in males include:

- Growth of body hair on abdomen and chest.
- Growth of facial hair.
- Enlargement of larynx (Adam's apple) and deepening of voice.

- Increased height and strength, and larger hands and feet than women.
- Change in body shape; broadening of shoulders and chest.
- Penis enlarges.
- Testes 'drop'.
- Production of semen.

Secondary sexual characteristics in females include:

- Enlargement of breasts.
- Widening of hips.
- Change in body shape; more subcutaneous fat and fat deposits especially near the buttocks, thighs and hips.
- Menstruation (periods) begins.

In later adolescence and adulthood, one norm is for individuals to become sexually active, should they choose to. Therefore a milestone associated with this time may be pregnancy and therefore issues around fertility and infertility, contraception and so on.

In later adulthood, or perhaps when individuals have had children, individuals may choose to stop their ability to have children and males may have a vasectomy, and females a 'tubal ligation' where the fallopian tubes are 'tied' or a hysterectomy where the uterus is removed.

In later adulthood, the sexual norms associated with aging are in women the menopause and in males possible issues around impotence. In both males and females, there may be a loss of libido.

However, many individuals are able to enjoy a happy, active sex life throughout their years, and regardless of the presence of a learning disability this should be accepted. Individuals should not face discrimination either because of their age or their learning disability.

9.2 What is happening to me?!

1.2 Milestones

Produce a report explaining main sexual developments throughout an individual's lifespan. Include norms at different life stages and development which may happen to males only, females only, or both.

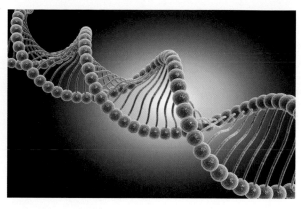

9.3 Genetic codes

LO2 Understand how the sexual development of individuals with a learning disability can differ

Everybody is different, and so every individual's sexuality is different. The reasons for this are not clear cut and have caused much debate and the 'nature–nurture' debate is often cited for many issues surrounding sexuality.

The sexual development of individuals with learning disabilities can differ between every individual as it does between individuals without a learning disability. Hence, we cannot categorise individuals with learning disabilities as all being 'the same', as their situation will be unique to them.

2.1 Describe how genetic factors can influence the sexual development, sexual expression and sexual health of an individual with a learning disability

There are two kinds of sex chromosome, the X chromosome and the Y chromosome, and they control whether a person is male or female. Females usually have two X chromosomes (XX). A female inherits one X chromosome from her mother and one X chromosome from her father. Males usually have an X chromosome and a Y chromosome (XY). A male inherits an X chromosome from his mother and a Y chromosome from his father. Hence sexual development is based on the genes.

Either as a result of the sperm, egg, conception or cell division while the embryo is developing, there could develop a variant combination such as XXY, XYY, XXX and so on.

- XXY is where a male has an extra X chromosome resulting in them having biological features often associated with females and often affecting fertility. It is also known as Klinefelter's syndrome.

- XYYs is a male with an extra Y chromosome leading to what is often referred to as a 'super male'. The presence of an extra Y chromosome may lead to increased height, speech delays, learning disabilities, mild to moderate mental retardation, and behavioural disturbance. It is also known as polysomy Y syndrome.

- XXX is a female with an extra X chromosome, leading to what is often referred to as a 'super female' often characterised by differing facial development, hair lines and usually being taller.

- It is worth mentioning that biology also helps to explain sexual development through hormones, as there is scientific evidence that there can be different levels of oestrogen and testosterone in the womb; often called a hormone surge. This could be due to the environment (e.g. diet) or stress levels. Some claim differing levels of hormones during development can alter an individual's sexuality.

Some argue that these genetic and hormonal variants are not only what drive our biological gender, but also our sexual orientation; although many contest this.

However, from a biological, evolutionary perspective some question the role of 'nature' 'assisting' homosexuality as there are no evolutionary benefits to this because reproduction is hindered.

Evidence activity LD 307

2.1 Genetic factors

Describe how genetic factors can influence the sexual development, sexual expression and sexual health of an individual with a learning disability. You may also want to research some of the genetic syndromes mentioned.

2.2 Describe how socio-cultural factors and religious beliefs can influence an individual's sexual development

Socio-cultural refers to the social and cultural factors which can affect development. These factors can affect how men and women are able to control the various aspects of their sexual development, for example when sexual experiences begin, public knowledge of such experiences, the conditions under which it takes place, and the use of contraception.

Time to reflect

2.2

Consider your own views on sexuality. Why do you think they are as they are? What socio-cultural or religious beliefs do you have that may have affected this?

Socio-cultural factors

Primary socialisation

Primary socialisation is what is learnt from parents and immediate family. Here, gender roles, the discussion and opinions voiced, can mean gender behaviour is punished or encouraged.

The expectations from parents can often affect sexual development. Parents' beliefs and lifestyles may encourage or discourage certain sexual developments. A known parental age of first sexual experience, thoughts on sex before marriage, sexuality, contraception, views on partners staying over in the home and so on may all be communicated within the family. Further actual family structures can create norms, such as single parenthood, cohabiting, marriage, teenage pregnancy and so on.

Secondary socialisation

Secondary socialisation is what is learnt from the wider world, school, friends, the media and so on. An individual's schooling can affect them greatly. Attendance at a single sex school could affect ability to mix with other sexes. Other experiences include smaller schooling experiences, time at residential settings, or pressure from loved ones to keep individuals 'safe' that mean reduced opportunities for individuals to meet members of the opposite sex. The media may present ideas about sexuality and may contribute to stereotypes and labels of people, such as the female roles in blockbuster movies. Cultural stigma and taboos (social bans) within socialisation, especially those related to sex and sexual activities, may affect what is deemed as normal for sexual development. Some desires that are deemed as outside the norms may be deemed 'fetishes' or 'alternative lifestyles'.

Specific factors due to having a learning disability

It may be that individuals with learning disabilities do not have the same exposure to sexual education or sexual material, perhaps in the media, films, magazines and so on, because their ability to access them has been limited.

Parents, carers and loved ones may feel the need to protect individuals with learning disabilities more than others and therefore 'wrap them in cotton wool' meaning they are more sheltered as regards sexual matters. Some individuals may have less experience in sexual matters possibly because individuals are more protected as regards sexual milestones earlier on in life, such as flirting or dating, and therefore knowledge and experience are lacking. Individuals may display less confidence than those without learning disabilities due to feeling they are 'different', and also because of the consequences of the above reasons.

9.4 'How can I talk to boys?'

Religious beliefs

Religion prescribes ethical guidelines for many aspects of daily life and also navigates belief systems and norms surrounding sexuality. Many faiths condemn premarital sex, contraception including condom use, and homosexuality. Some religions also advocate a more submissive role for women, with greater modesty in clothing and behaviour and indeed some may foster gender inequality in marital relations, and promote women's ignorance in sexual matters as a symbol of purity, indeed where virginity is even revered. Religions may also prescribe the dating rituals of individuals, the need for chaperones, parental involvement in the arranging of 'matches' and so on. Clearly some of these religious beliefs could be in conflict with an individual's wishes.

Evidence activity LD 307

 2.2 Socio-cultural factors and religious beliefs

Describe how socio-cultural factors and religious beliefs can influence an individual's sexual development. You may want to research specific religions and investigate some of the guidelines they provide about sexuality.

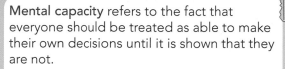 **2.3 Explain how mental capacity can influence sexual development, sexual experiences, sexual expression and sexual health**

Individuals with learning disabilities are protected under the law relating to **mental capacity**. The Mental Capacity Act (2007) states that everyone should be treated as able to make their own decisions until it is shown that they are not.

Key terms

Mental capacity refers to the fact that everyone should be treated as able to make their own decisions until it is shown that they are not.

According to Directgov someone can lack mental capacity:

> 'if they have an injury, disorder or condition that affects the way their mind works. This could mean they have difficulty making decisions all of the time or that it might take them a long time to make a decision.'

Because of this, a court may decide that an appointed deputy (appointed by the court of protection) or an individual's attorney will make decisions on their behalf. However, any decision made for an individual who lacks capacity must be made in that person's best interests. But it must be remembered that adults with learning disabilities have the capacity to make decisions about sexual matters unless the Mental Capacity Act 2005 deems this impossible.

It therefore follows that there could be occasions where the issue of mental capacity has to be raised in reference to sexual issues. This is particularly sensitive as the sexual life of any individual can be shrouded in embarrassment and secrecy, but for those with a learning disability there may be a greater sense of it being a taboo area and something that health and social care services should not interfere with. However, it must be remembered that any individual can have legitimate needs; these could include:

- a need for help in communicating an interest;
- individuals may need support achieving a satisfactory sexual function;
- a need for education, supervision from or restraint from an unintentional inappropriate sexual activity;

- a need to be protected from others' sexual interest;
- support with purchasing of clothing or underwear;
- a need for some privacy to be given in a healthcare or social care setting.

Individuals without mental capacity may well have difficulty expressing themselves appropriately, may not even understand what sexual acts themselves are, or if they have a physical desire for them. A clear balance between support, protection and rights is vital here.

Evidence activity `LD 307`

 Mental capacity

Explain how mental capacity can influence sexual development, sexual experiences, sexual expression and sexual health.

LO3 Understand the issues of sexual health and how these can be supported

3.1 Explain the key features of sexual health and well being and how these relate to an individual's overall health and well being

Every individual has the right to good sexual health, both physically and emotionally. There are many aspects to this including the following:

- Access to education on sexual issues and safety.
- Access to support and guidance on sexuality.
- Availability of contraception and safer sex.
- Access to fertility and infertility services.
- Pregnancy services including termination, adoption and fostering services.
- Information and testing for sexual transmitted infections.
- Legal pornography.

- Sexual aids and toys.
- Information on sexual abuse, sexual violence, safety and safeguarding (good/bad touching, public/private, saying no etc).
- Puberty, body awareness and changes.
- Breast and testicular checks and cervical screening tests.
- Relationships.

Each of these may be vital for an individual to be healthy sexually. It is not acceptable to consider one part of an individual's health. **Holistic** health and well being considers everything about the individual; physical health, intellectual health, emotional health, social health and also sexual health. Individuals have the right to have information, support and access to features which can ensure they enjoy their sexuality healthily and safely. Not doing so could call in to question the duty of care which care practitioners have as regards individuals in their care.

Key terms

Holistic means the 'whole' and the relationship between the 'parts'.

Evidence activity `LD 307`

 Key features of sexual health

Imagine you are producing a booklet on sexual health for a day centre for individuals with learning disabilities. Your supervisor has asked you exactly what features you will be including, so you need to produce a short report explaining the key features of sexual health and well being and how this relates to an individual's overall health and well being.

3.2 Identify sexual health issues that differently affect men and women

Individuals have the right to know what is happening to their own bodies and therefore need to know the specifics relating to their own gender.

However, it is also vital to remember that males and females have the right to understand what happens to members of the opposite sex to help them be as prepared as possible for any potential healthy sexual relationship.

There are some issues which may relate more specifically to males and females:

Males	Females
Wet dreams	Periods
Erections	Masturbation
Masturbating	Orgasm
Ejaculating, including premature ejaculation or inability to	Contraceptive pill, contraceptive injections, implants, IUD, diaphragms, caps and female condoms, etc
Impotence	
Condoms, including those specifically for anal intercourse	

Clearly each of these needs to be dealt with sensitively. Some individuals may be comfortable discussing sexual health with a member of the opposite sex, but some may desire a practitioner of the same sex. Further, an individual with transgender issues will need specialist support and advice.

It must also be noted that many sexual health issues are not only gender specific, but also culturally specific. For example many religions have menstruation-related traditions related to washing, gender separation, and rules on intercourse and these need to be noted and taken account of.

 Evidence activity LD 307

3.2 Gender specific differences

Produce two leaflets identifying sexual health issues that affect men and women differently for distribution to care workers specifically working with males and females.

3.3 Explain how sexual health issues can be supported within plans for healthcare

Any care assessment of any individual should include all facets of an individual's health, and that includes sexual health. The Health Action Plans which are produced for individuals with learning disabilities should make reference to the promotion of positive sexual health if applicable. Often, individuals with learning disabilities have not been able to access similar services to healthcare, which is poor practice, and Health Action Plans can help to reduce this. What is vital, however, is that Health Action Plans are fundamentally designed by the individual, not for them.

Health action plans are described by the Department of Health (2008) as:

> the actions needed to maintain and improve the health of an individual and any help needed to accomplish these. It is a mechanism to link the individual and the range of services and supports they need if they are to have better health... the plan is primarily for the person with learning disabilities and is usually co-produced with them.

And hence the term 'Health facilitation' is referred to as:

> a process that has evolved from roles developed by family carers, practitioners and others and from the wishes of people and families for support in accessing, navigating and using the NHS.

A Health Action plan should see the whole person, not just their learning disability. Individuals should be given the opportunity to request, question and demand sexual health services. And if they are not in a position to consider this, advocates or guardians can do so on their behalf. Not doing so could have significant consequences such as sexual abuse, pregnancy or sexually transmitted infections.

The sexual needs of an individual should be assessed and then action taken as to how they can be supported and advised.

Evidence activity **LD 307**

3.3 Health action plans

Speak to care practitioners and use the internet to research to explain how sexual health issues can be supported within plans for healthcare. You may choose to find an example of a Health Action Plan to help your explanation.

3.4 Identify local services that exist to support sexual health for individuals

Once sexual needs have been assessed, action needs to be taken to provide assistance to individuals.

Within education there will be lessons on Personal Social and Health Education (PSHE) which will specifically deal with sexual education taught by teachers and also guest speakers. But further sex education may also be a feature of Biology, Health and Social Care, RE and so on. There may also be a school nurse who can advise and offer support. Attendance in these lessons and access to a school nurse could be beneficial and just because an individual may not attend a mainstream school, this does not mean they should not have access to similar support in a different setting.

Sex education is also not just taught in secondary schools to teenagers. Individuals with learning disabilities also have rights to information about the body and relationships which children within primary school have access to through the national curriculum.

Within health services there are many services to support individuals. The GP's surgery will often be the place to start for many individuals with access to GPs and nurses (especially family planning or, more frequently titled, sexual health nurses). Here, advice and support can be given on many areas such as contraception, pregnancy and so on. This will also cover side effects and risks of contraception. It is vital that no person with learning disabilities is 'encouraged' to use a contraceptive method that is not their choice, but is more for the peace of mind of parents, care workers or health workers.

Sexual Health Clinics are often located within a hospital or other health service. They are often referred to as GUM clinics (genitourinary medicine) and can help with a range of issues such as contraception, emergency contraception, testing and treatment for sexually transmitted infections (STIs), testing and counselling for HIV and AIDS, help if you have been sexually assaulted, pregnancy and abortion advice and help and advice for people who are having problems with their sex life.

Another useful service is the C Card project. With a website (www.ccardfreecondoms.co.uk) to allow individuals to apply online too, the service provides a card or plastic key once there has been a discussion with your school nurse, youth worker or a range of other trained professionals about the use of condoms. This C Card key fob can be exchanged for free condoms.

However, one source of support and information which is increasingly used and which assures anonymity, is the use of the internet. Not only as a search engine for local services but also to access a range of professional support such as:

FPA **www.fpa.org.uk/**

NHS (for local services) **www.nhs.uk/servicedirectories/Pages/ServiceSearch.aspx**

NHS (for information) **www.nhs.uk/Livewell/Sexualhealthtopics/Pages/Sexual-health-hub.aspx**

Brook Advisory **www.brook.org.uk/index.php**

There is a wealth of information available for all individuals regardless of age, gender or abilities. In particular many groups target different issues at different times. For example, FPA focused on learning disabilities in its Sexual Health Week 2008 with the theme of 'It's My Right'. They claim 'some people in society, such as people with learning disabilities/difficulties, aren't always given the automatic right to have relationships and flourish as sexual beings. They have to persuade others to allow them to do it.' And hence they focused their campaign on the rights of people with learning disabilities to sex and relationships.

LD 307

(3.4) **Local services**

Investigate your local area, identify the local services which exist to support sexual health for individuals. Aim to consider all services, such as health, social and educational and also from various funding sources, such as statutory, private and voluntary.

LO4 Understand relevant legislation influencing the support of sexuality and sexual health for individuals with learning disabilities

(4.1) **Explain key parts of legislation relating to sexuality and sexual health for individuals and how this influences practice**

The Human Rights Act 1998 underpins rights of all people, including those with learning difficulties. According to the Equality and Human Rights Commission, the Human Rights Act sets out the fundamental rights and freedoms that individuals in the UK have access to. They include, amongst others:

- Right to liberty and security.
- Respect for your private and family life, home and correspondence.
- Freedom of thought, belief and religion.
- Freedom of expression.
- Right to marry and start a family.
- Protection from discrimination in respect of these rights and freedoms.

Which can all relate particularly to the rights of individuals with learning disabilities to a healthy, consensual sex life free from **persecution** or harassment.

Key terms

Persecution is hostility or cruel treatment because of an individual's beliefs.

Further, there are many laws which apply more directly to an individual's sexuality. These protect the individual's rights in employment, education and family life regardless of their gender, sexuality and so on. Some of these laws are:

- Equality Act 2006 & 2010
- Civil Partnership Act 2004
- Gender Recognition Act 2004
- Employment Equality (Sexual Orientation) Regulations 2003
- Sexual Offences Act 2003
- The Sex Discrimination Act (1975)
- The Children Act 1989 and 2004

Due to the nature of legislation, that is that it is often amended and updated, the Equality and Human Rights Commission is an excellent reference for up to date information and guidance on equality law.

Clearly, the effects of these laws are to promote the rights of all, but in practice it affects the care of individuals with learning disabilities in two specific ways:

Must integrate into own practice

- Every aspect of care must consider the legal implications. All care must be within the legal boundaries.
- Eg: The legalities of balancing good care and support in the provision of teaching sexual practice to an individual with learning disabilities and the showing of sexual images to individuals.

Must provide information to individuals about the existence of such laws

- Clearly dependent on the abilities of the individual, it may be that care practitioners need to help individuals be aware of their legal rights, if needed, this may be through the use of a guardian or advocate.
- Eg: Supporting a gay man with learning disabilities who is being discriminated against by other residents and also staff at the residental setting he stays at.

The Royal College of Nursing's *Sexuality and Sexual Health in Nursing Practice* provides an excellent range of case studies about situations that care professionals may find themselves in which require legal guidance. This can be found on their website.

Evidence activity LD 307

 Legislation influencing support for sexuality

Research the legislation mentioned and explain key parts of relevant legislation relating to sexuality and sexual health for individuals and how this influences practice. You may choose to consider practice in a care setting familiar to you, for example a residential home, hospital, day centre, school and so on. You may also want to ask your supervisors about legislation which they specifically have to refer to.

LO5 Know how to support the sexual expression of an individual with a learning disability

5.1 **Explain how own values, belief systems and experiences may impact on support for individuals with learning disabilities**

Everyone has values and beliefs and experiences, and at times individuals may think that 'they know best!' This may apply if the care worker is older than the individual who they are supporting and this could be exacerbated if the individual has learning difficulties. However, no one knows what is right for an individual, unless they are them. Further, it is an individual's right to find out for themselves, to make mistakes. It is good practice for individuals to ask others for their advice and support, as everyone does, but ultimately it is an individual's choice to make.

It needs to be noted that most parents do remain involved in their children's lives, be it finances, employment or relationships, and in the majority of cases, this is welcomed by the child. The perspectives of parents and carers of adults with learning disabilities may also be a valuable, welcomed input. Care practitioners may have experienced situations themselves or seen others in similar situations, but unless there are issues

It may also be the case that religious beliefs play a role here about what is the 'right' action to take. Clearly people take beliefs very seriously as, for many, their religion defines who they are, but it is important not to impose one's beliefs on others.

Evidence activity LD 307

5.1 The impact of your own beliefs

Explain how your own values, belief systems and experiences may impact on support for individuals with learning disabilities. You may want to consider a situation in a care environment you have been in where individual's wishes have clashed with the values, belief systems and experiences of others. What did the care workers do right, what do you think they may have done incorrectly?

5.2 Explain why the development of a meaningful relationship can be important to the development of an individual's sexuality

People with learning disabilities enjoy sex. It's a fact of life.

For more information and advice on sexual health, call **fpa**'s (Family Planning Association) confidential helpline on 0845 122 8690 or visit www.fpa.org.uk

9.5 Challenging stereotypes

with mental capacity, individuals with learning disabilities have the right to listen to values, beliefs and experiences of others, but then should be empowered enough to make their own decisions with all facts and perspectives presented in a way which suits them. There may be times when perspectives clash, but as in 'normal' family life, these should be voiced and discussed.

Relationships are a difficult 'game' for any individual, the 'rules' are never clear and may be subjective. From the early stages of 'flirting', to dating and expressing an interest, to being in a committed relationship, living together, engagement, marriage or children, the journey will be full of challenges, questions, compromises and

Case Study

5.1 John

John is 19 and is in love. John's mother suffered an injury whilst she was pregnant with John and, as a result, he has learning disabilities mainly affecting his problem solving, risk taking and logistical comprehension. John met Chloe 3 months ago. John is happy and wants to move in with Chloe. John's mother is adamant this will not happen. She tells John he is far too young to be moving out, 'Love?! You don't know what the word love means' ...

'In my day, you only lived with someone once you were married'. This has led to many family conflicts, as John is angry that she will not take his relationship with Chloe seriously. As John's main carer, you tend to agree with his mother.

How is John's mother using her own values, beliefs and experience to affect John's right to make his own decisions?

How could John's rights be promoted whilst still helping to support and care for him?

What could you do to assist John objectively and neutrally?

decision making. Even successful relationships may develop with periods of reflection and discussion.

For individuals with learning disabilities this could be even more problematic due to:

- A possible need for practical support to embark upon a relationship.
- Possible issues around independence.
- Possible issues if the partner also has a learning disability.
- Possible issues if the partner does not have a learning disability.
- Possible issues regarding assertiveness skills in order to be confident in making decisions relating to relationships and nature of their sexual activity.

9.6 Everyone needs to feel loved

However, it is imperative that care workers help with relationship development as it is key to sexual identity (and this is regardless of any specific sexual behaviour). Sexual identity can be expressed at any stage of a relationship. The actual act of penetration is only one way of expressing sexual identity. Close proximity, hugging, holding hands, body language (e.g. facial expressions and gestures) can all be used to

sexually express oneself without sexual intercourse. For some individuals with learning disabilities, this may be the only way they choose to express themselves sexually, as it may be that they do not feel comfortable with or understand anything further.

Care workers must accept however that, just like any adult, an individual does not have to 'be in' a relationship to express sexuality. And as long as that relationship, at whatever level – casual, monogamous, open, committed – is understood and consensual, individuals with learning disabilities have the same right to choose sexual expression as anyone else.

Evidence activity — LD 307

5.2 Meaningful relationships

Explain why the development of a meaningful relationship can be important to the development of an individual's sexuality.

5.3 Describe different ways and individual can express themselves sexually and how individual preferences can be supported

Individuals can express their sexuality many ways and, as explained earlier, the actual act of sexual penetration is only one element of this. As care workers, if an individual with learning disabilities requests your support in these matters, you need to do so sensitively and within the law. As a care worker, you should not judge, but support individuals to make choices that are right for them.

Clothing and underwear	Individuals with disabilities can dress in ways which they personally deem 'sexy' and this may involve underwear.
Grooming and appearance	The wearing of make-up, body lotions, aftershaves, perfumes etc and spending more time on grooming is part of making us all feel more positive about ourselves.
Masturbation	Private masturbation is a right of every individual and therefore privacy should be provided and encouraged. Practical advice should be provided about the practicalities e.g. timing, place, hygiene etc.
Pornography and sex aids	Legal pornography and sexual aids are a source of sexual expression used by many consenting adults. Care workers should never be judgemental or condemn its private use. If needed, care workers may need to support individuals to purchase items. It is important however, that care workers do stress that pornography is usually not a real representation of reality to help ground expectations and assist with self-esteem. Further, advice should be given about the storage of such items.
Dating	Dating is a normal part of expressing sexuality and can be as casual or intense as the individual would like. As for everyone, particular care may need to be taken regarding safety when dating. The need for a public place, letting others know, etc is vital. This is even more important if internet dating is being used. It may be that support is needed with transport, the making of reservations etc.
Sexual activities between two people	If it becomes apparent than an individual wishes for the relationship to develop further, care workers may need to support them e.g. with contraception, safety, hygiene, location, privacy etc.

Case study

 5.3 Sammi

Sammi is 42 and has met Richard at the Day Centre she attends for individuals with learning disabilities; Sammi also has mild visual impairments. Her carer Mags is shopping with Sammi for a winter coat at a large shopping centre. Over a coffee and a bun in a café when they are done, Sammi informs Mags that she would like to see more of Richard and that he asked her out on a date next week where he has invited her to his house where he will cook a meal, and they will watch a DVD. Sammi tells Mags that she wants to look nice for the date, and that she would like some new clothes and make-up, which make her feel nice, including some new underwear. She would also like to have her hair done.

Although initially Mags is a little shocked ('She hardly knows him?!'), she makes some suggestions:

1) How about they meet next week and Mags can shop with her again when they have more time?

2) In that time, Sammi can think about what she would like to wear.

3) In that time, Mags can gather her thoughts, remember her training, speak to her supervisor and book an appointment at the hairdressers.

4) Mags will also drop some sample items and some up to date magazines and catalogues into the Day Centre tomorrow when she visits another individual for Sammi to feel and see.

5) Mags is also planning to speak to Sammi's key worker about Sammi's knowledge of sexual expression, health, sexual abuse.

Sammi is very excited about next week. Mags is pleased that she will be able to deal with it better next week.

- How has Mags supported Sammi here to express her sexuality?

- How did she not judge Sammi?

- How is Mags ensuring Sammi is at reduced risk of harm?

Evidence activity LD 307

5.3 Expressing sexuality

Describe different ways an individual can express themselves sexually and how individual preferences can be supported. You may want to consider some of the issues Sammi expressed needing support with.

5.4 Explain how to support an individual to keep safe sexually, to minimise vulnerability and to avoid instances of abusive experiences

When working with individuals and providing information and opportunities for healthy sexuality, it is vital that at all times individuals are kept safe, are not sexually vulnerable and that abusive experiences are avoided at all cost.

Key terms

Vulnerable is being less able to take care of oneself or unable to protect oneself against significant harm or exploitation.

Sexual abuse can come in many forms and is not only rape. Inappropriate touching, kissing, holding, the showing of sexual images or films, viewing a person undressed or the exposure of their flesh, sexual harassment, sexual comments or sexual teasing are all forms of sexual abuse.

Unfortunately those with learning disabilities are more vulnerable to abuse because:

1. individuals may have less power
2. there may be increased need for personal care
3. there may be isolation from friends and family
4. individuals may be less able to physically defend themselves
5. there may be more language, speech or vocabulary barriers and impaired or limited cognitive abilities

6. there may have been less abuse prevention education
7. residing or attending care environments which may have poor protection and screening etc.

Mencap reports 1400 new cases of sex abuse against people with a learning disability per year in the UK, only 6% of which reach court and only 1% of these result in a conviction. More worrying is that most research into sexual abuse of those with learning disabilities concludes that most are sexually abused by those they know and trust.

Therefore at all times when supporting individuals staff should not break the law, but should protect individuals from any unreasonable risks. The balance between supporting an individual's rights with regards to sexual development, to the relationship becoming exploitative, degrading or even abusive is a delicate one. If in doubt carers should either speak to their supervisors or seek legal advice. Further, issues as regards confidentiality should also be dealt with sensitively. Clearly individuals with disabilities have rights to a private life, but this needs to be balanced with the need for good recordkeeping and documentation, for example should you record the use of soft pornography? Again, if this is a difficult decision, it may be best to seek legal clarification or speak to your supervisor.

A fundamental issue regarding sexual activity is consent, and this is a problematic area for every individual. However for people with learning disabilities, it is even more so due to their mental capacity to give consent.

Brown and Turk (1992) suggest that if a person is unable to think about or 'through' sexual behaviour in any of the following ways they are not in a position to consent to sexual activity. They highlight:

- making sense of what has been done to them and construing the sequence of behaviour as a sexual act;
- appreciating an inappropriateness of behaviour, for example, a woman with learning disabilities might not be told that sexual acts between fathers and daughters are not normal;
- appreciating the value accorded to a sexual act, for example, that having sex for a cigarette is not a fair deal;
- anticipating the possible consequences of sexual acts, such as pregnancy or sexually transmitted disease.

9.7 Protecting the individual is paramount

However, there may be times when even if consent has been given, there may still be issues that need to be considered and these usually relate to power and inequality. Cambridgeshire County Council in their document, *Adults with a Learning Disability - Interpersonal Relationships and Sexual Development'* state four reasons why this may be the case:

- the presence of a parental or familiar relationship between the person involved: this may of course involve in some circumstances the offence of incest
- the presence of a custodial or care-taking relationship between the persons involved
- the use of a weapon, threat or injury, or the use of force by the first person
- the presence of a power imbalance between them, which precludes consent by the weaker person.

The law relating to the sexual behaviour of people with a learning disability is complex. Some laws are outdated and do not represent society's more modern views, some laws have been subject to ad hoc amendments and some are not equal to both sexes (e.g. homosexuality laws for men, but not women) and therefore guidance and support for senior staff and legal advisors is advised.

Some simple steps which could be taken are:

- Organisational policies such as privacy, personal care and so on giving clear procedures to be followed.
- Full checks on all staff, whether direct carers or not (e.g. cleaners, porters, gardeners).
- Ongoing, high quality training for staff.
- High quality age and ability appropriate sexual protection education for individuals with learning disabilities.
- A clear whistleblowing policy to help highlight concerns.
- Clear guidelines for action to take in the event of suspicions or claims of sexual abuse.
- Excellent recordkeeping documenting allevents.

Evidence activity LD 307

 Keeping safe

Explain how to support an individual to keep safe sexually, to minimise sexual vulnerability, and to avoid instances of abusive experiences. You may want to use some of the measures highlighted above, but try to explain specifically how they will keep individuals safe from abuse.

Assessment Summary for Unit LD 307

To achieve the unit, your assessor will require you to:

Learning outcomes	Assessment criteria
1 Understand the development of human sexuality	**1.1** Define the terms: *sexuality, sexual health, sexual orientation, and sexual expression* See Evidence activity 1.1, p. 184.
	1.2 Explain main sexual development milestones throughout an individual's lifespan See Evidence activity 1.2, p. 185.
2 Understand how the sexual development of individuals with a learning disability can differ	**2.1** Describe how genetic factors can influence the sexual development, sexual expression and sexual health of an individual with a learning disability See Evidence activity 2.1, p. 186.
	2.2 Describe how socio-cultural factors and religious beliefs can influence an individual's sexual development See Time to reflect 2.2, p. 186 and Evidence activity 2.2, p. 187.
	2.3 Explain how mental capacity can influence sexual development, sexual experiences, sexual expression and sexual health See Evidence activity 2.3, p. 188.
3 Understand the issues of sexual health and how these can be supported	**3.1** Explain the key features of sexual health and well-being and how this relates to an individual's overall health and well-being See Evidence activity 3.1, p. 188.
	3.2 Identify sexual health issues that differently affect men and women See Evidence activity 3.2, p. 189.
	3.3 Explain how sexual health issues can be supported within plans for healthcare See Evidence activity 3.3, p. 190.
	3.4 Identify local services that exist to support sexual health for individuals See Evidence activity 3.4, p. 191.
4 Understand relevant legislation influencing the support of sexuality and sexual health for individuals with learning disabilities	**4.1** Explain key parts of relevant legislation relating to sexuality and sexual health for individuals and how this influences practice See Evidence activity 4.1, p. 192.

5 Know how to support the sexual expression of an individual with a learning disability	**5.1**	Explain how own values, belief systems and experiences may impact on support for individuals with learning disabilities See Case study 5.1 and Evidence activity 5.1, p. 193.
	5.2	Explain why the development of a meaningful relationship can be important to the development of an individual's sexuality See Evidence activity 5.2, p. 194.
	5.3	Describe different ways an individual can express themselves sexually and how individual preferences can be supported See Case study 5.3, p. 195 and Evidence activity 5.3, p. 196.
	5.4	Explain how to support an individual to keep safe sexually, to minimise sexual vulnerability, and to avoid instances of abusive experiences See Evidence activity 5.4, p. 197.

Further resources

Brook Advisory	**www.brook.org.uk/index.php**
Cambridgeshire County Council	**www.cambridgeshire.gov.uk/NR/rdonlyres/636B0452-E42B-4DFD-A72A-F111CB3D5651/0/disability51.pdf**
Directgov	**http://www.direct.gov.uk/en/Governmentcitizens andrights/Mentalcapacityandthelaw/Makingdecisions forsomeoneelse/DG_195206**
Equality and Human Rights Commission	**www.equalityhumanrights.com**
FPA	**www.fpa.org.uk/**
Health Action Planning and Health Facilitation for people with learning disabilities: good practice guidance 2008	**www.doh.gov.uk**
Mencap. (2002). *New bill to challenge sex abuse*. Retrieved December, 2002, from	**www.mencap.org.uk/html/news/sex_abuse_queens_ speech.htm**
NHS (for local services)	**www.nhs.uk/servicedirectories/Pages/Service Search.aspx**
NHS (for information)	**www.nhs.uk/Livewell/Sexualhealthtopics/Pages/ Sexual-health-hub.aspx**
Royal College of Nursing document	**www.rcn.org.uk/__data/assets/pdf_file/0004/184585/ 000965.pdf**

Brown, H & Turk, V. (1992) Defining sexual abuse as it affects adults with learning disabilities. Mental Handicap

Gunn, M. J. (1991 3rd Ed) Sex and the Law: Brief Guide for Staff Working with People with Learning Difficulties (Education & Training Resources) Family Planning Association;

'It Could Never Happen Here': ARC and NAPSAC 1993

10

Young people with a disability and the transition to adulthood

Unit LD 311K Principles of supporting young people with a disability to make the transition into adulthood
Unit LD 311C Support young people with a disability to make the transition into adulthood

What are you finding out?

Any teenager moving into adulthood has major adjustments they must make; from the changes in their bodies to new experiences of responsibility. These are changes that cause confusion and frustration. People with disabilities also have the transition from child to adult services to cope with. If someone with disabilities has been used to a key worker for a period of time, this person will change and trust needs to be built from scratch. As an adult you need to take responsibility for your actions, and we will explore the reasoning behind judgements and consequences with legislation and national practice guidelines. We will look at the resources and support available to ensure equality for persons with a disability especially around employment. We will identify possible risks and how to resolve these with the use of person-centred tools. This will give clear guidelines for the key person involved in supporting individuals with a disability.

The reading and activities in this chapter will help you to:

- Understand the steps and stages of moving from childhood into adulthood
- Understand how having a disability may affect the process of moving from childhood into adulthood

- Know the options for supporting a young person who has a disability to make the transition to adulthood
- Understand how to support a young person with a disability through a successful transition
- Understand the importance of supporting a young person and their family to reflect on the transition.

Key terms

Transition means change, movement.

10.1 Moving into adulthood

LO1 Understand the steps and stages of moving from childhood into adulthood

1.1 **Identify the range of physical, social and emotional changes which occur for young people as they move into adulthood**

Puberty is a time when physical, social and emotional changes occur. These are normal changes and prepare us to become adults. Physical changes for females involve breasts growing and periods starting. Males develop increased body hair and their voice deepens and both sexes experience an awareness of their sexuality. Most youngsters tend to get acne just when they are becoming more aware of their physical appearance. Emotions are heightened just as the body develops and many teenagers become uncomfortable with these changes.

Along with the physical changes that are occurring are emotional changes. Extreme behaviours are witnessed, moving from happiness to sadness in minutes. Hormones are released at irregular times increasing the frustration and confusion for the individual. Teenagers are not classed as adults yet are no longer children. They are moving into a new time of life with no guidelines.

Five stages of puberty were identified by child development expert Professor James Tanner and can be explored at:

> http://embarrassingbodieskids.channel4.com/
> men-in-white-coats/puberty/symptoms

Looking at these stages it is easy to identify with some of the emotional turmoil that teenagers experience.

The psychologist Piaget described emotional development from the age of 7 years to 11 years as the period of 'concrete thinking', the period when thoughts and beliefs are very focused on the object not the abstract.

While it is interesting to look at theories identified with development, it is very important to see these in the context of the society we live in, different cultures and family units. Most of these theories and concepts were developed some time ago in a different social environment. We need to explore the limited choices available for the younger person in today's world, including the lack of employment and career choices, the state of the economy and the reduced services available for the young person, the lack of community settings and the reality of dispersed families.

■ Research and investigate

1.1 Developmental stages

Identify the five stages of Tanner's development, the four stages of Piaget's cognitive development and the eight stages of Erickson's psychosocial stages.

	Tanner	Piaget	Erikson

1.2 Explain the changes faced by young people as they move from childhood into adulthood in relation to their freedoms, rights and responsibilities

As a child moves into adulthood they are expected to behave in a mature manner, to take responsibility for their actions and become a part of the social economy. These changes do not happen overnight and as every person is an individual development occurs at different times. As a society we identify the times we expect the individual to reach certain milestones. In general we expect the individual to have developed into an adult by the age of 18. Different cultures identify adulthood at different ages, for example Jewish families celebrate their children's coming of age when they are 13.

We agree that part of the process of becoming an adult involves the need to be independent. As an adult you need to make your own choices and take risks. This requires being responsible for your own actions. Whilst adolescents are expected to become self-sufficient they are also experiencing a variety of physical changes and dealing with surges of emotions and feelings. They are trying to identify where they belong in the world, their individual role. In their new world, they are starting to explore areas such as intimacy, developing new relationships, and possibly experimenting with drugs and alcohol.

Parents will probably try to allow them greater freedom and relax boundaries. Making decisions for yourself incurs risk and this requires the development of skills throughout childhood that allow us to contemplate and explore risk.

10.2 As children we have few responsibilities

1.3 Explain how culture may impact on the process of moving from childhood into adulthood

As previously discussed, different cultures have different ideas about age in relation to adulthood. We need to explore these differences to ensure we address individual cultures.

In English culture the legal age for marriage is 16 years old whilst the age for drinking and voting is 18 years of age. The age of consent used to be 13 years but this has been increased due to changes in attitude in our culture. Young people are now sexually active at a younger age while adult maturity appears more apparent at the age of about 18 years.

In America the legal age that you can consume alcohol is 21 years whilst in some states alcohol is banned. The age for sexual consent and marriage is 16 years except in one state, Texas, where the legal age to consent to marriage is 14 years old. The various ages of legal sexual consent around the world are listed below:

* Argentina – 15
* Bahamas – 16
* Canada – 14
* Colombia – male 14, female 12
* India – 18
* Indonesia – male 19, female 16
* Hungary – 14
* Peru – male 14, female 12
* Tunisia – 20
* UK – 16
* US – federal age 16

Time to reflect

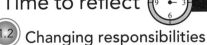

1.2 Changing responsibilities

Recall your own childhood and think about the changes that you underwent as an adolescent. Identify the changes in freedoms and the rights and responsibilities that went with this. Write about how you dealt with these changes, what went well and what did not.

The legal age for working is also set at different ages according to culture and country. In Bangladesh the legal age to work is 12 years old, in the UK 16 years, whilst in America the legal age is 18.

Becoming legally responsible for your actions and being able to be prosecuted is another age that varies from country to country, with a range of ages between 7 and 16 years.

Evidence activity

 1.3 Legal ages

Within your workplace identify policies and procedures relating to the transition for young persons and list areas that address the cultural issues that accompany these.

1.4 Explain theories about change and how this can affect a young person with a disability

Theorists and psychologists have spent years exploring the physical and mental changes that occur during this transitional age. Most main theories concur that there are several stages in the transition period.

- Erickson's theory relates to eight cycles in life, the first being birth to 18 months, classed as the ego development outcome. It explores the theory of trust development. If the infant is responded to effectively with touch and visual contact the foundation for trust and confidence is developed.

- The second stage is described as the time between 18 months and 3 years when we develop autonomy and explore our world. If negative responses are given when learning a new task, Erickson believed this would lead to self-doubt and a lack of self-esteem.

- The next stage is the play age from 3 to 5 years. This is where the child imitates adults and uses their imagination in play. If this period is not successful or encouraged, Erikson believed that the infant may become frustrated and display guilt.

- The stage between 6 and 12 years is the time of school. It encompasses a growing awareness of the outside world, peer pressure and changing views on the importance of parents. During this period new skills are encouraged and developed. This is a period where self-esteem will be highlighted or diminished and is also the beginning of social inclusion.

- Adolescence is classed as 12 to 18 years old. Erickson believed that this stage is more influenced by what is done to us, including the acceptance of peers and finding a role or purpose in life. This is a time of exploration. For any adolescent this is a testing time as it involves trying to find your own identity, creating your own boundaries and becoming responsible for your own actions.

- Stage six of Erickson's theory is from the age of 18 to 35 years, and is classed as young adult. This period is the time of developing relationships and planning a family. If we are not successful in developing these types of relationship, isolation will occur.

- The seventh stage of development according to Erickson is from the age of 35 years up to 65 years and is the time we choose to be in charge, active and settled within relationships.

- The final stage is from the period of 65 years to death: the wisdom years. This is a time for reflection, and frequently fear of our final days.

Time to reflect

 1.4 Stages of transition

Think of a time in your work setting when you have had to organise changes for an individual. Think of the process of change that was introduced, how this went and what you could have done differently. List the development stage of transition according to Erickson.

LO2 Understand how having a disability may affect the process of moving from childhood into adulthood

 Explain, giving examples, the potential effects of the transition process on young people with disabilities and their families

The transition from childhood to adulthood involves many changes that are difficult for any person, and when you have a disability these changes carry more intensity. For persons with disabilities, helping them understand the physical and emotional changes in order to prepare them and plan is very difficult, because all these changes are highly individual in terms of timings and emotion. Frustration and fear can be heightened and logical thinking tested. During the transition to adulthood many changes occur that require the individual to make choices and take risks. For a person with a disability these risks can be greater in terms of nature and intensity.

Any changes in routine can increase the anxieties of the individual, and this is why the planning and development of skills is generally achieved by small repetitive steps. As the transition is largely out of the carer's control, they need to spend time preparing the individual without knowing exactly when information will be necessary.

Parents of teenagers have extreme difficulties coping with the behaviour of a teenager who tests their boundaries and expresses their frustrations. For a parent of a young person with disabilities, their experience of parenthood has probably always been focused on protecting and shielding the individual from the risks of life. Sometimes parents of children with a disability have invested time and energy keeping their child away from the outside world due to anxieties about their abilities or the discrimination of others.

Case study

 Robert

Robert is 15 years of age and has cerebral palsy. He lives with his mother and 8 year old sister. They live in town and Robert goes to a special school that can manage his needs. He has a personal carer who assists him with daily tasks and supports him whilst at school. Robert attends school four days a week for five hours a day. At the school he has friends but has limited contact with anyone outside of school. Robert is going through puberty. His mother and support worker are trying to plan for the transition that Robert will go through to become an adult.

Write out the changes they will need to plan for and any difficulties this may cause.

Identify the effects of these changes on Robert's sister and mother.

10.3 Transition to adulthood can be a difficult time

2.2 **Identify challenges young people with a disability might have in understanding and coping with change**

When looking at the transition process, one of the areas we may need to explore is housing. This may be the first time an individual has lived on their own and they may require support with finding appropriate accommodation and managing that accommodation. Health is another factor they will need to manage and they need to recognise physical changes in themselves and understand the correct actions to follow. Employment and education are other areas that can be extremely difficult, and understanding the Disability Discrimination Act 1995 is essential. The individual needs to become a citizen and feel a part of this society. They may need practical help and support with necessities such as budgeting. Another area of transition is that of forming different types of relationships, including sexual, friends and support/carer relationships. Looking at all these changes, it is easy to see why the planning of this transition needs to be started by 13/14 years of age. If they are in school the child will already have Special Educational Needs [SEN] identified, which will assist the planning and support the transitional process.

Evidence activity

2.2 Transitional

Complete the table below by listing transitional changes and the possible difficulties these may incur.

Changes	Difficulties

2.3 **Outline the methods that can be used to support a young person with a disability to cope with change**

Support for people with disabilities has become available after many years of campaigning. Disabilities legislation has been passed to ensure fair access for all. This ensures rights and benefits are available so there is a clear package of care and support for the most vulnerable. The commencement of support begins with the SEN in schools to start planning the transitional period. This includes ensuring all relevant support services are involved, and should also include an advocate for the individual and family.

Financial support can be obtained in the form of personal budgets and housing benefits. Healthcare support is available from child services and adult services. Employment rights and support comes in the form of government sources such as the job centre and Connexions. Leisure is another important factor; help with travelling costs and leisure activities can be sought via the local authority. Leisure is an important aspect in becoming an active citizen who builds relationships. Housing support can be obtained from the community care assessment. There are also resources and support available from voluntary and charitable organisations.

We have outlined the physical resources available to the individual and their families. We now need to look from the carer and / or support worker's point of view.

Time to reflect

2.3 Using resources

Write about a time you assisted in the transition process for a person with disabilities. Identify what resources you used, what individual support you gave and what went well. Identify what you would do differently next time. Finish by explaining your feelings and perceptions during this process.

	What's working	What's not working
The person		
Family		
Staff		
What needs to happen next to build on what's working and change what's not working?		

10.4 What's working and what's not. Reproduced by permission of Helen Sanderson Associates.

2.4 Explain how legislation and local and national practice guidelines affect the planning of the transition for a young person with a disability from childhood into adulthood

We now need to look at current legislation and good practice guidelines. We have already identified some legislation: the Disability Discrimination Act 1995. This identifies the need for everyone to be treated on an equal basis and ensures that the person with disabilities receives the same opportunities as anyone else. This legislation was replaced in 2010 by the Disability and Equality Act. The main changes were the identification and clarity of the term disabled and reinforcement of the need to provide inclusion for the disabled person.

The SEN comes from the Education Act 1996, and guides local authorities in providing care for those with disabilities, including the protocol for transition into adulthood.

The government set up Aiming High for Disabled Children in May 2007, which led to the National Transition Support Team which ran until March 2011. This scheme identified the need for national support such as local authorities, named advisors and experts and Primary Care Trust [PCTs]. It also highlighted the need for support at a local level, which consisted of direct grants and named advisors.

http://www.transitionsupportprogramme.org.uk/

Research and investigate

2.4 Legislation and guidelines

Identify policies and procedures in your workplace and link them to relevant national and local guidelines.

2.5 Describe the legislation that affects the right of a young person with a disability to make decisions about their life

All children making the transition into adulthood need to take ownership and responsibility for their own decisions. Persons with disabilities can find this process very difficult, due to their level of understanding. To safeguard these individuals and to ensure their rights have been heard, legislation must be used. Any person, with or without a disability, can use the services of an advocate. An advocate is a person that will speak for you and advise you independently of your rights. This is useful for any person who has difficulties in expressing their views.

The Equality Act 2010 empowers individuals to the same rights and choices without discrimination.

Persons with a disability need to clearly identify their wishes and this is done through a period of planning. Every person involved in the planning has a legal duty to enable those wishes to be explored and if practical to be put into practice. Voluntary organisations and charities can assist in empowering the individual's choices. Local authorities have a duty of care to provide support for the individual to make their choices known and have them adhered to. In certain cases when the individual is unable to give informed consent, the Mental Capacity Act may be used. The Mental Capacity Act 2005 is legislation to protect informed consent. Informed consent can only be given if the individual understands the information given and understands the consequences of their actions. For those individuals who do not have capacity of understanding, the Mental Capacity Act 2005 is there to ensure support in making those decisions.

LO3 Know the options for supporting a young person who has a disability to make the transition into adulthood

(3.1) Explain how a young person with a disability can have equal opportunities to make life choices as a young person without disability

Disabilities in today's society should not put any restrictions on an individual's involvement with the planning or process of available opportunities. We have identified laws and legislation to ensure the individual has the same rights and responsibilities as others. If we did not ensure this the individual would be restricted in having their human rights addressed and could become isolated from society.

A young person with disabilities has access to healthcare and to support services from local authorities. They also have access to the government's job centre and all its resources. The individual has the right to direct payments, thus allowing them to manage their care independently. With direct payments, the individual becomes an employer.

If the young person wishes to leave home and live independently, financial support is available via disabilities facility grants for any adaptations that may be needed to living accommodation. There is also an independent living fund to assist with any extra support required to live independently and general benefits for housing, employment and education. With this financial support making choices is more achievable. Support groups are set up locally to enable the individual to gain understanding from others.

(3.2) Explain how to support a young person with a disability to explore the options available in relation to employment or continued education and development

With the economy undergoing a difficult time at present and the knock on effects this has on employment, the need for support in this area is paramount. Legislation ensures that persons with disabilities cannot be discriminated against. Some young people with disabilities may wish to explore further education and support for this can be found from education authorities, Connexions and through their social services network. Regarding employment, the local job centre has a duty to assist in finding employment for all. Apprenticeships are also an alternative way to get into employment, learning a skill whilst working. For a person with disabilities there are certain considerations that have to be made. They need encouragement to apply for positions they can fulfil. As the support worker you need to ensure they are able to carry out the tasks involved in the jobs they are applying for. Applying for a job requires the ability to demonstrate the skills they can bring to the role. Support may be needed to write a curriculum vitae [CV]. Practising interview skills may be required and there is the need to ensure that the job is in a location that will allow the individual to get there easily on a daily basis.

Case study

(3.2) Tracy

Tracey is 16 years old. She wants to leave education and get a job. Tracey has learning difficulties and wishes to work in a shop. She lives a mile outside of town but has a local shop nearby. Tracey has limited concentration and is not confident working with money, but feels able to stack shelves and tidy up. Tracey went to her local shop and asked if they would give her a job. They turned her down stating they have no work at present. Two weeks later a sign went up in the shop window asking for part time help with stock work.

- Write about what you could do to support Tracey to get this job and list the organisations you could use to support Tracey.

- Write what you would do if you identified that the owners had discriminated against Tracey regarding the job.

10.5 We need to support the young person to find a job

(3.3) Explain how personal budgets can be used with young people in transition

With changes in legislation and culture, the idea that the person receiving the care should have more direct control over their finances has become very popular. Personal budgets are set once a full assessment of needs has been undertaken. With personal budgets the individual is given sufficient monies to cover their expenses including care needs. The person can then decide if they wish to pay an individual directly for their care or commission the local services to deliver it. If they decide to pay for their care themselves with direct payments, they effectively become an employer with the responsibilities this entails. For some people with disabilities this can be very daunting and this is why personal budgets were implemented. With this form of payment the person is not directly employing another individual but is paying for services through a third party. The money paid as a personal budget ensures the individual lives at a recommended level and is able to afford food, household bills, and care and leisure activities. Managing the money requires clear budgeting skills that are assessed prior to budget being allocated. This may be the first time the young person has ever been involved in any form of money control and they will need the skills to manage this effectively.

Time to reflect

(3.3) Budget skills

Identify a time you assisted a young person with their personal budget. Describe the process of the assessment for personal budgets and how you helped the individual gain the skills of budgeting. Explain how this improved life for the individual, what went well with this process, what could have gone better and what you learnt from this experience.

LO4 Be able to support a young person with disability through transition into adulthood

4.1 **Explain the factors to consider, and types of support that a young person with a disability may need before, during and after the transition process**

We have already discussed the importance of planning as a young person begins their transition from childhood to adulthood. The government through the Special Educational Needs Coordinator [SENCO] have recognised the importance of taking steps towards this from the age of 13 to 14.

This is a very young age and ideas and plans may change several times before being actioned. Involving the right people from the start is critical for the success of this transition.

All children going through this transition will express anxiety. For persons with a disability this is heightened. Support should start with Child and Mental Health Services [CAHMS] and special educational needs [SEN]. These two services should have been involved in the individual's care for some time. Meeting and involving others in the planning for this transition is crucial. The most important factor that has been found to make the transition successful is the involvement of the parent. As with all care planning the individual should be at the centre of the process. From the outset of planning the key people involved in the care will be identified and agreed with the individual.

With any change, no matter how well planned, anxieties and changes will occur that may not have been anticipated. With changes in behaviour and physical development, unexpected events will occur. Having a basic plan allows us to help guide and support the young person. But because we are dealing with individuals we must ensure flexibility in our plans. As the support worker for the young person we may notice changes more frequently. It is our role to ensure we support the individual or are able to guide them to the most appropriate resources and support mechanisms.

The art of being an effective supporter is to understand the individual's choices and to be aware of the resources available to them. You must also be aware of your own limitations and know where to get any additional support required.

4.2 **LD 311C** **Support a young person to explore options for their future**

Young people may have many or no preconceived ideas for the future. Due to limited experiences of the adult world, the choices they make may not be practical or achievable. To reduce the negative impact of this and to ensure achievable goals the young person may need some help planning or exploring their options for the future. Although some choices or options may not be viable all choices should be explored before being discarded. The transition to adulthood is the time that exploring the risks and consequences of actions begins. Some choices may take time to achieve and this may be frustrating for the individual. Sometimes you may need to enlist help and resources from others and this may also create delays in the process and increase frustrations. Young people without disabilities do not have the same type of support and are encouraged to make these choices and deal with the consequences by themselves or with some support from family members. The most effective way to support a young person with disabilities with this transition and making choices is to implement person-centred planning. A useful tool during this process is to identify the individual's goals and dreams and work with the person to make these possible whilst accounting for any risks or restricting factors.

Case study

(4.2) LD 311C **Paul**

Paul has a physical disability and a history of epilepsy. He is now 20 years of age and wishes to leave supported living and move into a flat on his own. He has anxieties about this step but feels that in order to live a full and independent life he must make this change. Paul has no family members and limited relationships with people outside of his shared environment. He works part time in an office in the library but is seen as isolated and lacks some social skills.

As his support worker identify his possible goals and the small steps that would be needed to enable him to achieve these goals. Identify the support you would need to supply to help him achieve his goals.

(4.3) LD 311C **Use person-centred thinking to identify with the young person their needs and aspirations**

(4.2) LD 311k **Explain how person-centred transition reviews and person-centred thinking can be used as part of this planning process**

Person-centred thinking should be used in all our actions with the young person during their transition into adulthood. One tool of person-centred thinking is 'PATH': 'planning alternative tomorrows with hope'. Through this process importance is placed on the individual identifying their choices whilst the role of the carer is to enlist the appropriate help to achieve the individual's choices. PATH has eight steps: the first is to identify the long and short term goals; the second step is to identify what small steps can be made now to demonstrate movement towards the end goal. The third step identifies where they are now in relation to their final goal. The fourth step is to enlist all the people needed to achieve the goal: family, friends and so on. The fifth step identifies the need to keep the group together and to clarify responsibilities. The sixth step is making the full action plan to achieve these goals. The seventh step is the long term changes that need to be implemented to achieve those long term goals. The final step is the initial small steps to achieve the long term goal.

Once any plan is put into action the importance of review is paramount to ensure the goal is still in focus and discover any changes that need to be made. With the person-centred process there is the tool which identifies what is working and what is not, and the citizen review which clarifies the six areas for citizenship. Good practice says that six-month reviews should be booked when you commence the planning.

Evidence activity LD 311C

 (4.3) **Planning the future**

Draw a PATH for your own goals and ambitions.

Time to reflect

 (4.2) LD 311k **Transition reviews**

Identify a time within your work setting when you were involved in a transition review and planning session using person centred thinking. Describe what went well, what did not go so well and what you would do differently next time.

4.3 LD 311k Explain the difference in approaches to planning between children's and adult's support services

Children with learning disabilities are looked after by the children's section of social services. Social services have a duty to complete an assessment of the child's needs under the framework for the assessment for children in need and their families (Department of Health, 2000). This assessment relates to the Children's Act 1989. Following this assessment support and benefits can be made available and some of these are: short respite breaks, holiday play schemes and care at home. At school extra support will be given for learning and pastoral care. The involvement of professionals such as paediatricians, physiotherapists and so on will be necessary. Children and mental health services (CAMHS) coordinate the care for children. Young persons and adults are transferred to the adult services. In child care you have a consultant specialist, a paediatrician who will oversee all your health needs. In adult care you may see several different consultants. It is important to have a health assessment during the transition planning process to ensure all health needs will be met when the individual is transferred into adult services and will be required to apply for continuing care funds. Adult social services require an assessment of needs to identify the resources required. Some of the benefits that may be received are day centre care, a physiotherapist assessment to identify aids that may assist with daily living and support for transport.

The assessment for adult services focuses on community care whilst that for children is on education and ensuring all professionals are involved. Adult services have a variety of departments involved in delivering the care in the community.

▌Research and investigate

4.3 LD 311k Policies on transition

Identify in your own workplace the policies and procedures relating to transition. Research the differences between the children's/adult section.

4.4 LD 311C Use person-centred thinking to develop with the young person a plan to support them through transition

Person-centred thinking focuses on individual support and empowering the individual. Several tools and approaches are available. One of the most important factors when supporting the transition period is to identify the support the individual already has in place. Person-centred thinking identifies the important people in the individual's life. With this tool you can also identify the skills needed to help the individual achieve their goals.

Evidence activity

4.4 LD 311C Important people

Draw a relationship circle, identifying your close friends and people involved in your life. This process gives a picture of where the person is now and the support available to them.

4.5 LD 311C Involve families in the transition process according to the wishes of the young person

4.4 LD 311k Describe how to involve families in the transition process

We have discussed how it is important to plan the transition process at an early stage. We have also identified that parents have difficulties when any child begins the process of leaving and becoming independent. With individuals who have disabilities this transition increases anxieties. As parents/

family members they have actively been involved in the individual's care, ensuring they are protected from the outside world, as carers they have ensured all their needs have been met and they cannot suddenly switch this mindset off. Therefore it is imperative they are involved from the beginning of the transition period at the age of 13 to 14 years. With person-centred thinking we have identified the role of family, friends and carers in the planning process. The involvement of families in the process relies on the individual's wishes to include them in the process. This is their transition planning.

If families are involved in the process they can assist in many ways. They know the individual, their likes and dislikes and if involved they can help with tasks such as transport, which enables the parent/family member to feel they still have a role in their child's life.

Case study

 **LD 311k** **Janet**

Janet is 14 years old and has learning difficulties. Her mother Mary has managed her care and has been very active in supporting her choices whilst trying to protect her. Mary has never had a holiday as she has been concerned about leaving Janet in someone else's care. Mary's husband left her when Janet was born and Mary has invested all her energy into Janet's needs.

The SEN has organised a planning meeting for Janet and has invited Mary. Mary is anxious and feels this meeting is inappropriate because she believes Janet cannot leave home and she does not want to leave her.

How would you engage Mary and support her through this process?

What support mechanisms are available for Mary?

Evidence activity

4.5 Different viewpoints

In the case study above we looked at the situation from the mother's viewpoint. We need to look at the situation from Janet's perspective too. Write down how you would ensure Janet's choice to have or not to have her mother involved, and the process of planning this via person-centred thinking.

 LD 311k  **LD 311C**

Explain the role of key agencies and professionals likely to be involved in the transition process

The role of professionals and key agencies within this period is a complex one as we need to ensure communication and understanding between all agencies. Part of the transition process is to hand over from child services to adult services. As previously discussed adult services do not have one consultant in charge as with paediatric services. The needs of the adult individual are more complex and the individual has more choices and involvement. There is a need to ensure advocacy for the young person and coordination of their care throughout this transitional process. Good practice guidelines identify the need to have a care coordinator established to ensure all agencies involved communicate the needs of the individual. Resources that have been identified as useful include Connexions, youth programmes and charitable societies such as Mencap. To give effective support everyone needs to be informed of the process.

Research and investigate

 LD 311k LD 311C

The pathway for transitional care

Visit www.rcn.org.co.uk and read their adolescent transition guide. On page 21 they have a flow chart of the clinical pathway for transition. Using this as a model, devise a flow chart demonstrating your workplace's pathway for transitional care.

4.6 LD 311C **Identify ways to provide resources to meet needs**

4.7 LD 311k **Compare different methods of support to use with young people with disabilities who have varying abilities**

We have discussed the process of transition; within this section we are going to look at the types of resources available to facilitate this process and the different types/methods of support.

We know about the medical resources and child care services, CAMHS and the network of resources, educational psychologist, specialist doctors, physiotherapists and occupational therapists. All these people are part of the medical resource available and are accessible during this process. We also have social services that can assist with social needs and the local authority can help with resources such as housing. The other resources available are young person's advocacy services, Connexions for advice and guidance and careers services.

The type of disability dictates the services we may need; deaf persons, for example, may need the assistance of the audiology department or a translator.

Time to reflect

 LD 311C LD 311k

Arranging support

Identify a time when you arranged support for a young person during the transition process, what resources did you obtain and where from? How effective were these resources, what went well and what did not go so well? What you would do differently next time and what other resources could you have tried?

4.6 LD 311k 4.8 LD 311C

Outline possible areas of tension and conflict that may arise during the transition into adulthood

We have explored tensions from the onset of planning and transfer from child services to adult services. We have also looked at the need to engage families/carers and explored available resources. We can identify potential conflicts and tensions and the first way to reduce these is to have a good plan with good communication channels for all involved. Everyone involved should understand the process, and everyone should have an outline of their responsibilities and roles. Person-centred planning is paramount to identify potential tensions and conflicts before they arise. We have all had the experience of a carer/parent who does not want to let go and feels the goals being implemented are unrealistic. There may also be restrictions due to resource issues.

Research and investigate

 LD 311k LD 311C

Joseph Rowntree Foundation

Read the Joseph Rowntree Foundation report: Young people's transition report, and list some of the conflicts and tensions identified.

LO5 Be able to support a young person to reflect on the transition

5.1 **LD 311C** **Use person-centred approaches with the young person to review their transition plan and ensure it reflects their needs**

5.1 **LD 311k** **Explain why it is important to reflect on the transition with the young person and their family**

Person-centred approaches are the only effective tools to ensure the process reflects the young person's wishes and hopes. Person-centred planning focuses on the individual, their goals and ambitions, not on other people's views or beliefs regarding the individual's abilities. Part of this process is reflection. This is covered by the 'what's working what's not working' model. The importance of this part of the assessment is that it allows the individual to reassess whether what they want is still the same. This is important as we all can change our minds. As plans progress the outcomes may not be as we envisaged. This reflection needs to be communicated to all involved in the process to ensure the plan can be achieved. By reflecting with the young person, they can also see how far they have come with their individual plan and identify any difficulties still to come. Sanderson suggests five questions to focus this reflection:

1. What have we tried?
2. What have we learned?
3. What are we pleased about?
4. What are we concerned about?
5. Given what we know now, what is next?

Time to reflect

5.1 Identifying goals

Identify your goals and reflect on them using the questions above. How do you think you have done, what is good, how did the process make you feel about your own goals and achievements? Was this useful? Would it be useful for the people you care for?

5.2 **LD 311C** **Support a young person to record the transition and what has happened in their life in order to plan for the future**

5.2 **LD 311k** **Explain the importance of recording the process of transition**

The tools of person-centred thinking encourage recording of the plan and reviews. The importance of recording these events is to ensure clear communication, to identify what is working and what is not and to clarify who is responsible for what action. For the individual, the recording process makes this final and allows them to clarify how far they have come, the achievements they have made and the goals they still have to reach. These records can be in any format that enables the individual to understand what is meant by the record.

Anyone assisting with delivery of care has a legal duty to record activities. This requires knowledge of the legislation relating to recordkeeping. The format that this recordkeeping takes depends on the procedures relating to your workplace.

Research and investigate

5.2 **LD 311C** Planning for the future

Find the appropriate tool for recording an individual's development and life plan in your workplace. Write up a record for your own development.

Research and investigate

5.2 **LD 311k** Recording the transition

Find and review the policies and procedures in your workplace. From these policies and procedures explain the importance of recording the transition process.

Assessment Summary for Unit LD 311C

To achieve the unit, your assessor will require you to:

Learning outcomes	Assessment criteria
1 Understand the steps and stages of moving from childhood into adulthood	**1.1** Identify the range of physical, social and emotional changes which occur for young people as they move into adulthood See Research and investigate 1.1, p. 201.
	1.2 Explain the changes faced by young people as they move from childhood into adulthood in relation to their freedoms, rights and responsibilities See Time to reflect 1.2, p. 202.
	1.3 Explain how culture may impact on the process of moving from childhood into adulthood See Evidence activity 1.3, p. 203.
	1.4 Explain theories about change and how this can affect a young person with a disability See Time to reflect 1.4, p. 203.
2 Understand how having a disability may affect the process of moving from childhood into adulthood	**2.1** Explain, giving examples, the potential effects of the transition process on young people with disabilities and their families See Case study 2.1, p. 204.
	2.2 Identify challenges young people with a disability might have in understanding and coping with change See Evidence activity 22, p. 205.
	2.3 Outline the methods that can be used to support a young person with a disability to cope with change See Time to reflect 2.3, p. 205.
	2.4 Explain how legislation and local and national practice guidelines affect the planning of the transition for a young person with a disability from childhood into adulthood See Research and investigate 2.4, p. 206.
	2.5 Describe the legislation that affects the right of a young person with a disability to make decisions about their life See Time to reflect 2.5, p. 207.

Learning outcomes	Assessment criteria
3 Know the options for supporting a young person who has a disability to make the transition into adulthood	**3.1** Explain how a young person with a disability can have equal opportunities to make life choices as a young person without a disability See Research and investigate 3.1, p. 207.
	3.2 Explain how to support a young person with a disability to explore the options available in relation to employment or continued education and development See Case study 3.2, p. 208.
	3.3 Explain how personal budgets can be used with young people in transition See Time to reflect 3.3, p. 208.
4 Be able to support a young person with a disability through transition into adulthood	**4.1** Explain the factors to consider, and types of support that a young person with a disability may need before, during, and after the transition process See Evidence activity 4.1, p. 209.
	4.2 Support a young person to explore options for their future See Case study 4.2, p. 210.
	4.3 Use person-centred thinking to identify with the young person their needs and aspirations See Evidence activity 4.3, p. 210.
	4.4 Use person-centred thinking to develop with the young person a plan to support them through transition See Evidence activity 4.4, p. 211.
	4.5 Involve families in the transition process according to the wishes of the young person See Evidence activity 4.5, p. 212.
	4.6 Identify ways to provide resources to meet needs See Time to reflect 4.6, p. 213.
	4.7 Explain the role of key agencies and professionals likely to be involved in the transition process See Research and investigate 4.7, p. 213.
	4.8 Outline possible areas of tension and conflict that may arise during the transition into adulthood See Research and investigate 4.8, p. 213.

| 5 Be able to support a young person to reflect on the transition | 5.1 Use person-centred approaches with the young person to review their transition plan and ensure it reflects their needs
See Time to reflect 5.1, p. 214. |
| | 5.2 Support a young person to record the transition and what has happened in their life in order to plan for the future
See Research and investigate 5.2, p. 214. |

Assessment Summary for Unit LD 311K

To achieve the unit, your assessor will require you to:

Learning outcomes	Assessment criteria
1 Understand the steps and stages of moving from childhood into adulthood	1.1 Identify the range of physical, social and emotional changes which occur for young people as they move into adulthood See Research and investigate 1.1, p. 201.
	1.2 Explain the changes faced by young people as they move from childhood into adulthood in relation to their freedoms, rights and responsibilities See Time to reflect 1.2, p. 202.
	1.3 Explain how culture may impact on the process of moving from childhood into adulthood See Evidence activity 1.3, p. 203.
	1.4 Explain theories about change and how this can affect a young person with a disability See Time to reflect 1.4, p. 203.

Learning outcomes	Assessment criteria
2 Understand how having a disability may affect the process of moving from childhood into adulthood	**2.1** Explain, giving examples, the potential effects of the transition process on young people with disabilities and their families See Case study 2.1, p. 204.
	2.2 Identify challenges young people with a disability might have in understanding and coping with change See Evidence activity 2.2, p. 205.
	2.3 Outline the methods that can be used to support a young person with a disability to cope with changes See Time to reflect 2.3, p. 205.
	2.4 Explain how legislation and local and national practice guidelines affect the planning of the transition for a young person with a disability from childhood into to adulthood See Research and investigate 2.4, p. 206.
	2.5 Describe the legislation that affects the right of a young person with a disability to make decisions about their life See Time to reflect 2.5, p. 207.
3 Know the options for supporting a young person who has a disability to make the transition into adulthood	**3.1** Explain how a young person with a disability can have equal opportunities to make life choices as a young person without a disability See Research and investigate 3.1, p. 207.
	3.2 Explain how to support a young person with a disability to explore the options available in relation to employment or continued education and development See Case study 3.2, p. 208.
	3.3 Explain how personal budgets can be used with young people in transition See Time to reflect, p. 208.

4 Understand how to support a young person with a disability through a successful transition		Explain the factors to consider, and types of support that a young person with a disability may need before, during, and after the transition process See Evidence activity 4.1, p. 209.
		Explain how person-centred transition reviews and person-centred thinking can be used as part of this planning process See Time to reflect 4.2, p. 210.
		Explain the difference in approaches to planning between children's and adults' support services See Research and investigate 4.3, p. 211.
		Describe how to involve families in the transition process See Case study 4.4, p. 212.
		Explain the role of key agencies and professionals likely to be involved in the transition process See Research and investigate 4.5, p. 213.
		Outline possible areas of tension and conflict that may arise during the transition into adulthood See Research and investigate 4.6, p. 213.
		Compare different methods of support to use with young people with disabilities who have varying abilities See Time to reflect 4.7, p. 213.
5 Understand the importance of supporting a young person and their family to reflect on the transition	5.1	Explain why it is important to reflect on the transition with the young person and their family See Time to reflect 5.1, p. 214.
	5.2	Explain the importance of recording the process of transition See Research and investigate 5.2, p. 214.

Parents with disabilities
Unit LD 312 Support parents with disabilities

What are you finding out?

We will identify the barriers that parents with disabilities have had to overcome and we will look at the support mechanisms available to support parents with disabilities. A key area we will explore will be safeguarding and the role of the carer in supporting parents with disabilities.

In this unit you will need to analyse research and adapt it to the individuals you are working with

- Understand the legislative and policy frameworks that underpin good practice in the support of parents with disabilities
- Understand the support parents with disabilities may need
- Be able to support parents with disabilities
- Be able to support individuals with disabilities to overcome the barriers they may face in becoming parents and bringing up children
- Be able to develop positive working relationships with parents with disabilities
- Be able to work in partnerships with other workers, different services and informal support networks
- Understand how to maintain the primary focus on safeguarding and promoting the welfare of the child

LO1 Understand the legislative and policy frameworks that underpin good practice in the support of parents with disabilities

 Outline the policy, legislation and guidance relevant to supporting individuals with disabilities to have children and bring them up in a safe and nurturing environment

History of legislation

In the past the outcome for parents with learning disabilities was very bleak. Care for those with learning disabilities was in the form of 'work houses' or institutions. The belief was that people with learning disabilities could not look after themselves, therefore any children they had were taken away. Legislation changed this attitude. The first change came with the Human Rights Act 1998 and the Disability Discrimination Act 1995. This led to the government identifying what needed to change to comply with the law. The first difficulty they came across was identifying just how many citizens were classified disabled. When the government brought out the white paper 'Valuing people' in March 2001, estimates stood at 210,000 people with severe learning disabilities and approximately 1.2 million individuals reported to have mild to moderate learning difficulties.

Key terms

Legislation refers to the laws and changes in practice.

White paper means the guidelines devised to address issues of government and identify best practice.

Statutory responsibilities are legal duties.

Since this period, new white papers have been published and the law has changed regarding learning disabilities. Key milestones include 'Valuing people now, a three year strategy', 'Fair access to care services 2002', 'Framework for assessment of children in need and their families 2000' and the Children's Act 2004. All of these are white papers or legislation aimed at ensuring people with learning disabilities receive a fair choice and are able to enjoy a full and active life with support. All of these publications can be found on the department of health website:

www.dh.gov.uk

An important part of legislation is the statutory guidance on making arrangements to safeguard and promote the welfare of children under section 11 of the Children Act 2004.

All of these acts and legislations identified the need to adjust thinking to ensure fairness. It is not acceptable to believe that experiencing disability means you have limited life expectations, and this includes the ability to parent children.

Research and investigate

1.1 Legislation

Read through the frameworks and relevant legislation. Identify within them the good practice guidance for supporting parents with disabilities. Note the changes in legislation and identify the correct policies and guidance within your work environment.

1.2 Explain the statutory responsibilities placed on organisations towards families and children who are in need

With all these policies and guidance, support for the individuals should be great, but unfortunately due to different agencies being involved the communication between partners has not always been successful. The need to improve communications required an agreed standard of good practice; the 'Good practice guidelines on working with parents with a learning disability' produced in 2007 by the Department of Health addressed this issue. Identifying the statutory responsibilities of individual agencies with a major emphasis on communication was done with full acknowledgement of the statutory guidance on inter-agency cooperation to improve the wellbeing of children, such as Children's trusts. The law aims to ensure support for parents with disabilities.

1.2 Statutory responsibilities

Identify the responsibilities placed on organisations towards families and children in need by completing the table below:

Area of need	Legislation
Housing	
Antenatal care	
Health access	
Education	
Rights	
Assessment	
Finance	
Support / advocacy	

LO2 Understand the support parents with disabilities may need

2.1 Explain the support provided by adults and children's services to a family receiving support from both

Everyone has anxieties about becoming a parent. All new parents rely on friends and family to support them through this process, and being a parent requires us to increase our knowledge of parenting and learn new skills. Becoming a parent requires extra money to enable us to buy resources to provide for the child. Housing and employment may be additional issues. We are also anxious about our own health and that of our unborn child. For individuals with learning disabilities these fears are heightened. Individuals with learning difficulties require extra support to build their confidence and learn many new skills. There is a good chance that they will require long term support to deal with this major change in their life. The sooner a person with disabilities knows they are pregnant the sooner the support can be put in place. It is not uncommon for people with disabilities to be frightened of informing people because they fear their child may be taken away from them. It is important for everyone involved to emphasise that the aim of social workers is to keep the child with their parent. Research has demonstrated that a child who stays with their parent has a more enriched life, which is why courts will always ensure that if the child is safe it remains in the custody of the natural parent.

Within adult services the support available to parents with disabilities is exactly the same as that offered to parents without disabilities. The health authority has a responsibility to ensure the same assistance, and therefore an assessment is required. This is not an assessment to identify parenting skills but one that aims to identify any support necessary to enable successful parenting, for example help with housing if the individual's home requires adaptation. Support may be needed in preparing a nursery or obtaining resources to enable more effective formula measurement. This assessment from the adult services is to support the parent. If there are concerns for a child then they need to be referred to the children's services.

Case study

2.1 **Rose**

Rose has had learning difficulties since she was born and for most of her life she has been raised in an institution. Recently Rose has been seeing a boyfriend and has announced that she is pregant.

Explain the process of referral for Rose and the time scales for this to occur. What information you would give to her?

 Time to reflect

2.2 **Sources of support**

Think of a time when you needed some support. Who did you ask for support, did they give you advice on how to achieve your wishes, what would you do next time? How helpful was this support?

2.2 **Explain the ways in which independent advocates can play an important role in the support of parents with disabilities**

Recall a time when you, a friend or family member found out they were pregnant, what did you do? Many people would inform friends and families of the good news and different people would tell you what to expect and what services were available. For people with disabilities pregnancy may be a frightening time. They may not understand the physical changes that are happening to them and may be concerned about keeping their child. We all have choices about keeping a baby and generally we make our decision by looking at all the factors and asking family and friends for support. Sometimes people with disabilities do not have these resources open to them and may not have supportive family or friends available to guide them. Advocates can be most useful at these times. Advocates can assist with explaining procedures and ensuring the rights of the individual are heard. There are three terms used in advocacy:

- self-advocacy, which is giving the skills to the individual to ensure they know how to be heard effectively,
- advocacy, where an individual identifies a person to speak for them, and
- independent advocates who are generally appointed for the individual.

Key terms

An advocate is a person who ensures your voice is heard and enables your choices to be implemented.

2.3 **Explain the benefits of providing support to families at the earliest stage possible**

Supporting a person from the earliest stages of pregnancy helps the process of building trust. Every new parent finds the first stages of pregnancy a frightening time: the baby is at the most vulnerable stage and many new mothers lose their babies within the first three months of pregnancy. The mother's hormones are changing and they may experience morning sickness and tiredness. Frequent tests and check-ups are required. Sometimes the health professions use jargon or medical terms that the new mother may not be familiar with. This is why we so frequently rely on friends and family members who have experienced pregnancy and childbirth to support us through this period. Persons with disabilities can feel even more anxious, especially if they feel unsure of what is happening to their bodies and are worried that they will not be able to keep their baby. Early intervention by support and information will reduce these anxieties and enable the learning process and any adaptations that are required to be addressed.

11.1 Pregnancy can be a worrying time for any new parent

LO3 Be able to support parents with disabilities

3.1 Assess the needs, strengths and preferences of the parent(s) and child(ren) to form the basis of any support

When offering any support to parents, we need to identify the skills the individual already has and the support circle available to them. If we do not identify these areas we cannot be sure of the additional support individuals require. This is why it is important to use a person-centred plan. With person-centred planning you can easily identify the types of support already available through their circle of friends, the skills the individual already has and identify the means of positive communication and their likes and dislikes. By doing this you will be able to build a relationship and the trust that will enable the best outcome for the individual.

Every pregnant person has the right to support, and this process ensures you have a clear idea of the type of support required. Sufficient notice makes it easier to ensure the resources are in place to enable the parent to cope and enjoy their parenting time. The parent may already have a child and may need assistance to ensure this new delivery will not impede on the sibling's care and needs.

Person-centred planning will give clear indications of risks and obstacles to overcome and the sooner this is implemented the sooner any obstacles can be removed.

Assessments need to be carried out when we know the individual is pregnant. The amount of assessment a person with disabilities has to go through has been criticised. Good practice suggests that assessments should be kept to the minimum. This may be the Common assessment framework or Framework for the assessment of children in need and their families. Good practice also states that these assessment tools must include the family and environmental factors.

It is important to emphasise that preconceived ideas of persons with disabilities being unable to parent are negative, untrue and cannot exist within person-centred planning and thinking. We as professionals must demonstrate and reinforce the fact that these assessments are not about testing parenting capability. While there are some tests to identify the level of learning disability and the individual's ability to learn new skills, these tests have not been identified or proven to demonstrate the individual's abilities to parent.

Case study

3.1 Rose

Rose has told her support worker she is pregnant. A trip to the GP has confirmed that Rose is 12 weeks pregnant. Her boyfriend has epilepsy and is a few years younger then her. Her boyfriend does not want the baby and his parents have decided to leave the area, with no contact available for Rose. Rose has clearly identified she wants to keep the child and has no family members to help her. Rose has limited knowledge of parenting and has difficulties expressing herself.

Describe how you would assess her needs and strengths. How would you present the information to Rose and why would you present it in that format?

3.2 Develop flexible support strategies to meet families' needs at the different stages of the child's development

When supporting parents with disabilities we have already recognised the importance of the child remaining with the parent, but we must also recognise that the child's welfare is a central concern of any planning. If any requirements are identified for the child it is important to involve the children services so that the child's needs are assessed and supported. This assessment should not be in isolation of adult services but in conjunction with it. Adult and children's services need to work together for the family.

To meet the individual's needs we need to identify the available strategies to help the process. Some of the support strategies available are:

- advocacy
- different formats to enable understanding, such as picture formats and audio
- repetition
- signposting to support
- support worker
- time
- small meetings
- less jargon.

Child development goes through several stages that will all require different support mechanisms. A baby will cry when it is hungry, a child may need support starting school and socialising. Teenagers experience confusion and frustration. Specialist skills are needed throughout the child's development.

Research and investigate

3.2 Flexible support strategies

Identify what support and resources would be available for a parent with learning disabilities whose teenage daughter has just started her periods.

3.3 Implement support strategies to ensure they continue to meet the needs of the family

While a family's need for support may be apparent, implementing support strategies can be made difficult because of individuals' perceptions or unfounded fears. Effective support requires the building of a trusting relationship, and when working with individuals with learning disabilities this relationship is paramount. For any strategy to be effective it needs to be implemented as soon as possible to reduce risk. An example of this might be a parent feeling able to discuss and ask for help on educating their child about contraceptives. If this was not explored prior to the child becoming sexually active, unwanted pregnancy might occur.

Time to reflect

3.3 Implementing support strategies

Identify a strategy you have implemented with a parent with disabilities. Describe the scenario of the implementation of the strategy, write about what went well, what you would do differently next time and whether it was implemented at the correct time. Write a statement of the benefits of implementing the strategy at the earliest time possible.

3.4 Evaluate support strategies to ensure they continue to meet the needs of the family

Sometimes when we put strategies in place they do not have the desired outcomes. We need to evaluate the effectiveness of our strategies on a regular basis. If the strategy did not work there may be difficulties in adapting the strategy. This is where you as the care worker must increase your support and re-clarify what the outcomes should be and what the individual wants to achieve. You may have to explore different partners to work with, possibly in the voluntary sector.

Sometimes when we evaluate a plan we can see that the strategies in place are effective and need to continue; this is great, but we still need to check frequently to ensure this success is maintained. Remember, especially when children are involved, these needs change on a regular basis due to the child's development and the parent's coping skills' development. Sometimes changes can occur rapidly such as when a child develops an illness. Every parent would be anxious, but parents with disabilities may need particularly high levels of support and this should be explored in the strategy.

Time to reflect

3.4 Evaluating support strategies

Identify a support strategy you have been involved in at your setting. Write down the review process and identify what worked well and what did not. Identify any practice you would do differently next time.

11.2 Everyone should be involved in planning support strategies

LO4 Be able to support individuals with disabilities to overcome the barriers they may face in becoming parents and bringing up children

4.1 Analyse the positive and negative implications for parents with disabilities of having their child assessed as being 'in need'

To ensure the support that some parents with disabilities may need, they are required to agree to an assessment. As previously stated, many parents have concerns about assessments due to misconceptions and the fear of having their child taken away from them. The courts already acknowledge that a child flourishes more with their natural parent and will not take a child away from their parents unless the child's safety is compromised. We need to emphasise that the assessments are there to help and support the parent with disabilities. Assessments can be reduced if information is shared between partnerships following the individual's agreement. The child/ children may be assessed as being 'in need'. To dispel fears surrounding this label we need to fully understand what 'in need' actually means. A child in need is defined in the Children's Act 1989 by the following statement:

A

- He is unlikely to achieve or maintain, or to have the opportunity to achieving or maintaining, a reasonable standard of health or development without the provision for him of services by a local authority under this part.
- His health or development is likely to be significantly impaired, or further impaired, without the provision for him of such services or
- He is disabled

B

- Children who are experiencing, or at risk of experiencing, significant harm and where the children's services authority then has a duty to make "such enquiries as they consider necessary to enable them to decide whether they should take any action to safeguard or promote the child's welfare"

C

- Children who take on a caring role to the extent they meet the definition of carer within Carers Legislation, that is, "someone who provides or intends to provide a substantial amount of care on a regular basis" to a person who has been assessed as needing a service under the NHS and Community Care Act 1990 or the Chronically Sick and Disabled Persons Act 1970.

D

- Disabled children who are not only covered by obligations towards children in need but might also meet the definition of disabled person as laid down by the Disability Discrimination Act 1995 and the Chronically Sick and Disabled Persons Act 1970. They may also have special educational needs, as defined by the Special Educational Needs Code of Practice 2001 or the Code of Practice on the identification and assessment of educational needs 1989.

The concept of early intervention was highlighted by the Every Child Matters publication. Every Child Matters is the framework devised from the Children's Act 2004. Sometimes when legislation has been passed, a framework is devised to put the law into practice. The framework tells us what actions we need to take to enforce the legislation.

Every Child Matters has five outcomes to ensure children and young people remain well. These are:

1. Being healthy
2. Staying safe
3. Enjoying and achieving
4. Making a positive contribution
5. Achieving economic wellbeing

Reviewing this information, it is clear that the main objective of assessment is to ensure the child is safe and protected. Legislation states that persons with disabilities should have equality in the services and support they receive. In the government white paper, Valuing people 2001, there was a specific aim relating to the support disabled parents should receive to enable a parenting role.

for Excellence identified many factors contributing to barriers for disabled parents to receiving the support required to raise their child. This evolved into 'Supporting disabled parents and parents with additional support needs' by Jenny Morris and Michele Wates published 2006. The factors they highlight include poor housing, finance/ poverty, negative attitudes and lack of information.

Research and investigate

 Barriers to parenting

Identify the reasons why parents with disabilities are more likely to have their children put into care, and the support that can be implemented to reduce this outcome.

Evidence activity `LD 312`

 Positives and negatives

In the table below, identify the negative and positive outcomes for a parent with disabilities having their child assessed as being 'in need'.

Positives	Negatives

11.3 Parents with disabilities face additional challenges when parenting

Key terms

Barriers are any type of obstacle that prevents progression.

4.2 **Explain why parents with disabilities are more likely to have their children removed from their care than parents who do not have disabilities**

Research has demonstrated that parents with disabilities are more likely to have their children removed from their care due to lack of support services (60 per cent of parents with disabilities are not living with their child). The Social Care Service

4.3 **Support individuals with disabilities to overcome barriers to successful parenting**

The barriers that were identified by the Social Care for Excellence include, for example, poor housing. To overcome this obstacle the support worker needs to involve other partnership services. There is a need to ensure that the accommodation is adapted to enable the disabled parent to complete tasks, a lowered sink so the parent is able to wash items and keep a clean area is one suggestion. Identifying the obstacle preventing good parenting is of paramount importance.

 Time to reflect

 4.3 Identifying obstacles

Identify a parent you support, look at the barriers they faced initially and identify what resources / support you were involved in. Did these make the desired difference, what went well, what would you do differently next time and what difference did this make to the parent?

4.4 Work in a way that promotes individuals' self-determination and self-confidence in their role as parents

Case study

4.4 Peter

Peter is the father of Abbey who is 11 years old and is about to start secondary school. Peter has learning difficulties and lives with his mother and daughter. His mother is very supportive and Peter has a package of care. His anxieties have emerged since his daughter is due to start secondary school. The school she needs to attend is 5 miles away. Peter cannot walk that distance and is not confident around roads. His mother is elderly and does not drive either. Peter has a sister who lives near the school who has offered to let Abbey stay with her. Peter does not want to give up his role as parent.

Looking at the case study, identify what resources can be put into place to enable Peter to maintain his role as parent. What are the benefits of Peter maintaining his parental role?

4.5 Support parents with learning, communication and/or sensory disabilities to acquire the skills and knowledge they need, using methods adapted to their learning needs and circumstances

Disabilities come in many forms and require different tools to enable the individual to live an equal lifestyle. To ensure we can support all individuals we must identify the correct resources for each individual. One of the factors parents with disabilities identified as a crucial problem was a lack of information. While there is a huge amount of literature to be found in communal areas, such as Doctor's surgeries and libraries, this is in written format, and for someone whose disability is lack of vision this type of information is of no use. A parent with learning disabilities may need support on a frequent basis and this may take the form of repetitive reinforcement of a process. They may need step by step guiding either by being shown a task or through a pictorial guide. Various teaching programmes have been explored to assist parents with disabilities in gaining valuable skills. An example of this would be the Bristol Education and Lifelong Learning which has a specific fund for British sign language, to enable interpreters for local authorities to meet the cost of interpreting for deaf parents.

Time to reflect

 4.5 Support in acquiring skills

Identify a disabled parent who has a learning, communication and/or sensory disability that you have supported to acquire skills or knowledge. What resources did you use and what methods needed to be adapted? Did this go well? What could you have done differently? What was the outcome of your intervention?

LO5 Be able to develop positive working relationships with parents with disabilities

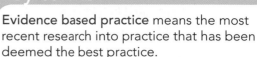

5.1 **Analyse the findings of research into the wishes of parents with disabilities about the qualities, attitudes and approaches they would like those working with them to have**

We have previously discussed the barriers and difficulties parents with disabilities face. We have identified some tools and services that can overcome these issues, empowering the parent and improving their confidence levels. Most of this information has come through research. It is important to listen to parents with disabilities to discover what they would like to happen and their experiences of past interaction.

Research and investigate

5.1 The wishes of parents with disabilities

Research the experiences parents with learning disabilities have had regarding the attitudes and approaches they have encountered and identify the ways they have expressed they would like to be approached with.

5.2 **Use evidence based approaches in developing positive relationships with parents with disabilities**

We have identified the barriers to parents with learning disabilities and the need to reassure the parents that we are there to support them, not to put them in an institution or take their child away. To do this we have discussed the importance of knowledge and the need to change attitudes. Research has concluded that there is a need for support workers to look at their practice and their sharing of resources. When we are arguing over best practice we need to check what is the most recent research identifying best practice. Since the publication of 'Valuing people now' the issue of disability has been highlighted and examined. The issue of parents with disabilities has been explored and findings can be found in a variety of sources, including Social Care for Excellence. Mencap have some excellent publications including advocacy and the white papers are available from the Department of Health.

Research and investigate

5.2 Current research

Find the most up to date research on approaches in developing positive relationships with individuals with disabilities.

LO6 Be able to work in partnerships with other workers, different services and informal support networks

 6.1 Plan how to involve relevant services to support parents with disabilities and/or their children

Key terms

Other workers does not refer to your colleagues, but to workers who have an input and are paid for that input but do not come from the care services.

In previous sections we have explored the need to reduce assessments and for services to work together. This is primarily the adult social services and the children's social services, where assessments have been organised for joint assessment. The children's social services work within the national services framework for children, young people and maternity services, and have an agreement about sharing information with adult services and a core assessment of needs has been agreed. With the 'Fair access to care' (2003) policy guidelines the needs of the adult and child need to be assessed independently in a person-centred plan. Adult services have a duty under the Children's Act 1989 to ensure the wellbeing of children.

Evidence activity   LD 312

6.1 Involving relevant services

Within your workplace identify the process and plan for informing services in order to support parents with disabilities and/or their children. Complete a blank plan with the actions you would take. Do not put in any names.

 6.2 Access relevant services to support parents with disabilities and/or their children

When a parent with disabilities is first referred to you, your workplace has guidance and procedures you must follow. These policies and procedures ensure you are working within the legislation and good practice guidelines. Following these procedures also ensures that no one falls through the net and does not get access to the support they require. Protocols have been developed to address the issues of partnership working. Protocols are drawn up by the multi-agencies and are agreed locally.

Time to reflect

6.2 Access relevant services

Think about the last time you were involved in working with another agency to support a parent with disabilities. Identify what the process was, how it went, the outcomes of joint working and whether there was anything you could have done differently to improve the outcome.

6.3 Demonstrate ways of helping to create, enhance and work with informal support networks

Hopefully parents with disabilities have a network of family and friends that can support them. This would be identified through the person centred planning process. It is important to support these informal networks and ensure they are fully aware of the services being delivered. Informal support workers need recognition of their importance in supporting the individual. This is why they should be included in any meetings and planning for the individual.

Case study

(6.3) Peter

Revisiting the case study of Peter in case study 4.4, we identified two informal support workers, his mother and sister. From the study we can see the sister wanted to help but maybe had not realised that taking his daughter away from him would have been detrimental to his confidence and the skills he already demonstrates. His mother is less able to help physically but is still an important part of the support network.

How could you involve them in the planning and implementing of the support planning for Peter, ensuring that they felt they were supporting well whilst Peter remains in control? Your assessor will need to see this demonstrated in their observations.

11.4 Informal support networks are very important

LO7 Understand how to maintain the primary focus on safeguarding and promoting the welfare of the child

Key terms

Safeguarding means protecting from harm.

(7.1) Explain own role and responsibilities in relation to safeguarding children

Children's welfare is paramount. The child is the main focus of anything we do, even if this means the outcome is then detrimental to the adult or parent. The Children's Act 1989 places a legal responsibility on local authorities to ensure the safety of children first. The Every Child Matters guidelines can be found in Working Together to Safeguard Children: A Guide to Inter-agency Working to Promote and Safeguard the Welfare of Children.

Every Child Matters states that we must ensure the child is:

- Healthy
- Safe
- Enjoying and achieving
- Making a positive contribution
- Achieving economic wellbeing

When working with parents with disabilities it can be difficult to keep the focus on the child / children due to our primary role of being involved with the parent. We have spent time ensuring all the support services are there to give the parent equal rights to care and to bring up their child/children. We have explored how important it is for the individual to be a parent and we may have arranged a variety of support services to enable this process. Therefore, when you notice a possible risk to the child/children it can be hard to address this knowing the effects it will have on the parent. But the child/children are the focus. Their wellbeing is paramount. Our role in supporting the parent needs to change to support them through this transition and ensure they are able to access services such as advocacy.

Research and investigate

7.1 Safeguarding

In your workplace identify the policies and procedures for safeguarding children or child of parents with disabilities and explain your role in safeguarding child/ children.

7.2 Identifying processes

Identify in your work setting the policies and procedures regarding the safeguarding of children. Describe your role within that procedure, and identify when you as the worker need to intervene.

7.2 Identify the processes set up under child protection legislation, policy, procedures and guidance to establish whether action is required to safeguard or promote the child's welfare and to intervene if necessary

Safeguarding is never taken lightly. If you believe a child is at risk this needs to be reported straight away. When the social team has been alerted a process begins. This action causes section 47 of the Children's Act to be implemented. Section 47 is classed as Enquiries. Once actioned, Section 47 starts the process of assessing whether the child is at risk or likely to be at risk. The case manager, generally a social worker with relevant knowledge in this area, will follow the guidelines/ protocol of assessment to identify any risk to the child. During this process support is needed for both the parent and child. They must have information in a format they can understand.

Following this assessment, if the child is deemed not at risk, support is still required for the parent and child.

7.3 Describe the action to take in response to any concerns regarding safeguarding children

While working with the parent, you need to be aware of the signs and symptoms of a child in need. Below is a list of possible signs of neglect:

- The child is hungry/loss of weight.
- The child appears unkempt, clothes are dirty, signs of poor hygiene.
- Baby's nappies are not changed frequently, resulting in nappy rash, broken skin, infection.
- Clothing not appropriate for climate/ activity.
- Medical attention not sought when child is ill.
- Frequent accidents occur with regular signs of bruising.
- Developmental delay, not reaching the milestones expected.
- Left with unsuitable carers.
- Home has dangerous items within reach, no protection for the child.
- Lack of attendance at school.
- Develops strange behaviours, e.g. head banging.

This is not an exhaustive list and cannot be used as the sole piece of evidence that a child is in need. The list is indicative of problems too. For example, a child who is frequently absent from school may have a health problem that prevents them from attending.

Case study

(7.3) Mary

Jasmine is the daughter of Mary, who is deaf and has learning disabilities. Jasmine is six years old and has been behaving differently at school. The staff have reported that she sometimes wets herself and say that though they have told Mary, the problem persists. The school is worried about Jasmine and feels she may be at risk.

As the support worker for Mary, and the person who has been informed by the school, what actions would you take?

On further investigation it transpires the school did indeed tell Mary, but she was unable to hear. Jasmine had tried explaining the situation to her mother but Mary did not understand what her daughter was trying to say. The support worker was able to communicate the problem to Mary in a format she could understand. The support worker then involved the children's team who identified the problem as having a medical cause. With the correct medication the infection was cleared and the incontinence stopped.

11.5 Legislation aims to protect and support families

(7.5) Describe the adjustments and additional support that parents with disabilities may need at different stages during the child protection processes and procedures

The child protection process is actioned by the children's services team, who have a legal duty to act when a child is under police protection or if they feel a child in their area is suffering or likely to be suffering significant harm. This is known as Section 47. This section is for social workers to investigate if there is any cause for concern and to identify if any further action is required.

Following Section 47 if the child is not found to be at risk, the local authority will provide support for the parents, called family support services. Whilst these enquiries are going on the child may stay in their home if this is assessed as safe. The policy works within the Working together to safeguard children strategy in order to complete the initial assessment; this is called the Framework for the assessment for children in need and their families. The process is in six stages:

1. Initial assessment
2. Core assessment
3. Strategy discussions
4. S47 Child protection enquiries
5. The child protection case conference
6. The child protection review conference

Throughout the process support for the parents and the child should be available, with the possible need for an independent advocate for both the parents and the child. This is an ordeal for any parent or child. This process is only activated

(7.4) Explain the types of support the child may need in his/her own right

Time to reflect

(7.4) Supporting the child

Identify from your work environment a situation when concerns for the child of a parent with disabilities were raised. What support was needed for the child, what support were you able to give and what other services were involved? Was the outcome good, what could have been done differently? What other support services are there available for children?

to safeguard the child, and the child must remain the focus at all times. Parents with disabilities will naturally find this process very stressful, and as their support worker you need to ensure that they understand the process fully and the reasons why this process has commenced.

 Research and investigate

7.5 **Additional support**

Research what additional support and resources you may need to support a parent with disabilities during the process of child protection. Explore local resources and voluntary services.

Assessment Summary for Unit LD 312

To achieve the unit, your assessor will require you to:

Learning outcomes	Assessment criteria	
1 Understand the legislative and policy frameworks that underpin good practice in the support with parents with disabilities	**1.1**	Outline the policy, legislation and guidance relevant to supporting individuals with disabilities to have children and bring them up in a safe and nurturing environment See Research and investigate 1.1, p. 221.
	1.2	Explain the statutory responsibilities placed on organisations towards families and children who are in need See Evidence activity 1.2, p. 222.
2 Understand the support parents with disabilities may need	**2.1**	Explain the support provided by adults and children's services to a family receiving support from both See Case study 2.1, p. 223.
	2.2	Explain the ways in which independent advocates can play an important role in the support of parents with disabilities See Time to reflect 2.2, p. 223.
	2.3	Explain the benefits of providing support to families at the earliest stage possible See Evidence activity 2.3, p. 224.
3 Be able to support parents with disabilities	**3.1**	Assess the needs, strengths and preferences of the parent(s) and child(ren) to form the basis of any support See Case study 3.1, p. 224.
	3.2	Develop flexible support strategies to meet families' needs at the different stages of the child's development See Research and investigate 3.2, p. 225.
	3.3	Implement support strategies to ensure they continue to meet the needs of the family See Time to reflect 3.3, p. 225.
	3.4	Evaluate support strategies to ensure they continue to meet the needs of the family See Time to reflect 3.4, p. 226.

Learning outcomes	Assessment criteria
4 Be able to support individuals with disabilities to overcome the barriers they may face in becoming parents and bringing up children	**(4.1)** Analyse the positive and negative implications for parents with disabilities of having their child assessed as being 'in need' See Evidence activity 4.1, p. 227.
	(4.2) Explain why parents with disabilities are more likely to have their children removed from their care than parents who do not have disabilities See Research and investigate 4.2, p. 227.
	(4.3) Support individuals with disabilities to overcome barriers to successful parenting See Time to reflect 4.3, p. 228.
	(4.4) Work in a way that promotes individuals' self-determination and self-confidence in their role as parents See Case study 4.4, p. 228.
	(4.5) Support parents with learning, communication and/or sensory disabilities to acquire the skills and knowledge they need, using methods adapted to their learning needs and circumstances See Time to reflect 4.5, p. 228.
5 Be able to develop positive working relationships with parents with disabilities	**(5.1)** Analyse the findings of research into the wishes of parents with disabilities about the qualities, attitudes and approaches they would like those working with them to have See Research and investigate 5.1, p. 229.
	(5.2) Use evidence based approaches in developing positive relationships with parents with disabilities See Research and investigate 5.2, p. 229.
6 Be able to work in partnership with other workers, different services and informal support networks	**(6.1)** Plan how to involve relevant services to support parents with disabilities and / or their children See Evidence activity 6.1, p. 230.
	(6.2) Access relevant services to support parents with disabilities and / or their children See Time to reflect 6.2, p. 230.
	(6.3) Demonstrate ways of helping to create , enhance and work with informal support networks See Case study 6.3, p. 231.

7 Understand how to maintain the primary focus on safeguarding and promoting the welfare of the child	Explain own role and responsibilities in relation to safeguarding children See Research and investigate 7.1, p. 232.
	Identify the process set up under child protection legislation, policy , procedures and guidance to establish whether action is required to safeguard or promote the child's welfare and to intervene if necessary See Evidence activity 7.2, p. 232.
	Describe the action to take in response to any concerns regarding safeguarding children See Case study 7.3, p. 233.
	Explain the types of support the child may need in his/her own right See Time to reflect 7.4, p. 233.
	Describe the adjustments and additional support that parents with disabilities may need at different stages during child protection processes and procedures See Research and investigate 7.5, p. 234.

Further resources

Department of Health, Home Office and Department for Education and Employment (2000) *Framework for Assessment of Children in Need*, The Stationery Office.

Department of Health (1970), *Chronically sick and Disabled Persons Act*, Department of Health.

Department of Health, (2001), *Valuing People: A New Strategy for Learning Disability for the 21st Century*, The Stationery Office.

Department of Health, (2002), *Fair Access to Care Services: policy Guidelines, Department of Health.*

Emerson, E, Malam, S., Davies, I. and Spencer, K.(2005), *Adults with Learning Disabilities in England 2003/2004.* www.ic.nhs.uk/pubs/learndiff2004

Department of Health (1999), *Working Together to Safeguard Children: A Guide to Inter-Agency Working to Safeguard and Promote the Welfare of Children*, The Stationery Office.

SCIE (2005), *Helping Parents with Disabilities in their role as parents.* http://www.scie.org.uk/publications/briefings/briefing14/index.asp

Department of Health (1998), *Human Rights Act*, The Stationery Office.

Department of Education and Skills(2003) *The Children Act report 2002,* London: Department for Education and Skills

Children Act 1989

Carers (Recognition and Services) Act 1995

Department for Education and Skills and Department of Health (2004) *The National Service Framework for Children, Young People and Maternity Services,* London: Department of Health

Morris.J, and Wates.M. (2006), *Supporting disabled parents and parents with additional support needs,* York: Joseph Rowntree Foundation

Human Rights Act 1998

Children's Act 2004

Children's Act 1989

Index

Index

Index